Introduction to PRECIS
for
North American Usage

Introduction to PRECIS
for
North American Usage

By
Phyllis A. Richmond

1981
Libraries Unlimited, Inc.
Littleton, Colorado

LIBRARIES UNLIMITED, INC.
P.O. Box 263
Littleton, Colorado 80160

Library of Congress Cataloging in Publication Data

Richmond, Phyllis A
    Introduction to PRECIS for North American usage.

    Includes bibliographical references and index.
    1. PRECIS (Indexing system)   I. Title.
Z695.92.R52   025.4'82   80-25977
ISBN 0-87287-240-8

Libraries Unlimited, Inc. books are bound with Type II nonwoven material that meets and exceeds National Association of State Textbook Administrators' Type II nonwoven material specifications Class A through E.

PREFACE

The Preserved Context Index System, PRECIS, was designed by Derek Austin to combine human intellectual effort with the labor-saving capability of the computer. Index terms in PRECIS are made up of sets of words in variable patterns as needed to convey informational content of materials being indexed. The indexer determines the logical sequences, while the machine makes the actual entries. In presenting this system, emphasis has been placed on the decision-making factors involved.

The text is written for North American users. Social and cultural differences in the use of the English language have resulted in variation in idiomatic usage. Such variation appears in the choice of index words. North American terminology has been selected where needed in order to allow PRECIS to stand on its own merits.

The system is presented here in medium level completeness. Complex formats, such as those for following differences, intake into a system and the export-import problem, have been omitted, along with routines specific to practice in the British Library. It is expected that this method of indexing will be most useful to information specialists whose collections are hard to handle with methods designed for books.

This book could not have been written without the receipt of a Mid-Career Fellowship from the Council on Library Resources and a sabbatical leave from Case Western Reserve University. The opportunity to work with Derek Austin and his staff in the Subject Systems Office of the British Library was invaluable. The hospitality of Joan Austin is gratefully acknowledged. Brian Holt and Martin Nail of the Bibliographic Services Division provided access to materials. Permission to publish samples from the *British National Bibliography* has been extended by Joel C. Downing on behalf of the British Library. The cheerful assistance of all with whom I came in contact is remembered with pleasure.

A very special note of thanks is owed to Janet Waters, of the Subject Systems Office, whose painstaking review and patient explanations of the more complex aspects of PRECIS made possible the accuracy and clarity of this presentation. Both she and Professor Margaret Kaltenbach of Case Western Reserve University, read the entire manuscript twice and offered many valuable suggestions. Any remaining inaccuracies or obscurities are, of course, my own.

Correspondence with Jutta Sørensen of the Danmarks Biblioteksskole has been enlightening. James C. McDonnell, Judy Wood, and Gale Manson helped with critical comment. Shahrokh Afsharpanah aided in proofreading and made the index.

Phyllis A. Richmond
December 1980

To

James Hugh Richmond

TABLE OF CONTENTS

LIST OF FIGURES

1
INTRODUCTION

PRECIS IN CONTEXT

The Preserved Context Index System—PRECIS—is a methodology for indexing created by Derek Austin of the Bibliographic Services Division, British Library, in the early 1970s. The system was designed for use as the subject index to the *British National Bibliography* when that *Bibliography* adopted the 19th edition of the Dewey Decimal Classification. After an initial experimental period ending in 1973, the index entries began to appear in their current form. Since January 1974, thousands of books and other materials have been indexed using PRECIS.

It is an unusual system in several respects. In the first place, as its name suggests, it provides the user with the context of all major indexing words. One or more of these words are included in a larger unit, the Term. The Term is designed to convey the concepts denoted by the words as well as the relationships between them. By means of a string arrangement, the Terms place each other in context in certain formats. The chief claim to originality of PRECIS lies in the ability of the system to manipulate words and Terms in order to preserve *meaning*, especially in cases where the context alone could be misinterpreted. The upshot is that chances for misunderstanding and ambiguity are greatly reduced. The actual index entries are somewhat longer than in most indexes because of the necessity to preserve meaningful context. They are also proportionately more informative.

In the second place, PRECIS is a fully computerized system that may also be used manually. This book will describe the system in manual terms, but the reader should keep in mind that prices and sizes of computers have been drastically reduced with the introduction of large scale integrated circuits so that what was once handled by a huge machine can now be done by mini- and micro-computers. At the same time, the need for general purpose computers is not as crucial as it once was because proliferation of these electronic machines has made the special purpose computer economically feasible.

As a system, PRECIS was designed to be used with a computer because, quite obviously, this is the wave of the future for bibliographic systems. PRECIS does not stop at merely being an indexing process with special features designed to ensure that meaning is not lost. Rather, it allows a high degree of variability, combined with accessibility, so that when Terms are joined, their meanings are as secure as they were in the original string. This is a very important asset because there are indexing systems whose value is limited to the subjects or disciplines for which they were prepared, and their words cannot be used freely for other subjects. An example is the *Thesaurus of Scientific and Engineering Terms*, which contains many words that have entirely different meanings in other disciplines. These cannot be merged into a total system without adding explanatory matter for purposes of differentiation among terms.[1] Even disciplines as closely related as education and psychology have thesauri that list identical index words, but examination of their hierarchical and associative relationships shows that they are not necessarily given the same structural interpretation in each discipline.[2] Keyword-in-context systems attempt to make meanings clear by supplying context, but in those systems the context is normally the title of a book or article, with all the advantages and disadvantages of this form in conveying content. The most exact way of providing words in context for giving precise meaning is, of course, the concordance, but making concordances for every document is, at the present time, like using a shotgun to kill mosquitoes. For indexing purposes, a concordance is an intellectual overkill.

PRECIS, besides providing enough context to achieve unambiguous meaning for its Terms, also can be used for almost any kind of material. The word "documents" is generally associated with "indexing" because indexes are usually made up of words either in the natural language of the document[3] or taken from a controlled listing, as with subject headings. PRECIS, however, does not have these limitations. Anything that can be described in words can be indexed with PRECIS. This is because the starting point is neither a title nor the indexer's translation of the words in a text to the words in a prescribed list. The indexer begins by making one to four title-like phrases describing the content of whatever is being indexed. From each phrase, a string of lines, called "Terms," is derived. The Terms are manipulated one-by-one in string order to make the actual index entries.

The title-like phrase is distilled from the subject matter of the item being indexed. If new terminology is required, new terminology may be used. Semantic features of PRECIS permit the introduction of new Terms at any time, or the changing of terminology when words become obsolete or take on different meanings in different contexts. The system is open-ended to the extent that there are no barriers to introduction of Terms or change in existing Terms *if* the subject requires it.

PRECIS, therefore, is both flexible and usable in a wide variety of contexts. This kind of system is especially useful where normal indexing or classification systems cannot be applied in a satisfactory manner. It can be used with most kinds of audiovisual materials, special collections, archives, and even for office files in cases where exacting circumstances call for special subject treatment, as perhaps, in legal materials or where the presence of multiple disciplines requires indepth indexing of a type not found in standard thesauri or classification systems. Examples of the latter situation occur in space, environmental and energy sciences, mission-oriented research, and in cross-disciplinary areas, such as the ethics of cloning or the rights of the individual as the object of an experiment.

One advantage to PRECIS is that it can be used without the bibliographic apparatus required for centralized and standardized systems of subject headings or classification. That is, the user builds his or her own files and is not dependent on a national or international authority to provide a controlled vocabulary. This, in effect, makes it a "portable" indexing system. The indexer learns the method, decides where it is applicable and then applies it. One could, for example, have a situation where an archivist manages several different archives on different subjects and located in different places. PRECIS could be used for each one with only such carry-over as the archivist needs for generalities. Furthermore, since the system can be used manually or with a computer, the archivist could, depending on the circumstances, use both of these outputs. In Toronto, for example, a school librarian used PRECIS manually until she had access to a computer. Then she converted her system to a computerized one.[4] In designing PRECIS plans were made to use it as a computerized indexing method from the very beginning, so that the tags and codes used for identification of elements also serve as triggers in programming instructions. Therefore, the user who begins manually can switch to automatic production of entries without having to re-learn an additional set of rules and operations.

The learning process in PRECIS is easiest if it is possible to take a short, intensive course given by experienced personnel at or borrowed from the Bibliographic Services Division of the British Library. However, not all potential indexers are able to take advantage of these courses. It is the purpose of this book to assist those who wish to learn the system without leaving home. At this point, therefore, the materials needed to embark on learning PRECIS will be described briefly.

BACKGROUND MATERIALS NEEDED
FOR LEARNING PRECIS

The logic used in PRECIS is classical and based largely on Aristotle. Those readers who wish may even use the works of this philosopher directly, especially his *Categories* and *Topics*. Or, one step removed, the basics may be read through Cohen and Nagel's *Introduction to Logic and Scientific Method*, itself a classic. An unusually clear text including logic and language is available in Black's *Critical Thinking*. (Exact references to these and other works mentioned here may be found at the end of the chapter.)

A clear text in English grammar will also be needed, preferably at the high school level. Two are listed, but many more are available. The reader will find it necessary to review an elementary explanation of the parts of speech in the English language, with examples and definitions. In addition, a description of how syntax puts them together and the various constructions used will be needed, including transformation from active to passive voice. Perusal of Chomsky's classic *Syntactic Structures* will not come amiss. A glossary of terminology used in PRECIS is to be found in Appendix A. The reader should glance over the whole list at the earliest opportunity and refer to it as may be necessary during the reading of this book. Since some of the terminology used by Derek Austin in describing this indexing language has special connotations, the reader would be well advised to use the glossary freely until the definitions are familiar.

For this book as a working tool, directions for individual processes have come from various parts of Austin's *PRECIS: A Manual of Concept Analysis and Subject Indexing* (hereafter referred to as the *Manual*), from handouts used in the training courses for indexers of the *British National Bibliography* and elsewhere, and from communication with staff of the Subject Systems Office, Bibliographic Services Division of the British Library. New or augmented instructions have been added to update parts that may be out of date or only partly available in the *Manual*. References will be given at the end of each chapter in this book to sections in the *Manual* for pertinent rules, by section number if possible.

Since PRECIS is a living system and research, particularly on its multilingual aspects, is continuing to produce new insights and revised applications, the reader should not regard either this text or the rules as cast in stone. New or revised procedures are still being added, as greater understanding takes place. During the writing of this book, for example, the differencing operators were changed from a letter code to a numerical one, greatly increasing their scope and at the same time removing a source of confusion with some of the letter tags used as typographical instructions.

In addition, suggested readings on PRECIS itself are given at the end of the chapter. The most important single work is the *Manual*, which should be obtained if at all possible because it includes much more detail than could possibly be used here. It also has, for the most part, a different set of examples. In case an illustration is not clear in one place, it may, perhaps, be more lucid in the other. Several helpful titles, mostly articles, are included to give background or extension to the description of the system. The reader should begin to watch the literature for articles describing progress, the adoption of new and better techniques, and information on the use of the new MERLIN system, which is expected to come on line in the British Library when circumstances permit.

THE COMPUTER ASPECT OF PRECIS

Use of the computer as part of indexing with PRECIS will be minimized in this book in order to place the emphasis on intellectual aspects of the system without distraction. This does not mean that the importance of the computer in implementation of PRECIS should be ignored. In fact, to use PRECIS entirely manually, while possible, is doing things the hard way. The system was designed to have the indexer do the brain work and the computer do the drudgery of routines, an admirable division of labor. It is probably one of the first functional (as opposed to experimental) index-classification systems created to take full advantage of this electronic tool.

The computer, as employed in PRECIS, creates actual index entries from Terms in the string made by the indexer. It first validates each line of the string, checking to be sure that all instructions and forms of inputs are legal for the system. The operations performed are specific to each tag used in coding the parts of the string. These codes cover typography as well as manipulations. In addition, the actual series of operations performed is written in the form of an algorithm (pattern) for each code. A summary of the algorithms is to be found in Appendix 3 of the *Manual*. They are extremely useful, and it is recommended that the reader apply them when checking to be sure that all operations attached to and invoked by the tag for each code have been accomplished in the process of creating index entries from the string. Algorithms, though helpful for the computer, were designed by people. The computer is the servant of the system and not its master.

THE BASICS OF PRECIS

In addition to being based on logical rules, with linguistic overtones, augmented in application by a computer, PRECIS has its own rationale. The reader interested in understanding PRECIS may find that a little un-learning of familiar systems is needed. PRECIS is a logical, syntactical system. Librarians and indexers who use subject headings or the equivalent will be accustomed to looking for the most *important* aspect of a work, the most *important* concept and its verbiage. This kind of approach has been developed for assigning the class number and the corresponding first subject heading.

In PRECIS, one looks for syntactical roles of concepts (to be explored more fully in later chapters) and, to start off, for the presence of an action. This may be expressed as a noun such as "management" representing the process and/or product of action, or a gerund describing action, such as "teaching." The rest of the words describing a work follow (or precede) the action, according to the logical sequence of normal English syntax in putting grammatical terms together or the logic of hierarchy when it is called for in certain concepts. For example, in a subject described as "the razing of buildings by fire," the action is "razing"; the object is "buildings," and the agent performing the action is "fire." The syntax of the passive voice, which is used in PRECIS, gives the order. The passive voice requires the past participle of a verb:

buildings — razed [by] — fire

However, in indexing, verbs are replaced by nouns, if possible, or, if there is no usable noun form, by gerunds. Since there is no noun form for the verb "to raze," in the above case the gerund would apply:

buildings — razing — fire

The active voice for the same action would be "fire razes buildings," but for indexing purposes the passive, using a noun equivalent of the verb or a gerund, functions better.

In dealing with concepts, the logic is strictly that of hierarchy, as in a case such as "the bones in the tails of cats." A librarian assigning subject headings to a book on this topic would use "bones" as the most important term. In PRECIS, however, the *logical* format is required:

cats — tails — bones

The bones are within the tail which is part of the cat. Hierarchically, as in a classification table, these terms would be displayed as:

```
100   cats
110       tails
111           bones
```

The notation has been added here because, in a classification system made by logical division, the notation can be very helpful in conveying the format of the hierarchy.

Where concepts are related to each other by *association*, rather than by one representing a form or a part of another, there is not the same problem with logic, provided the indexer does not try to make a hierarchy where none exists. For example, three related terms are "malacology," which is the branch of zoology dealing with mollusks, "conchology," the branch dealing with their shells, and "shell collecting," which is an activity that can be done by anyone who can bend over. Conchology is conceivably a branch of malacology, but shell collecting is more closely related to other kinds of collecting than to the specific objects collected. While a collector acquires much knowledge about what is collected, the collections tend to be recreational. A serious, scientific shell collector or one whose collection is related to the way he earns a living would be called either a conchologist or malacologist.

These points are raised here because PRECIS indexing is not quite like any other kind. The reader should be prepared for some unfamiliar concepts of indexing, which, while not unknown, may not previously have been applied in traditional indexing processes.

The basic order of "actions" in PRECIS is the classical, Aristotelian one:

to be   (predicative, essence, existing)
to have   (possessive)
to do   (interactive)

In case of doubt, one asks the questions:

What is it?
What does it possess? What are its properties?
What does it do?

Furthermore, the same term may play different roles in different circumstances, which is, in part, where the logic comes in. It was easy, in the case given earlier, to see the bones in the tail of the cat as a logical sequence. It is less easy, but no less valid, to see a similar relationship in "the career prospects of social workers in hospitals." For the visually-minded, a diagram may be a good differentiating method for showing what belongs to what:

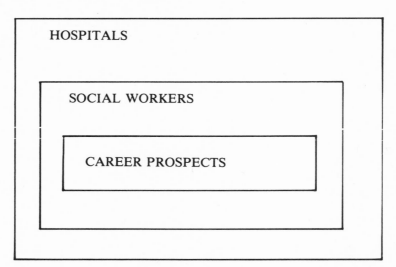

An alternative type of emphasis might bring together the career prospects of members of various professions in a given geographical area, as in a discussion of job openings for accountants, foresters, social workers, and geologists in the United States:

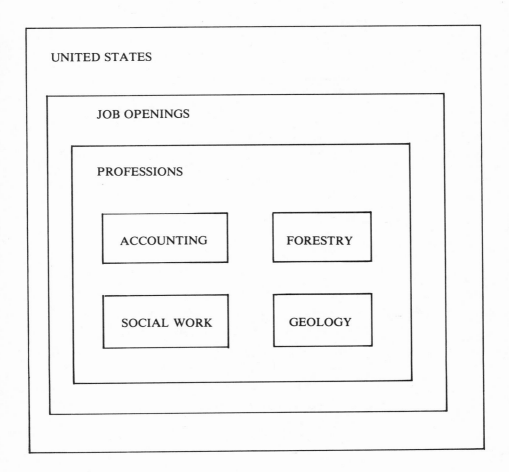

The art of subject analysis is always dependent upon the ability of the analyst to distill the content of the material being classified or indexed into concepts. PRECIS further requires the analyst to indicate accurately the relationships among the concepts.

To some extent this is done in classifying with a standard system such as the Dewey Decimal Classification because the classifier searches the schedules for the combination of concepts recognized in the work in hand. For a book on physiology of newts, a search will be made for a more specific spot than that implied by either general heading, "newts" or "physiology." In the Dewey classification, the classifier is working with a set of pre-coordinated entries. The same is true in using subject headings; the indexer will hope to find a heading in the prescribed list, such as "Newts — Physiology." In PRECIS, the *indexer* makes the connection between concepts, as a rule. This is most advantageous in dealing with a new subject or a new relationship. One does not have to wait for it to appear in a class schedule or a new list of additions and changes to an existing subject heading list. To this extent, PRECIS is open-ended.

Once Terms have been selected, they will be established in the form required by the context and will be used in this established form unless or until a varying context requires a different configuration. "Establishment" covers individual formats such as single word Terms, multiple word Terms, compound Terms (in which each word is potentially a headword in the index), Terms as synonyms, Terms structured as cross-references and special Terms used according to logic, custom, or other requirements. The methodology of PRECIS assists in differentiating among these various possibilities.

THE METHODOLOGY OF PRECIS

The PRECIS methodology consists of the following steps:

- Examination of the material to be indexed
- Preparation of one to four title-like statements to describe its content
- Conversion of statements to passive voice if required
- Analysis of each statement to determine the relationships involved
- Conversion of words in the statement to Terms for a string, according to the function of each word and its position in the phrase
- Determination of suitable tags or "operators" for each Term
- Rearrangement of tagged Terms into a logical string
- In a manual system, the indexer will write out the results (index entries), looking for errors, ambiguity or omissions with regard to concepts or contents
- If the system is computerized, the indexer will write "manipulation codes" for each string and put the results into the computer. In this situation, the computer printout would then be checked for errors, ambiguity, and so forth.

Though this process may sound complex, actually the hardest part is the analysis of the content of the item being indexed and selection of representative Terms. Everything else depends on this.

The string, with its components and the relations between them, is the *syntactic* factor in PRECIS. With this string in proper order, making entries becomes sufficiently mechanical to be entrusted to a computer.

Syntax, alone, however, is hardly an adequate base for such a system. *Meaning* (semantics) is only derived from juxtaposition of words if their grammatical structure is supported by a relational structure conveying the broader, narrower, and associated concepts attached to each word or words used for indexing.

Clarity and unambiguous usage call for some structural means of handling the collective vocabulary of an index. This structure is found in a list of some kind, such as a thesaurus.

KEEPING TRACK OF WORDS:
Thesaurus and Vocabulary

During the indexing process, the indexer will need to create files to aid in exact definition of Terms. These files, called a "thesaurus," perform the normal cross-referencing function of handling relationships between words, including synonyms, and result in "see" and "see also" references. As with any other well-designed indexing system, the reference thesaurus is an integral part of PRECIS. In PRECIS, however, the relationships between Terms are not limited to making cross-references. Instead, they represent a careful analysis of the description of the subject being indexed.

Relationships are recognized as being of three main types:

I.   HIERARCHICAL Relationships
      (a)   *Generic*
              Animals
                  Invertebrates
                    Bivalves
                    Worms
                    Insects
      (b)   *(Hierarchical) whole-part*
          (i)   Geographical regions
                  United States
                    New England
                      Massachusetts
                        Boston
                          Back Bay

         (ii)   Systems and organs of the body
                Skeleton
                  Spine
                    Vertebrae

         (iii) Areas of discourse (disciplines)
                Humanities
                  Literature
                    Poetry
                    Drama
                    Prose, etc.

II.   ASSOCIATIVE Relationships
         Those with a defining or explaining function; subjects commonly coordinated, where the relationship is not hierarchical, as given above, but of a less formal type:

Teeth / Dentistry
Cattle / Animal husbandry
Books / Libraries

III. EQUIVALENCE Relationships
    (a) Synonyms
        Woods *see* Forests
        Oceanside *see* Seaside
    (b) Quasi-synonyms
        Height / Depth

Ideally, the reference file should not be made by the same person who does the indexing. Preferably, this should be done by a specialist whose job is to draw up the relationships among the indexer's strings of Terms. This specialist would use dictionaries, encyclopedias, gazetteers, and other bibliographic tools, including textbooks, to create family trees for each Term used. The degree of complexity and form of terminology would depend on the needs of anticipated users. The actual family trees are created inductively, working upward from the lowest Term to the highest, with branches as needed. There may be parallel trees of hierarchical relationships connected with associative relationships. Polyhierarchy (multiple hierarchies) is common in thesauri, so that this feature of the PRECIS thesaurus should not be regarded as unusual.[5] Building the reference structure while defining Terms as used by the indexer is a classification process. This is the *semantic* feature in PRECIS.

THE PLAN OF THIS BOOK

Most of this book will deal with the syntactic factor in PRECIS — how strings are made and interpreted. However, the backup reference file is so closely related to the whole process that it cannot be ignored. In PRECIS, it provides the cross-references that users of the index will need if they approach with a vocabulary not necessarily the same as that used in indexing the materials in collection. It holds the system together structurally.

Procedures for PRECIS will be described in full detail following a chapter on the background of the system, its origins and early usage. Readers anxious to start on the methodology immediately may skip to the section in chapter 2 entitled "PRECIS Format."

PRECIS will be presented here primarily as a system of techniques. If possible, solutions to any single type of indexing problem will be avoided. Examples from the *British National Bibliography* appear here and there in illustration of some kinds of problems.

In all chapters except the second, the reader will be referred to pertinent sections of the *Manual* as explanations unfold. For convenience, these references are placed at the end of each chapter. References to exercises in the *Manual* are added to the list in some cases. Since these are somewhat different from the examples used in this book, the reader is urged to try them. Though in some cases normal British terminology is unlike that used in North America, readers will find they can decipher the meaning from the context in most instances. Answers, in case of confusion, should be studied carefully in order to discern the techniques involved. If the vocabulary is completely a mystery, the *New Oxford Dictionary* or updated versions of it should prove helpful. Background reading will also be advisable.

READING LIST

Sources of Information about PRECIS

Derek Austin. "The Development of PRECIS: A Theoretical and Technical History," *Journal of Documentation*, v. 30, no. 1 (March 1974), pp. 47-102.
This long review article gives the history of the system in considerable detail.

Derek Austin. *PRECIS: A Manual of Concept Analysis and Subject Indexing.* London: Council of the British National Bibliography, 1974.
This reference manual is virtually indispensible; no PRECIS indexer should be without it. It provides not only directions for all kinds of situations which may be encountered, but also the rationale behind most of the decisions made. This is extremely important for both beginner and expert, because one must understand the reasoning to be able to function well in cases where there is no exact equivalent to the case described. The *Manual* includes a description of the system (pp. 1-244), manipulation coding to translate the indexer's decisions to computer format (pp. 245-67), description of the method used to construct the files of references needed for backup (pp. 268-355), special problems and other details (pp. 356-422), flowcharts (pp. 425-35), algorithms for entry construction (pp. 437-80), notes on programming and verification of strings (pp. 481-85), and a most valuable PRECIS index to all the examples used in the text (pp. 487-502). The *Manual* includes exercises at the end of each major section and their answers. Since it is basically a reference tool, it is not particularly easy to read from cover to cover, but rather should be used for information on how to handle problems as they arise. Parts are now out of date, but most of it is still highly pertinent.

Derek Austin. "The Role of Indexing in Subject Retrieval." In *Major Classification Systems: The Dewey Centennial.* Kathryn Luther Henderson, ed. Urbana/Champaign, IL: University of Illinois, Graduate School of Library Science, 1976. pp. 124-56. Papers presented at the Twenty-first Allerton Park Institute, Nov. 9-12, 1975.
This paper adds a few comments not in earlier or later ones.

Derek Austin and Veronica Verdier. *String Indexing: PRECIS. Introduction and Indexing.* London, Ontario: University of Western Ontario. School of Library and Information Science, 1977.
PRECIS used for indexing a set of articles from the *Journal of the American Society for Information Science.* Since the articles themselves deal with research studies, most of the strings are long and complex.

Derek Austin et al. "PRECIS in a Multilingual Context," *Libri*, v. 26, nos. 1-4 (1976). Pt. 1, Derek Austin, "PRECIS: An Overview," pp. 1-35; Pt. 2, Jutta Sørensen and Derek Austin, "A Linguistic and Logical Explanation of the Syntax," pp. 108-139; Pt. 3, Jutta Sorensen and Derek Austin, "Multilingual Experiments, Proposed Codes, and Procedures for the Germanic Languages," pp. 181-215; Pt. 4, Germaine Lambert, "The Application of PRECIS in French," pp. 302-323.

The first part is an excellent brief introduction to PRECIS and is recommended without reservation. The remaining three parts should be read after acquiring some experience in indexing with PRECIS. The series updates the *Manual* and introduces new concepts. In fact, the application of PRECIS to French and German has produced new methods which turn out to be applicable in English and they have added new dimensions to PRECIS in this, its original language.

Larsen Poul Steen. *A Bibliography of PRECIS*. Aalborg, Denmark: Royal School of Librarianship, 1976. (Obtainable from: Danmarks Biblioteksskole, 6 Birketinget, DK-2300 Copenhagen S.).

A new edition is being prepared by Jutta Sorensen.

The PRECIS Index System: Principles, Applications, and Prospects. Proceedings of the International PRECIS Workshop Sponsored by the College of Library and Information Services of the University of Maryland, October 15-17, 1976. Hans H. Wellisch, ed. New York: H. W. Wilson, 1977. "I. The PRECIS System," pp. 1-97.

The first three sections of part I summarize PRECIS and are extremely helpful. The reader who can obtain this book is strongly urged to do so. The fourth section is of interest and supplements the *Libri* articles mentioned above.

Background Material

Black, Max. *Critical Thinking: An Introduction to Logic and Scientific Method*, 2nd ed. Englewood Cliffs, NJ: Prentice-Hall, 1952. pp. 117ff, 194-95, 198-99, 216, 281, 299-303, 439, 443.

Chomsky, Noam. *Syntactical Structures*. Janua Linguarum Nr. 4. The Hague: Mouton, 1964.

Cohen, Morris, and Ernest Nagel. *Introduction to Logic and Scientific Method*. New York: Harcourt Brace, 1934. pp. 30-41, 63, 80-81, 113-26, 234-37, 256-59.

Hodges, John C., and Mary E. Whitten. *Harbrace College Handbook*. New York: Harcourt, Brace, Jovanovich, 1977.

John, Mellie, and Pauline M. Yeates. *The New Building Better English II*. Evanston, IL: Row, Peterson, 1956.
High school level.

McKeon, Richard, ed. *The Basic Works of Aristotle.* New York: Random House, 1941. *Organon,* "Categoriae," Ch. 2, 3, 5, 7, 12, 14, 15, pp. 7-14, 19, 34-37; "De Interpretatione," Ch. 3, p. 41; "Topica," Book I, Ch. 4, p. 190, Ch. 5, pp. 191-93, Ch. 9, p. 195, Ch. 15, pp. 202-204.

PRECIS MANUAL REFERENCES

In addition to the general historical sections mentioned above, the relationships between concepts are discussed on pp. 19-27, Sections 4.1-4.14 of the *Manual.* For a glimpse of what lies ahead, the reader should also read the brief introduction to the PRECIS system on pp. 28-35, Sections 5.1 to 5.16.

REFERENCES

[1]Phyllis A. Richmond, "A Thesaurus within a Thesaurus: A Study in Ambiguity," in *Toward a Theory of Librarianship: Papers in Honor of Jesse Hauk Shera,* Conrad H. Rawski, ed. (Metuchen, NJ: Scarecrow, 1973): 268-301.

[2]Sue Sahli, "The Conceptual Framework of Thesauri: 'Cognitive processes' in ERIC [Educational Resources Information Center] and the Psychological Abstracts Information Services." Unpublished manuscript, incorporated into an ongoing dissertation, Case Western Reserve University, Cleveland, Ohio.

[3]"Natural language" is defined here as the language of the work, as opposed to the normalized, standardized, controlled language found in subject headings or thesauri. In information science usage, "natural language" is a special case of natural language in the linguistic sense; it is a subset (a writer's own personal expression) of the English language as a natural language.

[4]Audrey Taylor, "Manual Applications of PRECIS in a High School Library," in *International PRECIS Workshop, University of Maryland, October 15-17, 1976* (New York: H. W. Wilson, 1977): 157-68.

[5]By "standard" is meant those thesauri that follow either the *American National Standard, Z39.19-1974: Guidelines for Thesaurus Structure, Construction and Use* (New York: American National Standards Institute, 1974), or the *International Standard ISO 2788-1974: Documentation—Guidelines for the Establishment and Development of Monolingual Thesauri* (Geneva: International Organization for Standardization, 1974).

2
THE BACKGROUND OF PRECIS

There are two special needs for bibliographic organization and control which have become critical in the later twentieth century. These needs are, first, a better distribution system for centralized cataloging copy and, second, a new and more modern classification system.

Cataloging copy has been produced at the Library of Congress and national bibliographic organizations elsewhere as a part of the National Program for Acquisition and Cataloging. For this, two technological instruments were available: the computer, which has rapidly become an all-purpose tool, and telecommunications equipment, which permits rapid transmission of data in machine-readable form. Successful development at the Library of Congress of a methodology for producing machine-readable cataloging was speedily followed by an equally successful delivery system, the Ohio College Library Center (now OCLC, Inc.).

The second need, a New General Classification system, has not met with the same degree of accomplishment as the first. The Classification Research Group in London was able to secure funding for a major research project, with a full-time investigator, for the purpose of discovering a fundamental system upon which to base the classification of the future, but this effort was unsuccessful at reaching its goal. The research itself confirmed the insights of Aristotle with regard to classification, but did not produce the desired system.[1] Both of these responses to clearly perceived needs deserve a brief description in more detail because of their significance in the eventual development of PRECIS.

THE DEVELOPMENT OF
MACHINE-READABLE CATALOGING

A format for machine-readable cataloging (MARC) was developed at the Library of Congress in 1964, the year following issuance of the King Report.[2] This report outlined the requirements for putting records at the Library in a form suitable for computer usage. At the same time, it was recognized that the computer offered the possibility of replacing the catalog card and its distribution system with something that eventually would be less costly and more versatile. British authorities on cataloging were consulted during the experimental stages, which ran from about 1964 to 1970. Additionally, as a part of the general cooperative program of "shared cataloging" (National Program for Acquisition and Cataloging), an office was established in London in 1966 to produce records from British sources in the format used in the *National Union Catalog* produced at the Library of Congress. However, it seemed rather wasteful to change British cataloging into American format when, under cooperative methods, British librarians could do the job once, both for themselves and for North American libraries, particularly since both groups by 1968 were operating, at least theoretically, under the *Anglo-American Cataloging Rules*.[3]

In the process of developing a British version of machine-readable cataloging (U.K. MARC) for use with the *British National Bibliography* (BNB), it was decided that, in the interests of greater compatibility, the latest edition of the Dewey Decimal Classification should be adopted.[4] Up to this time, the BNB had been made with a variant of the Dewey classification, the variation partly being a necessity for chain indexing, which was the terminological subject approach to the classification. Chain indexing needs a considerable degree of accuracy in logical division, and although the Dewey system was created by logical division in theory, in practice the logic has become somewhat battered. Thus, achieving greater bibliographic compatibility between British and North American cataloging required a retrograde step in that the current version of the decimal classification was less usable for the relatively automatic indexing possible with chain procedures. Since a computer-produced subject index was desired above all, this meant finding a new method of indexing to replace the chain type.

At this point, it should be recalled that the BNB is a classified catalog. That is, an item listed in it may have as many classification numbers as necessary to cover its subject content. A user would look in the schedules of the Dewey Decimal Classification and find the exact class number of the topic desired. With this, it was possible to go directly to the same class number in the BNB for an instant bibliography on that topic. However, direct access to the Dewey schedules is not easy for the person unfamiliar with their layout. The chain index, used with BNB's own version of Dewey, was able to catch every level in a hierarchy to make a sort of rotated index based on class description. The chain index was highly satisfactory because it picked up most of the steps in the logical division process and therefore offered better chances at finding material if the user's vocabulary or logic did not fit that of the system.

Therefore, if the BNB was to appear with the eighteenth edition of Dewey, worked out in North America, a satisfactory replacement for chain indexing was urgently needed. The BNB staff had already begun to prepare for assuming the responsibility of adding all British bibliographic records to the MARC data base. This was part of an international effort to provide machine-readable cataloging at source in each country, to be shared among all nations.[5] (The international version is now called UNIMARC.)

THE CLASSIFICATION RESEARCH GROUP PROJECT

The Classification Research Group's activity had centered on a search for basic principles to underlie a new general classification system, taking into account the improvements and advances made during studies and experiments in faceted classification.[6] Faceted classification, which was originally developed by the Indian librarian, S. R. Ranganathan, and used in his Colon Classification, formed the basis for much of the research carried on by the Classification Research Group during the past 30 years. The group accepted Ranganathan's ideas, but not his implementation of them.[7] Most of the following description is based on the group's work.

Faceted classification is made by a process of analysis and synthesis. A subject is analyzed into its basic categories (facets) by asking a set of questions:

What is it? (Thing)
What are its parts? (Part)

What is it made of? (Constituent)
What properties does it have? what does it do? (Property)
What object has been acted upon? (Object, Patient)
What action has taken place? (Action)
Who or what performed the action? (Agent)

This analysis results in a collection of data called "foci," which are arranged in schedules hierarchically. Each group of foci forms a facet of the subject. The method is essentially inductive. In skeleton form, a faceted classification looks like a list of terms in schedules — a list of things in one schedule, a list of parts in another, a list of constituents in a third, properties in a fourth, and so on. But, practice produces schedules that are partitioned and not as simple as this. Categories for geographic space and chronological time, as well as auxiliary terms that may be applied to all works being analyzed (form divisions, etc.), are added. A faceted classification consists of a group of partitions for a subject, with all terms of a given type collocated. In classifying, a classifier goes to the schedules and picks out what is needed for the item being classified, putting selected class terms together in a prescribed order.

The process of analysis and synthesis may be made clearer by use of an analogy. Suppose that some old houses are being torn down and all usable parts are saved and put into separate piles. Thus there would be a pile of usable bricks, another of usable boards, one of cinder blocks, one of usable pipes, one of wires, one of window frames, and so on. A builder with a new design selects what is needed from these piles and uses it to create a new house. The new house will be different from the old houses, but its constituents will have been drawn from the piles of material from the old houses. The materials will be the same, but the design totally different. This is basically what happens with faceted classification. Instead of classes being listed in one grand schedule in some pre-coordinated order, they are made up from the terms in the various facets by a method called "post-coordination," meaning put together as the material being classified requires. The actual classification for any item is made up on the spot. In this type of classification, no one has decided in advance what the classification shall be. The chief advantages are flexibility and freedom to accommodate new subjects, particularly those derived from combinations of old subjects. Where standard classification systems fail to find a spot for interdisciplinary subjects, for example, a faceted system can manage.

Classification research showed that the following things were essential to a new system:[8]

1) An outline or some sort of a thesaurus giving a general system of categories, with a hierarchical notation (to be made by experimentation).

2) A set of tags ("operators") indicating the relationships between index terms, and set down in a predetermined filing order corresponding to the logical arrangement of the terms.

3) Rules for classifying which would identify the initial concept for subject-building.

In order to understand these essentials, it is necessary to consider their context in terms of research in indexing as well as classification research. The "outline or some sort of thesaurus" is a merging of two processes: faceted classification and current notions of the indexing process.

RESEARCH IN INDEXING

In contrast to classification research, research in indexing (here defined as word arrangement in alphabetical form) was an attempt to escape the "carved in rock" qualities of pre-coordinated classification systems such as Dewey, Library of Congress, Universal Decimal, Bliss, and others. Indexing, however, fell afoul of the ambiguities caused by multiple meanings of words. The freest coordination, any word with any other word, as used in the early Uniterms system, gave way to "bound terms." (Food fish and fish food are not the same thing and each pair must be "bound" and used as a single term.)† Gradually, experience with experimental indexing methods led to the development of thesauri. These lists of terms in alphabetical order are characterized by provisions for the presence of synonyms ("number" USE "numeral"), hierarchy in terms (BROADER TERM, NAROWER TERM) and word association (RELATED TERM). The thesaurus is a semi-classified word list and is very useful in many ways. Its terms, for example, can be post-coordinated to make class descriptions. The system is probably easier to keep up to date than any classification system, even a faceted one. It does, however, have the weakness of ambiguity if each and every word is not defined, a factor pointed out many years ago[9] and still not fully appreciated. Each class in a classification carries its family tree around with it. In contrast, almost every word has more than one definition.

COMMON GROUND FOR MARC, RESEARCH IN CLASSIFICATION, AND THE THESAURUS

Faceted classification and the thesaurus both require hierarchy for convenience in building class definitions. In addition, there should be a set of tags for indicating relationships between words. When classes are made from schedules or terms selected from thesauri, it is necessary to indicate what acts on what or is acted upon by what; meaning is often dependent upon knowing this order. The mere juxtaposition of classes or terms can be totally ambiguous. The predetermined combining order used in faceted classification helps on this, but does not completely solve the problem. Therefore, tags have to be added for purposes of identification. These tags are called "role operators" to suggest their operational characteristics and the function they perform. Thus there are role operators to indicate dependent elements:

part of

property of

member of a group, aggregate or collection

and there are operators to define roles (for linking concepts), to show coordination of two or more things taken together, to define a key system, and so on.

All systems have rules for classifying, whether written, as in the case of the Dewey Decimal Classification, or largely learned through experience, as with the

---

†A thesaurus "term" may consist of one or more words. In this book, the capitalized word "Term" is used in the specific sense of one or more words describing a concept. In this sense, Term, as used throughout this book, is a direct adoption of thesaurus usage.

Library of Congress Classification. In a faceted system or its equivalent, role operators called "facet indicators" are applied according to five general rules for analysis:[10]

1) Analyze a compound subject into its component parts, using the set of questions given earlier, but omitting any that do not apply. Terms usually are given in the plural, except in cases where the singular is conventional in indexing (steel, water, air) or where the meaning may change with number (glass, glasses).

Example

Repairing necks of broken glass bottles with epoxy cement

Questions: What is it? bottles
                         What are its parts? necks
                         What is it made of? glass
                         What properties does it have? broken
                         What object has been acted upon? [the pieces]
                         What action has taken place? repair
                         Who or what performed the action? epoxy cement

The answers to the questions are lined up in Vickery's "Standard Order,"[11] resulting in the following rough outline:

THING — PART — CONSTITUENT — PROPERTY — OBJECTS —
bottles   necks   glass   broken   [the pieces]†

            ACTION — AGENT
            repair   epoxy cement

The faceting process allows great latitude in making a class number to fit the subject — any subject — but the standard order sometimes must be modified to suit particular subjects or disciplines. Ranganathan, in his Colon Classification, used a different formula for each of his main classes.[12] In specialized schedules, such as those developed by members of the Classification Research Group,[13] the *thing* category would have to be modified in its schedules to permit indication of *kinds* of things, e.g., beer bottles, milk bottles, pill bottles, perfume bottles, carboys, and the like.

2) Look up each component in the schedules of the faceted system being used and get its class number. In the example above, a number like this might result:

THING — PART — CONSTITUENT — PROPERTY —
 22   4   568   470

            ACTION — AGENT
            3864   102

Put together, they might look like this:

22.4.568.470.3864.102

---

†Since the broken bottle's pieces are the direct object of the action, they are listed here. However, normally one speaks of repairing bottles, with "pieces" being understood.

The parts of the number are separated here by decimal points, but where schedules use numerals and letters repetitively, a facet indicator (role operator to tell which facet is which) is necessary before each facet other than the first. These indicators are often tagged with punctuation marks:

   . indicates what follows is a part
   @ indicates what follows is a constituent
   # indicates what follows is a property
   $ indicates what follows is an action
   %indicates what follows is an agent

This example, redone with facet indicators, is given below in three forms: numeric notation, alphabetical notation, and mixed notation. The "schedules" from which they were taken are purely imaginary in each case, but the subject represented by coding in each facet is presumed to be the same one (*see* Figure 1).

Figure 1
Some Types of Notations for Faceted Classifications

	Thing	Part	Constituent	Property	Action	Agent
(numerals)	22	.4	@568	#470	$3864	%102
(letters)	Xz	.A4	@tsb	#eTn	$KloR	%DsV
(mixed)	X22	.4	@5C7	#84p	$A6798	%34

These notational parts *can* all be run together, but if people rather than machines will be using them, they should be separated. The point here is that the tag or operator that identifies each part is independent of the notation for the individual items *within* each part. The notion of a facet indicator obviously has a common feature with the tag for an element in a string. From such a class number above, one would know that @ indicates a CONSTITUENT is to follow, # foretells PROPERTY, $ shows an ACTION is next, and % means that the following facet represents an AGENT. The *whole*, THING, is separated from its PART by a decimal. There are many different versions of faceted classifications. The above is by no means the only one.

   3) The principal component would be determined by the rules for classifying. At this point the types of faceted classification based on the Ranganathan model and the experimental types developed by the Classification Research Group begin to be less important. The "principal component" is not necessarily the term that librarians may consider to be the most important. Instead of a subjective decision as to what is important, the rules for classifying have been changed. The classifier looks for the action, meaning the verb or verb phrase. In the example, the action is *repairing*. To get the principal component, one asks:

"Repairing what?" (At least this is possible in cases where a transitive verb is present.) The "what" is the bottle, and so "bottle" is the principal component.

4) After the principal component is found, the roles of the other components are ascertained, and each subsequent component is tagged with a facet indicator for identification purposes.

5) Finally, the whole group of terms is listed in an order based on the tags. In the example given, the string begins with the object of the action, with such descriptive matter as is needed, followed by the action and its agent:

bottles (principal component, key system, object)
(.)   necks
(@) glass
(#) broken
($) repairing
(%) epoxy cement

The value of the facet indicators starts with the principal component and rises through .,#, and $ to %, the highest. These are equivalent to 1,2,3,4,5,6 or a,b,c,d,e,f. For a faceted classification, the role of the facet indicator is a major one. It is a code for indicating what each facet is, and at the same time it is used in a specific sequence so that one knows where this facet stands in relation to other facets above or below, for ordinal purposes.

THE PROBLEM OF MEANING (SEMANTICS)

With this type of classification, it is possible to define all the parts of a class number and get them into a standard order, but it is not possible to show exactly what effect one has upon another. Saying that "this comes before that" is not the same as saying "this acts upon that" or "this is acted upon by that." Even in a faceted classification with term order carefully delineated, ambiguity is possible because the prescribed order does not necessarily define relationships exactly.

The faceted classification string is a very telegraphic type of representation of the subject analysis of a document. The same thing is true for post-coordinate indexing with multiple terms selected from a thesaurus. The problem of meaning has been a very difficult one for indexers, particularly those who are trying to develop systems of automatic indexing from various kinds of texts,[14] or who want to combine individual index terms (descriptors) by logical means such as Boolean algebra. This algebra has turned out to be indispensible for putting together integrated circuits for the components of a computer.

In the electronic situation, meaning has only two states, 0 and 1 (on-off, high-low, positive-negative, true-false). Words are not so cooperative. Most have multiple meanings, and even the most lucid ones can change their semantic content by virtue of their context. The subject analyst, therefore, has a serious problem in fulfilling the obligation to be unambiguous. This applies whether classification or indexing is involved, but it is a much more serious problem in indexing because words do not have a visible family tree structure to carry them. A *class* description is made up of words, but these stand in some kind of a schedule, even in faceted classifications. Index terms, however, are usually presented in alphabetical order. Thesauri may have appendixes that show hierarchies of terms, to assist in establishing meaning, but the main part of the thesaurus follows the index pattern, from A to Z.

Words themselves have to be defined in some way, and their relationships with other words help in the definition. There are many ways of studying words and their usage. The science of linguistics is most valuable in this respect. Serious research in indexing has brought with it the necessity for attention to linguistics.

THE ROLE OF LINGUISTICS

Classification and indexing research were the major but not the only factors leading to the development of PRECIS. Another factor was linguistics. This is the factor governing how the language is put together, and it is based on the principle of context dependency. If I say, "The ..." the listener waits for the word following. If I say, "the dog ..." and pause, the listener, depending on my tone of voice, either looks around to see if he is about to be bitten or waits for more words. If I say, "The dog bit ..." he continues to wait for the next term because what I have said so far does not convey much in the line of a message. If I say, "The dog bit the mailman and ..." he has received some information but knows that more is coming. Finally, if I say, "The dog bit the mailman and the mailman hit him with the mailbag causing letters to be scattered all over the lawn," he has received the full message, but the message was not complete until the last word had been spoken. In delivering this message, I also have several methods of expressing it. I could have said, "The lawn was all covered with letters because the dog bit the mailman, who then hit him with the mailbag," or "the mailman was bitten by the dog. He hit him with the mailbag and letters fell out all over the lawn," or "The lawn was covered with letters because the dog was hit by the mailbag after he bit the mailman."

This message, however relayed, conveys four actions that take place consecutively:

> The dog bit the mailman.
> The mailman hit the dog with the mailbag.
> (The force of hitting with) the mailbag released the letters.
> (Force of gravity) scattered the letters across the lawn.

Somehow the sequence of actions, which are each dependent upon the previous one, has to be maintained in describing what happened. The four ways in which the event was described are not the only ones that could be used, but they are sufficient to show two things. First, there is more than one syntactical method of conveying the same message. And, second, in some cases the whole of the action is not expressed, but parts of it are understood by the hearer because the context permits filling in details from everyday experience. Causing letters to be scattered all over the lawn assumes familiarity with observational experience of the laws of gravity, force, scattering, and such. And " ... covered with letters because ..." makes the same assumption. The parenthetical parts of the third and fourth statements explicitly say what caused the actions. Parentheses are used because in normal speech one would tend to say, "The letters fell out of the mailbag and were scattered across the lawn." In all, there are at least ten possibilities:

Active Voice	**Passive Voice**
The dog bit the mailman.	The mailman was bitten by the dog.
The mailman hit the dog with his mailbag.	The dog was hit by the mailman with his mailbag.
The mailbag hit the dog.	The dog was hit by the mailbag.
The mailbag released the letters.	The letters were released from the mailbag.
Letters covered the lawn.	The lawn was covered by letters.

At this point, all these paths to PRECIS come together in the person of Derek Austin.

THE CATALYTIC ROLE OF DEREK AUSTIN

At the time when international cooperation on the MARC format and adoption of the eighteenth edition of the Dewey Decimal Classification were under discussion, the *British National Bibliography* staff included Derek Austin, Subject Editor and later Principal Investigator for the PRECIS Project. Austin had just spent a year as special full-time investigator on the Classification Research Group's New General Classification Project. In the process of developing a replacement for chain indexing (which did not work with the eighteenth edition of Dewey because of logical inconsistencies among classes), various alternatives were examined until, in 1970, it became apparent that the approach developed during Austin's work on the project offered enough advantages to merit a serious trial. This trial period, from 1971 to 1973, showed the general strength of Austin's index as well as its weaknesses, which were corrected. By the end of 1973, the experimental period was over and the final, permanent version had been made. This was adopted for the BNB in January 1974.[15]

During the process of trying to work out a new general classification, Austin discovered that if a class description was put in the passive voice, it was easier to determine the object, action and agent. Thus a document dealing with the process of sealing leaky wooden barrels with pitch fitted Vickery's "Standard Order" better if it was in the order: barrels — wooden — leaky — sealing — pitch, which correspond to THING — CONSTITUENT — PROPERTY — ACTION — AGENT. This reversal of order was not unlike the order developed for transformational grammars.[16] Note that the passive form of the verb, which would have been "sealed [by]," has been replaced by the gerund, "sealing." Therefore, Austin began to look into linguistics, particularly those parts of the subject dealing with grammar and syntax. It is the syntax, in particular, which came to be associated with PRECIS.

In the mailman example, the following listing shows both the passive voice and the equivalent gerund:

mailman	(OBJECT)	
bitten (by)	(ACTION)	biting
dog	(AGENT)	
dog	(OBJECT)	
hit (by)	(ACTION)	hitting
mailman's bag	(AGENT)	
letters	(OBJECT)	
released (by)	(ACTION)	releasing
mailbag	(AGENT)	
lawn	(OBJECT)	
covered (by)	(ACTION)	covering
letters	(AGENT)	

Notice, however, that in each case the word "by" has had to be added to distinguish the object from the agent. This illustrates the problem mentioned earlier: the word order does not necessarily indicate actual word meaning. Though unlikely, the mailman could have bitten the dog; the dog could have hit the mailman's bag. The letters could not have released the mailbag, but, given time, the lawn could have overgrown the letters. The principle of context dependency by itself would not necessarily solve the problem any more than predetermined word order, but when combined with the notion of syntactical structure and the passive voice, as developed in transformational grammars, and making use of "function words" for clarity, a string of terms could be set down in a relatively unambiguous form for indexing purposes.

Thus the path to PRECIS led from classification research, which produced a tagged word order for faceted systems, to the underlying principles of structural grammars. In PRECIS, as will become apparent, the initial *analysis* is both syntactical and classificatory while the initial *activity* (string writing) is primarily syntactical. The backup files are almost purely classification, and hierarchical at that. The results are an index with the following features:[17]

- Each entry expresses all of a compound subject.
- Each entry is specific enough to be assigned to its "most obviously correct place" in any classification scheme.
- Each entry may be made by computer, using the indexer's coded strings.
- Each entry is reasonably unambiguous to the normal reader.
- Each entry has a necessary and sufficient backup component in the form of adequate cross-references.
- Each entry's meaning should not have been distorted in the course of computer manipulation.

THE PRECIS FORMAT

In PRECIS there are two main kinds of relationships between concepts. These are:

SYNTACTICAL — relations between terms which, taken together, express the subject matter of a document.

SEMANTIC — relations between terms in index entries and other, unstated terms. For example, "computer systems" implies data processing; "kangaroos" implies marsupials. (There are also semantic relationships between some words in strings.)

The syntactical relationships appear in PRECIS index entries:[18]

East Lancashire†
Environment planning. Structure plans. Plan making.

Guinea pigs
Colour. Genetic factors.

Mathematics
Understanding by students. Influence of intellectual
development

Tribal societies.   Africa south of the Sahara
Influence of Western civilization, *to 1974 — Study regions:
Angola, Dahomey & Lesotho*

The semantic relationships appear in the cross-references:[19]

1)   Equivalence relationships (synonyms, near-synonyms, and, rarely, antonyms)

Algorisms *See* **Algorithms**

Disturbed *See* **Maladjusted**

2)   Hierarchical relationships (generic, whole/part)

Dogs
See also
Beagles
Greyhounds
Labradors
Terriers

Recreation land
See also
Golf courses
Playgrounds
Race courses [Race tracks]
Wildlife parks

---

†An explanation of spacing used in PRECIS entries and cross-references may be found in Appendix B.

3) Associative relationships (mentally associated, one term entails or explains another)

Intellectual development
See also
Cognitive development

Travel
See also
Books on travel

Eating
See also
Feeding

The "see" or equivalence function in the PRECIS reference system is not unusual. The other two relationships, however, bear explanation. **Dogs** *See also* (kinds of dogs) is a broader Term to narrower Term solution for a generic relationship. Higher Terms, such as the one covering dogs, wolves, and foxes, would also have a *See also* leading to **Dogs**. The PRECIS reference structure has a tagging system that is used to attach the lower Term to the next higher. This appears in the *tracing* on the file cards:

Zoology $o **Biology**

The tag, ($o) creates the reference:

Biology
See also
Zoology

These tags appear to go from the top down as in any deductive system, but because the reference system is built inductively from the bottom up, the lower-to-higher method is used in the tracing.

Associative relationship references are the equivalent of RT (related term) in modern thesauri. In PRECIS, as in subject headings, *See also* is used for hierarchical and associative relationships alike. (Please recall that in this book Term with a capital T means one element or line of a string, whether one or many words are in it. An uncapitalized "term" is a generic form or synonym for "word(s).")

THE SUBJECT INDEX ITSELF

A PRECIS-made index is usually used in a two-stage system. That is, the subject index is separated from full descriptive detail. All subject terms lead into the descriptive catalog (or list) by means of a call or class number. This is in contrast to a card catalog where the full descriptive data are on unit cards. Entries for subject, editors, and so on are typed in the space at the top of the card, and these are filed alphabetically. The user of the card catalog gets all the descriptive data plus the class or call number in one step when looking up the subject. The user's time is saved by repeating the data at each possible entry point. All this information is available whether the user wants it or not.

With the computer-produced book catalog, bibliography, or finding list, a record system is made so that full data are given only at one point and other entries lead into that point. When more storage space becomes available and an on-line time-sharing system is used, the user, in dialog with the machine, may select the amount of data needed. With on-line terminals, one may expect the two stages described above to be merged into one. Eventually, the state of the art will permit this to be done at a fraction of its present cost.

SUMMARY

In summary, PRECIS is a syntactical-semantic system which was developed out of the necessity for a new subject index to the *British National Bibliography*. It was strongly influenced by research in classification and indexing, with an added application of linguistics. What had been an either-this-or-that situation in subject analysis became a *both* situation. The combination added the *meaning* aspect from modern classification with its built-in family trees to syntax as represented in structural grammar. The resultant mix has produced an index with content dependency features, which resolve much of the ambiguity found in less sophisticated systems. In the chapter following, description of the actual process of indexing with PRECIS will begin.

PRECIS MANUAL REFERENCES

The historical account of the development of the system is briefly covered in the "Foreword," by A. J. Wells, pp. iii-v, and on pp. 11-13 of the text. The journal articles mentioned in chapter 1 of the *Manual* also include historical information. The most detailed is in Austin's article, "The Development of PRECIS: A Theoretical and Technical History," *Journal of Documentation*, v. 30, no. 1 (March 1974), pp. 53-84. Historical notes in the *Libri* articles may be found in the beginning sections of parts I and III. There was a running barrage of letters to the editor of the *Journal of Documentation* in 1975-76. These are amusing, but not particularly enlightening.

REFERENCES

[1]Thomas V. Sullivan, a classicist and librarian at Freiberger Library, Case Western Reserve University, notes that "Even in PRECIS, for example, the notion and use of *role operators* may be compared to a type of form shaping the matter examined into certain patterns. The use of such terms as *object of transitive action, agent of transitive action, action/effect, agent of intransitive action, aspect, target/form, part/property,* etc. [is] distinctly Aristotelian in description and idea." (unpublished paper)

[2]Gilbert W. King et al., *Automation and the Library of Congress* (Washington: Library of Congress, 1963).

[3]William S. Budington, "Access to Information," *Advances in Librarianship* 2 (New York: Seminar Press, 1971): 60-71; Barbara Schrader and Elaine Orsini, "British, French and Australian Publications in the National Union Catalog: A Study of NPAC's Effectiveness," *Library Resources & Technical Services* 15 (Summer 1971): 345-53.

[4]Derek Austin, "The Development of PRECIS: A Theoretical and Technical History," *Journal of Documentation* 30 (March 1974): 64-65.

[5]Austin, "Development of PRECIS," pp. 63-66.

[6]Austin, "Development of PRECIS," pp. 70-71.

[7]Classification Research Group, "The Need for a Faceted Classification as the Basis of All Methods of Information Retrieval," *Library Association Record* 57 (1955): 262-68. Papers of the group are listed in issues of the group's *Bulletin* published in the *Journal of Documentation* 12 (Dec. 1956): 227-30; 14 (Sept. 1958): 136-43; 15 (March 1959): 39-57; 17 (Sept. 1961): 156-72; 18 (June 1962): 65-88; 20 (Sept. 1964): 146-69; 24 (Dec. 1968): 273-98; 29 (March 1973): 51-71; 34 (March 1978): 21-50; International Study Conference on Classification for Information Retrieval, *Proceedings of the International Study Conference on Classification for Information Retrieval Held at Beatrice Webb House, Dorking, England, 13th-17th May 1957* (London: ASLIB, 1957).

[8]Austin, "Development of PRECIS," p. 62.

[9]Calvin Mooers, "The Indexing Language of an Information Retrieval System," *Information Retrieval Today: Papers Presented at the Institute Conducted by the Library School and the Center of Continuation Study, University of Minnesota, September 19-22, 1963*, Wesley Simonton, ed. (Minneapolis, MN: Center for Continuation Study, University of Minnesota, 1963): 34.

[10]Austin, "Development of PRECIS," p. 62.

[11]Brian C. Vickery, *Information Systems* (London: Butterworths, 1973): 104-106; and his *Techniques of Information Retrieval* (Hamden, CT: Archon Books, 1970): 110, 115-16.

[12]S. R. Ranganathan, *Colon Classification*, 6th ed. (New York: Asia Publishing House, 1960).

[13]Quite a number of publications and sample faceted classification systems were made during the 1950-1965 period by members of the Classification Research Group. Samples may be found through the group's *Bulletin* (see reference 7 above). "How to" instructions are in Brian Vickory's *Faceted Classification: A Guide to Construction and Use of Special Schemes* (London: ASLIB, 1960). A second edition is available, but is not much different from the first. Another source is Douglas J. Foskett, "The Construction of a Faceted

Classification for a Special Subject." In *Proceedings of the International Conference on Scientific Information, Washington, D.C. November 16-21, 1958* (Washington: National Academy of Sciences—National Research Council, 1959), v. 2: 867-88.

[14]Karen Sparck Jones, "Automatic Indexing," *Journal of Documentation* 30 (Dec. 1974): 393-432. Another publication covered earlier material in detail: Mary Elizabeth Stevens, *Automatic Indexing: A State-of-the-Art Report*, National Bureau of Standards Monograph 91 (Washington: GPO, 1965).

[15]Austin, "Development of PRECIS," pp. 71, 77-78, 96.

[16]Noam Chomsky, *Syntactic Structures*, Janua Linguarum Nr. 4 (The Hague: Mouton, 1964).

[17]Derek Austin, *PRECIS: A Manual of Concept Analysis and Subject Indexing* (London: Council of the British National Bibliography, 1974): 11-12. (Freely paraphrased, with additions).

[18]Taken from the *British National Bibliography, Interim Cumulation* (London: British Library, 1975): May-Aug. 1975. Reproduced courtesy of the Bibliographic Services Division, The British Library, London, England.

[19]*British National Bibliography.*

3
SUBJECT ANALYSIS:
The Title-Like Phrase

THE NATURAL LANGUAGE OF PRECIS

In most subject analysis processes, the purpose is to condense the subject matter of the work or item and extract a terse, concise statement of its subject content. For this purpose, the classifier or indexer† will examine the formal parts of a work — the title, table of contents, preface — and may skim through the text or other content to get a general notion of the subject and its presentation. The illustrations and tables are often helpful, as may be appendixes and bibliographies. The intellectual level is usually not too difficult to ascertain, although for purposes of indexing or classification, one is mostly concerned with whether it is material for adult or juvenile use. The subject indexer is neutral with regard to the material being indexed and avoids any critical assessment of it. The job is to present the subject in concise form, to distill its essence into a few words, which will enable its subject matter to be understood by the potential user of the index.

In general, for information retrieval purposes, there are two main kinds of indexing. The first uses the exact wording of the text being indexed. In such cases, where the document's language is used exactly, it is called "natural language." This language may not be natural to the indexer, but it is natural to the text. The second kind of indexing occurs when the terms to be used by the indexer must be taken from a prescribed list. Here the language is called "controlled." The purpose of a controlled language or vocabulary is to assure that the same subject is described in exactly the same words every time it appears. When the language is replaced or incremented by terms not used in the text or taken from a list, it is neither natural nor controlled, and should be regarded as new text. To some extent, PRECIS fits this latter pattern.

The index terms in a Keyword-In-Context (KWIC) or Keyword-Out-of-Context (KWOC) entry are in natural language. Library of Congress subject headings are a controlled vocabulary. Some thesauri are a mixture of the two. The terms in such thesauri are controlled, but new terms may be added, provided they follow the rules of the standard for thesaurus-making.[1] In many cases, the controlled or prescribed terms will coincide with those used in the title or table of contents and no problem arises. Problems appear when an existing term is being used with a new meaning or when one meets colloquialisms or equivalents.

The indexer is free to use any dictionaries, encyclopedias, or other bibliographic tools in ascertaining the proper subject for an item. Where general indexing of all subjects is being done, as in an academic or public library or for a national bibliography, the indexer needs the broadest possible background of knowledge. No subject is useless; no bit of information is wasted. Not only are

---

†"Indexer" is used here in the sense of a person making an analytical form of subject listing, not the type of indexer who collects terms from the text and uses them to make a back-of-the-book index.

formal qualifications important, but also incidental knowledge acquired through hobbies or pastimes. Even in situations where the indexer is supposedly covering only one subject, related information may turn out to be extremely interesting. The indexer whose breadth of interests approaches those of the fabled "Renaissance man," with considerable depth in some areas as well, is a most valuable person. For general indexing, as for general classification, there is no such thing as too much knowledge. Even if the breadth is shallow to start, continuing in this type of work will deepen it, provided the indexer is reasonably intelligent and ambitious enough to want to do a better job.

PRECIS requires breadth of knowledge. Natural language may be used when a subject is new, such as the case of training films in which a new technique is described. Controlled language is used where the subject is already in the system and where no change in meaning or context is involved. The major difference with PRECIS is the linguistic or *context*-dependent feature, which requires entries to be written in string format. This will be discussed in the next chapter. The present chapter will include a brief introduction to the process of subject analysis, followed by more detailed explanations of the title-like phrase from which strings are derived. Examples of various kinds of written records shall serve as sources.

SUBJECT ANALYSIS

Subject analysis should not be confused with descriptive analysis (descriptive cataloging). Subject analysis covers the content of the item, what it is *about*. Descriptive analysis covers choice and form of entry words and the physical attributes of the item (a description of what it looks like) and is used to locate or identify the specific item. For books and other materials going into library collections, this description may be the standard *Anglo-American Cataloguing Rules*, second edition (AACR2).[2] For non-book materials, AACR2 is supposed to be the standard, although several other usable ones exist.[3] For rare books[4] or for archival materials,[5] there are certain descriptive methods that are customarily followed. Although the physical description may differ according to the rules followed or the format of the material or both, the *subject matter* of all of them can be described with PRECIS. If the subject content can be described in words, the item can be indexed with PRECIS. So far, no one appears to have tried PRECIS for museum objects; nevertheless, even these may be amenable to such indexing.

In developing a series of examples of title-like phrases to illustrate this aspect of PRECIS, pamphlets, paperbacks, assembly manuals, and other materials will be used, because these are normally harder to handle than books, serials, music, maps, films, or other items that fit clearly into one genre or other.

WRITING THE TITLE-LIKE PHRASE

The title-like phrase is absolutely vital. The content of the item being indexed must be expressed faithfully. Concepts and their relationships should be given clearly and as the author apparently intended. Of necessity, this part of the process is somewhat subjective. Though attempts are being made to index automatically, in the interests of greater objectivity, so far these have not been particularly impressive and reliance upon the human indexer still is necessary. In the examples to be used in illustration here, greater detail will be used than might appear necessary, but this is done to indicate what should be considered during the process of formulating statements. The responsibility of the indexer in the process cannot be overestimated. The analytic process may go through the head of the experienced indexer like greased lightning, but here it is slowed down so that various pros and cons may be discussed. The normal indexer arrives at the outcome by what is almost a Gestalt (aha!) process. Actually, it is a form of induction whereby clues are put together in the human brain and the answer is drawn from them unconsciously, based on all previous learning and reasoning. The cognitive processes involved are of great interest to psychologists and educators in particular.

Three examples will be used. The first is a pamphlet, the second a paperback book, and the third a paperback printed entirely by computer. In each case, enough detail will be given to arrive at one or more title-like statements describing the content. Following these three, some equipment leaflets will be used to describe a type of material normally difficult to fit into standard indexes.

EXAMPLES

1) **Pamphlet**: *How to Buy a House* [by] the Editors of the Family Handyman Magazine. New York: Universal Publishing and Distributing Corporation, 1969. 62p.

Chapter headings:

1. How this book will help you choose your home wisely.
2. The exterior
3. The interior
4. The basement
5. The attic
6. The plumbing system
7. The utilities — electricity and gas
8. Heating
9. Insulation
10. Fixtures and appliances
11. Is it a buy? [neighborhood, price, rating]
12. The business of buying
13. Cooperatives and condominiums
    Glossary
    Master checklist

This pamphlet is illustrated with diagrams to show the prospective buyer the appearance of things to look at, such as the basic framing structure, flooring, insulation, leaks, termites.

The title-like phrase would be reached by running (mentally) through a few possibilities until a suitable one appeared:

> Physical characteristics of houses
>
> Examination of a house for defects in structural details
>
> Informed house buying

All but three chapters are on the physical characteristics of a house and how to recognize them. The main thrust of the pamphlet is on acquiring sufficient data to be able to make an informed decision about buying a house. The above phrases describe the pamphlet, but the title would preclude the last phrase. The first phrase is a possibility but does not seem specific enough for this case. It could just as well cover an architectural or historical account of houses of different composition through the ages. The second phrase seems more promising, but the emphasis on defects is not warranted. In the process of reaching a decision, the potential buyer will be weighing the assets against the defects. Also, what is a defect to one person (other than things like water in the basement or termites) may be an asset to another. Therefore, a more neutral phrase seems in order:

> Examination of houses in terms of their physical soundness
> and structural stability; for the prospective buyer

This would cover all the parts of the book except those involving taste and economics, which actually are very important but not something that can be rated like the roof or the plumbing. In this case, the title page gave the purpose of the book from a very practical point of view. Not all titles are as helpful. Note that the last part of the statement had to be added because index words will be separated from the title and one has to indicate that the pamphlet is for the buyer, not the seller or appraiser.

2) **Paperback** (30 x 21-1/2 cm.): *The World of M. C. Escher.* With texts by M. C. Escher, J. L. Locher. New Concise NAL Edition. New York: Harry N. Abrams, Inc. Distributed by New American Library, 1974. 151p.

This work has no table of contents, but it consists of

> J. L. Locher, "The Work of M. C. Escher," p. 5-14 — describing the content.
>
> M. C. Escher, "Approaches to Infinity," p. 15-16 — indicating what he was trying to do.
>
> "The plates," p. 16 — one paragraph on sequence, content, ownership and availability. 184 plates, 8 in color.
> (Plate #5 is also on the cover)

Obviously, since this is about the work of an artist, the index made with PRECIS will have an entry under his name:

> Escher, Maurits Cornelis, 1898-1972.

Escher was a Dutch artist who specialized in drawings of a very distinctive type. The indexer can read Locher's description in a very short time and probably would be well advised to do so. Locher uses the term "graphic" to describe the media in which Escher worked. The indexer, therefore, would follow this lead and consider as an entry:

Graphic arts

or more specific forms of graphic art if the paperback was being added to a special collection on art. In most indexing, the degree of specificity of index terms depends, in part, on the type of collection into which the item is to be fitted. If this work were to go into a small public library, the above term with a qualifying addition might suffice:

Graphic arts — Dutch drawings in the 20th century

In an art collection, however, more would be needed, such as an entry under each of the media in which Escher worked. The format of most of Escher's drawings was the print; he made woodcuts, lithographs, wood engravings, a few stencils, and mezzotints. This paperback also includes reproductions of drawings made in pencil and watercolor, India ink, and even crayons. At the least, therefore, one would expect the title-like phrase to be something like this:

Drawings of the Dutch artist, Maurits Cornelis Escher

Prints of the Dutch artist, Maurits Cornelis Escher

Again, depending on the collection, the specificity of the index entry would depend on the degree to which the hierarchy was broken down:

Graphic arts
    Drawings
    Engravings
      Prints
        Woodcuts
        Lithographs

In a collection of prints, for example, the phrase leading to the entry would be in the nature of:

Wood engravings of the Dutch artist, Maurits Cornelis Escher

Although in PRECIS the number of permissible phrases is four, it still would be advisable to give several formats in one entry where possible:

Drawings, engravings, and prints of the Dutch artist, Maurits
Cornelis Escher

Aside from his technical competence as an artist, interest in Escher's work also is a result of his artistic rendering of the mathematical technique called "tiling the plane."[6] He often used real or imaginary zoological creatures, some of which were exquisitely drawn. An art library might want an entry under "mathematical techniques" to add to its other entries under specific techniques. A mathematical library purchasing this paperback might require an entry under:

The mathematical technique of tiling the plane

Another type of publication is the non-commercially printed specialist work. This kind of book usually is issued in paperback, but unlike the items above, it is done in offset or equivalent from a computer-printed manuscript, in upper- and lower-case type.

3) **Computer-produced manuscript "printed" on Xerox-9700 machine**: *Speakeasy Manual: The Speakeasy III Reference Manual*. Level Nu, OS/VS version, by Stanley Cohen and Stephen Pieper. Chicago: Speakeasy Computing Corporation, 1979. 269 p.

This book is a manual for users of an advanced computer language called "Speakeasy." It includes explicit directions on how to use this computer language plus a detailed description of the routines available for use in it. The title-like phrase is much simpler than either of the preceding examples:

Programming languages for digital computer systems, Speakeasy, level Nu

The level has been added because in this area, users generally need the latest version. Since this is a reference manual, a form division for that should also be a part of the string, yielding:

Programming languages for digital computer systems, Speakeasy, level Nu
— Manuals

As a rule, the shortest title-like phrase that covers the content of the work is preferred. One can analyze to great depth, but usually this is only needed if the topic itself is very complex. In later chapters, some of these complex types will be discussed in explaining the PRECIS techniques developed to handle them.

Turning to another kind of title-like phrase, three examples will be used, this time of a type of material that is very hard to index by most methods other than PRECIS. This ephemeral material includes equipment manuals, assembly manuals, manufacturers' catalogs, how-to-do-it sheets, and equipment specification sheets. These and their equivalents in nontechnical collections are either single sheets, throw-away-next-year (season, month) catalogs, or small, easy to lose leaflets. Some samples are:

4) **Assembly manuals**: "Assembly Manual for Holstrom Associates Preselector, Model SK-20, for Radios in the 3-30 mHz. Range"

This statement is fully descriptive and can be used as is.

5) **Manufacturers' catalogs**: "Miniature Strip Chart Recorders — Rustrak"

The statement is made up from the content of the catalog in this case. Presumably the company name would be sought.

6) **Practical information**: "Tips on Using Field-Effect Transistors — Motorola Semiconductor Products"

There is more than meets the eye in this case: applications have to apply to something — in this case, electronic circuits.

In the above examples, the name of the manufacturer may be needed as an access point in some collections, such as those in an industrial laboratory or an engineering school.

Almost identical types of ephemeral literature exist for gardening and planting and for woodworking and many other crafts. With gardening, for example, there would be nursery or seed catalogs; planting, watering, and feeding directions; highly specialized instructions for particular items such as bonsai trees, lilies, roses, dahlias, African violets, and so on; equipment; tools; and even the equivalent of specification sheets.

While the experienced indexer undoubtedly does most of this process unconsciously, it is recommended that beginners write down the analysis. Before discussing this analytic process in greater detail, it is necessary to mention those aspects of PRECIS which are derived from language usage, especially grammar and syntax.

LANGUAGE AND THE LINGUISTIC FEATURES OF PRECIS

The Passive Voice

The title-like phrases given above are written in a telegraphic style, with great economy in wording that still conveys as much information as is desirable. One feature of PRECIS, which undoubtedly was influenced by the research on faceted classification carried on by members of the Classification Research Group, was the combining order of terms.[7] As mentioned in the previous chapter, in an interactive situation such as "the dog bit the mailman," the telegraphic form:

dog bit mailman

was found to index (and classify) in a more satisfactory manner if written in the passive rather than the active voice:

mailman bitten (by) dog

A sentence in the active voice is written as subject and predicate (with the predicate containing the verb and its object)

(the dog) (bit the mailman)
subject   predicate

In the passive voice, without losing the meaning of the statement, the *object* (grammatical) would be the focus of the action (its recipient). This becomes the "key system" in PRECIS. Emphasis is placed on the *recipient* of the action rather than on the agent that performed the action. Thus, in indexing order, the grammatical subject becomes the logical "agent," while the grammatical object becomes the logical "key system."

The same type of order turns up in Brian Vickery's "Standard Order":

THING (product) — PART — CONSTITUENT — PROPERTY — PATIENT — ACTION — AGENT.[8]

This order, translated to fit the subject, would reduce a very complex descriptive title to manageable proportions. Something like "sealing leaky wooden barrels with pitch" would emerge from the faceted classification analysis process as

barrels — wooden — leaky — sealant — pitch

All are words that could be put directly into classification schedules or indexes. Derek Austin, in the research undertaken for the Classification Research Group, made use of similar word order to handle very complex descriptions of highly technical materials.[9] His experience finally led him to turn to linguistics in search of further justification for procedures discovered empirically. More recently, with the assistance of linguist Jutta Sorensen in particular, the value of case grammar has come to be appreciated.

Application of Case Grammar and Syntax

To a considerable degree, arrangements in PRECIS conform to case grammar. For this reason, a very short review of this grammar will be given for those readers who need a quick update. Cases in grammar, particularly in languages other than English, are helpful for distinguishing the syntax of a language. The most common examples of modern languages that use cases extensively are German and Russian. When everyone studied Latin, case grammar was much more familiar than it is now.

Case in the English language largely is restricted to personal pronouns. Words like I, me, mine, etc. are inflected, but most words are not. The table below (*see* Figure 2) shows names of cases, examples of English equivalents, and identifying questions useful for identifying cases. In using English, we tell case by word order, not by word ending, with some exceptions. When using the passive voice, as in Standard Word Order mentioned above, in English the syntax is rearranged, but the actual words retain the same spelling (except in the possessive). The contrast with inflection can be shown with personal pronouns:

Dog bit *man*	*I* hit *him*
Man bit *dog*	*He* hit *me*

Comparison with our biting dog and mailman example, shows only a change in the form of the verb plus the word "by" as indicating the change in voice. This makes English easier to index because the spelling does not have to be changed from the accusative case to the nominative when "mailman" moves from predicate in the active voice to grammatical subject (key system) in the passive voice. This advantage in indexing is a distinct disadvantage in understanding English grammar.

Figure 2
Elementary Outline of Cases, Based on Latin, but with English Interpretation

The Vocative Case has been omitted because it did not appear
likely to be used in PRECIS.

CASE	NAME	FUNCTION	EXAMPLE	IDENTIFYING QUESTIONS
Nominative	Subject	Doer of action	The cat ate the mouse	Who/What did something?
Accusative	Direct object	Recipient of action	The dog bit the man / Jane wrote a letter	Did what?
Genitive	Possessive	Possessor of some thing or quality	John's hat / Mary's temper / Its tail	Whose? What's?
Dative	Indirect object	Recipient of an indirect action	John gave the bone to the dog / Mary bought a spoon for her collection	To whom? To what? / For whom? For what?
Ablative	Instrument of action	Indication of something used in action	Mary washed her hair with detergent / Peter hit John with a baseball bat	What was done with / with what instrument?
Locative	Location (in space and time)	Place where, time when	It is in Paris / It happened in 1948	Where? When?

THE BASIC RELATIONSHIPS IN PRECIS: RULES

The basic relationships in PRECIS may be stated by three general rules:[10]

(a) *predicative relationship*: the kind or category is stated before the individual member.

(b) *possessive relationship*: the whole or possessor is stated before the part or thing possessed.

(c) *interactive relationship*: the thing affected (object) is stated before the action, and the action before the agent (subject): that is, the passive construction is preferred.

Three examples of each:

a) predicative

category:	gastropods	rodents	buildings
member:	cowries	rats	houses

b) possessive

whole:	plants	bicycles	gardens
part:	leaves	wheels	flowers

c) interactive

key system:	libraries	bridges	man
action:	administration	washouts	diseases
agent:	directors	rain	viruses

In the PRECIS *Manual,* in courses, and in some of the articles written recently, we are told emphatically that "Whatever reference is made to the object or performer [agent] of an action, this invariably means the logical, not the grammatical object or performer."[11] Later research, including discussion of deep structure in syntax and case grammar, suggests very strongly that language and logic, though not exactly going hand in hand, must have enough in common for language to convey information. If language were illogical, how could communication take place? In PRECIS, top priority goes to procedures that *ensure* that index words make sense and are unambiguous. It is the job of the indexer to retain enough of the context to achieve this aim.

The title-like phrases developed earlier in this chapter will now be rewritten in telegraphic form and then in list order as a string in preparation for identification and tagging. Strings made at this time will be in downward reading order. These strings are as yet incomplete because they do not take into account details in the rules of PRECIS necessary for exact production of satisfactory index entries. The actual rules and role operators will be defined and assigned in the next few chapters.

The first title-like phrase was:

Examination of houses in terms of their physical and structural stability: for the prospective buyer†

This can be restated in telegraphic form as:

Houses, physical soundness and structural stability, examination, for prospective buyers

In string form this would be written:

houses

physical soundness and

structural stability

examination

for prospective buyers

Note that since the pamphlet is designed to instruct a prospective buyer on how to assess the physical condition of a house, this is retained to indicate the target at which the work is aimed—the person who is considering buying a house.

The title-like phrase in the second example is a type used for artistic, literary, musical, and similar works. Entries will be called for under each genre, the country of the artist (suggesting style) and the artist's name. In cases where the date is needed, it may go either with the artist's name or with the type of art work, depending on the emphasis of the item indexed.

Drawings, engravings and prints of the Dutch artist, Maurits Cornelis Escher (1898-1972)

Graphic arts will be made a thesaurus entry, as follows:

Graphic arts
See also
    Drawings
    Engravings
    Paintings
    Prints

This is done to avoid a multiplicity of entries that would come under "Graphic arts." Separation of the various genres makes three strings out of one at this stage. Later a technique will be shown for getting the same entries from a single string. The telegraphic format and strings follow:

---

†Bold italic face type will indicate title-like phrases from this point on.

Drawings, Dutch drawings, Escher, Maurits Cornelis (1898-1972), illustrations (as a form)

        drawings   (whole)

        Dutch drawings   (part)

        Escher, Maurits Cornelis (1898-1972)

        illustrations (as a form)

Engravings, wood engravings, Dutch engravings, Escher, Maurits Cornelis (1898-1972), illustrations

        engravings

        wood engravings

        Dutch engravings

        Escher, Maurits Cornelis (1898-1972)

        illustrations

Prints, Dutch prints, Escher, Maurits Cornelis (1898-1972), illustrations

        prints

        Dutch prints

        Escher, Maurits Cornelis (1898-1972)

        illustrations

In an art library or collection, Terms like "Engravings" and "Prints" would be even further subdivided, with more cross-referencing, so that entries would be more specific, thus saving the time of the user.

The added entry for:

The mathematical technique of tiling the plane

probably would be described as:

Mathematics, geometry, techniques, tiling the plane

        mathematics

        geometry

        techniques

        tiling the plane

A mathematics library would use a thesaurus reference rather than an index entry under "mathematics":

Mathematics
> *See also*
> > **Geometry**

The third example, the *Speakeasy Manual,* converts to the telegraphic format as:

> ***Digital computer systems, programming languages, Speakeasy III, level Nu, manuals***

In string form:

> digital computer systems
>
> programming languages
>
> Speakeasy III, level Nu
>
> manuals (as form)

Note that the form of the work has been added. This is to give the reader an idea of what type of book it is. A person looking for a textbook would not want this one as a rule. The version of Speakeasy III is added because the user would want to know which version the manual covers. This would not, however, be needed as an access term.

The various operation and assembly manuals, catalogs, how-to-do-it instructions, and specification sheets would translate telegraphically and convert into strings relatively easily:

1) ***High frequency shortwave radios, preselectors, Holstrom Associates model SK-20, assembly manuals***

> high frequency shortwave radios [3-30mHz by definition]
>
> preselectors
>
> Holstrom Associates model SK-20
>
> assembly manuals (as form)

2) ***Miniature strip chart recorders, Rustrak, manufacturer's catalogs***

> miniature strip chart recorders
>
> Rustrak
>
> manufacturer's catalogs (as form)

3) *Transistors, field-effect transistors, Motorola, applications, practical information*

> transistors
>
> field-effect transistors, Motorola
>
> applications
>
> practical information (as form)

4) *Circuits, inductors, J. W. Miller Company: coils, chokes, toroids, specification sheets*

> circuits
>
> inductors, J. W. Miller Company
>
> coils
>
> chokes
>
> toroids
>
> specification sheets (as form)

In the above examples, the name of the manufacturer has been included. Depending on the needs of users, this might or might not be necessary. The indexer should know the clientele and decide accordingly.

These examples will require thesaurus references. They will have to be made so that the user will be led to kinds of field-effect transistors from the general term. Acronyms like J-FET and MOSFET will have to be taken care of. These references are made to keep the string from getting too bogged down in levels of hierarchy. Unnecessary hierarchy is avoided for very common words in any given subject area. This has to be done with some care. Too many cross-references can clutter an index unnecessarily. Too few may leave the user mystified. To make or not to make a reference is one of the finer arts of the indexer, and one of the most vital.

SUMMARY

The analysis of a document and compilation of a title-like phrase or statement begins the PRECIS indexing process. A statement may initially be somewhat vague and imprecise, but by the time the indexer has begun to think in terms of action, recipient of action, and doer of action, and has actually started to set these out in order suitable for a string, the thinking should sharpen up considerably. The end point is to be a string with tags denoting the type of information contained in each Term in the string. The tags are called "role operators" because they not only identify the various parts of the final statement, but also indicate what manipulations are to be made with Terms in the string and what the order of the final index entries is to be.

In the process of string-writing, elimination of all vagueness, imprecision, and ambiguity should be the major objective. The trick is to construct a string so well designed that its execution—the actual making of index entries—should exactly represent the analysis of the particular document being indexed. Only on very simple subjects is there much chance of success if one starts immediately to write the string, even with experience. On topics of any range or complexity, a systematic analysis of requirements and an overall design of the structure of the string should precede any attempt to write strings. The top level is the initial title-like statement and the bottom level is the complete set of index entries. The number of intervening levels depends on the complexity of the subject of the document and the skill of the indexer.

The rest of this book will supply details of the means to be used to achieve the desired results. When the string has been compiled it should be tested term by term and line by line to be sure that the resultant index entries represent an accurate analysis. At this stage the indexer should be aware of the possibility of errors in interpretation and double check to be certain that the entries are so constituted that they represent a faithful analysis of the content of the item being indexed.

The next step in the learning process is to understand the manipulation features of PRECIS and then begin the writing of tagged strings, in logical order.

PRECIS MANUAL REFERENCES

The "Introduction" to the *Manual* (pp. 1-6) discusses the process of analysis in general terms. Very little is available here or in other descriptions of PRECIS on the analytic stage, and almost no examples of the title-like phrases that must have been used. This was probably because those working with PRECIS were experienced in subject analysis from previous work as catalogers or indexers. However, since PRECIS does not function like either subject headings or ordinary indexing for lists and abstract journals, it would be advisable, at least for the first few months, to take care with the analytic process and write out the title-like statement(s) before making the strings. Such a process would also be an aid in teaching others, provided these phrases were retained for this purpose.

REFERENCES

[1] In the United States, this is: *American National Standard Z39.19-1974: Guidelines for Thesaurus Structure, Construction and Use* (New York: American National Standards Institute, 1974).

[2] *Anglo-American Cataloguing Rules.* Second Edition (Chicago: American Library Association; Ottawa: Canadian Library Association, 1978). The earlier edition and its revised parts were in use up to January 1981.

[3] Alma M. Tillin and William J. Quinly, *Standards for Cataloging Nonprint Materials: An Interpretation and Practical Application*, 4th ed. (Washington: Association for Educational Communication and Technology, 1976); Jean Riddle Weihs, Shirley Lewis, and Janet MacDonald, *Nonbook Materials: The Organization of Integrated Collections*, 2nd ed. (Ottawa: Canadian Library Association, 1979); Library Association Media Cataloguing Rules Committee,

Non-book Materials Cataloguing Rules (London: National Council for Educational Technology, 1973); John Horner, *Special Cataloguing with Particular Reference to Music, Maps, Serials and the Multimedia Computer Catalogue* (London: Clive Bingley, 1973).

[4]Ronald B. McKerrow, *An Introduction to Bibliography for Literary Students* (Oxford: Clarendon Press, 1927); A. Esdaile, *Esdaile's Manual of Bibliography*, rev. ed. by Roy Stokes (New York: Barnes & Noble, 1967); Fredson T. Bowers, *Principles of Bibliographic Description* (Princeton: Princeton University Press, 1949); Paul S. Dunkin, *How to Catalog a Rare Book*, 2nd ed. (Chicago: American Library Association, 1973).

[5]Hilary Jenkinson, *A Manual of Archival Administration*, 2nd ed. (London: Percy Lund, Humphries, 1965); Samuel Muller, J. A. Feith, and R. Fruin, *Manual for the Arrangement and Description of Archives*, 2nd ed., transl. by Arthur H. Leavitt (New York: H. W. Wilson, 1940); Theodore R. Schellenberg, *Management of Archives*, Studies in Library Science, no. 14 (New York: Columbia University Press, 1965); and his *Modern Archives: Principles & Techniques* (Chicago: University of Chicago Press, 1975).

[6]See Martin Gardner, "Mathematical Games," *Scientific American* 204 (April 1961): 171-75; 214 (April 1966): 110-21; 233 (July 1975): 112-15; 233 (August 1975): 112-14; 236 (Jan. 1977): 110-21.

[7]Classification Research Group, "The Need for a Faceted Classification as the Basis of All Methods of Information Retrieval," *Library Association Record* 57 (1955): 262-68; Papers of the members of the group as listed in the group's *Bulletin* published periodically in the *Journal of Documentation*: 12 (Dec. 1956): 227-30; 14 (Sept. 1958): 136-43; 15 (March 1959): 39-57; 17 (Sept. 1958): 156-72; 18 (June 1962): 65-88; 20 (Sept. 1964): 146-69; 24 (Dec. 1968): 273-98; 29 (March 1973): 51-71; 34 (March 1978): 21-50; International Study Conference on Classification for Information Retrieval, *Proceedings of the International Study Conference on Classification for Information Retrieval Held at Beatrice Webb House, Dorking, England, 13th-17th May 1957* (London: ASLIB, 1957); Classification Research Group, *Classification and Information Control: Papers Representing the Work of the Classification Research Group, 1960-1968*. Library Association Research Publications No. 1 (London: Library Association, 1969): 81-130.

[8]Brian C. Vickery, *Classification and Indexing in Science* (London: Butterworths Scientific Publications, 1958): 25, 33, 98, Appendix B. More recent editions of this work are available, but this first edition is still excellent; his *Techniques of Information Retrieval* (Hamden, CT: Archon Books, 1970): 110, 115-16; and his *Information Systems* (London: Butterworths, 1973): 104-106; *Faceted Classification: A Guide to Construction and Use of Special Schemes* (London: ASLIB, 1960): 30. A second edition is available, but the first is still quite adequate. An earlier analytic system of relationships may be found in James W. Perry, Allen Kent, and Madeleine M. Berry, *Machine Literature Searching* (New York: Western Reserve University Press—Interscience Publishers, 1956): 86.

[9]Classification Research Group, *Classification and Information Control*: 96-130. A number of earlier articles about various aspects of classification and

PRECIS appeared between 1969 and the "final" statement in Reference 1. These are now mainly of historical interest: Derek Austin and Peter Butcher, *PRECIS: A Rotated Subject Index System* (London: Council of the British National Bibliography, 1969); Derek Austin, "Prospects for a New General Classification," *Journal of Librarianship* 1 (July 1969): 149-69; his "Development of a New General Classification: A Progress Report," *Information Scientist* 3 (Nov. 1969): 95-115; his "Subject Retrieval in U.K. MARC." In *U.K. MARC Project: Proceedings of a Seminar on the U.K. MARC Project ... University of Southampton 28-30 March 1969* (London: Oriel Press for the Cataloguing and Indexing Group of the Library Association, 1970): 30-51; his "PRECIS Indexing," *Information Scientist* 5 (Sept. 1971): 31-51; and his "A Conceptual Approach to the Organization of Machine-held Files for Subject Retrieval." In Ottawa Conference on the Conceptual Basis of the Classification of Knowledge, October 1st-5th, 1971, *Conceptual Basis of the Classification of Knowledge*, Jerzy A. Wojciechowski, ed. (Pullach/München: Verlag Dokumentation, 1974): 371-98.

[10]Derek Austin, *PRECIS: A Manual of Concept Analysis and Subject Indexing* (London: Council of the British National Bibliography, 1974): 24.

[11]Austin, *PRECIS: A Manual*, p. 26.

4

BASIC ORDER IN PRECIS:
Standard Format

CONTEXT DEPENDENCY

Context dependency is the fundamental feature of PRECIS. That is, the order of the elements in a string of words describing a subject is arranged so that each Term is dependent upon the Term before it and sets the stage for the Term following it. Consider the following string, first represented by the letters A, B, C, D and then by actual Terms:

A >   B >   C >   D

California >   sea otters >   protection >   wardens

Each Term sets the context for the ones that follow. California, the geographic context, is the most inclusive. The sea otters are in California. The protection is for the sea otters. The wardens do the protecting. It is possible to have all kinds of index entries in this basic form. For example, "California" might be replaced by any other geographical entity, "sea otters" by any other object of action, "protection" by any other action, and the "wardens" by any other agent. The sense of the string would be different, but the format identical. Several examples are given to show this:

Canada >   caribou >   hunting >   Indians

Kenya >   elephants >   observation >   tourists

Lake Erie >   ice >   formation >   low temperatures

California >   earthquakes >   causation >   San Andreas Fault

A type of string without an agent may also be demonstrated in context-dependency form:

New York >   skyscrapers >   offices >   rentals

In this case, the relationship between "skyscrapers" and "offices" is one of the whole to the part, and the final Term expresses an action. Strings similar to this might be:

Japan ＞ electronics industries ＞ computers ＞ marketing

Kentucky ＞ folk dancing ＞ Virginia Reel ＞ photography

Cleveland ＞ peripheral metropolitan parks ＞ paths ＞ bicycling

All of these strings are a briefer restatement of title-like phrases. There can be considerable variety to the grammatical format and there is a necessary human factor involved in turning them into strings. The originals might have been something like the following:

Protection of California Sea Otters by Wardens

Indian Caribou Hunting in Canada

Observation of Elephants by Tourists in Kenya

Formation of Ice in Lake Erie by Low Temperatures

Earthquakes in California [role of] San Andreas Fault

Rental of Offices in New York Skyscrapers

Marketing in Japanese Electronics Industries: Computers

Photography of Folk Dancing in Kentucky: The Virginia Reel

Bicycling on Paths in Cleveland's Peripheral Metropolitan Parks

The important thing to notice here is, first, the "function" words: of, by, in, from, on. In the last example the possessive has been used instead of "the peripheral metropolitan parks of Cleveland." "Electronics industries: computers" has been substituted for the more descriptive "computers made by electronics industries." Second, the way a thing is said or written is not necessarily the clearest way to represent its meaning in grammatical terms. The order of spoken or written words, the omission of "understood" connections, and the varied meaning of a word in different context all cause problems in writing strings. These problems are the chief reason for the various methodologies developed in PRECIS for retaining the meaning of the original statement. For the moment, only the order of strings will be considered.

BASIC ORDER OF TERMS IN THE SHUNTING PROCESS

The production of PRECIS word order in entries is based on the

A ＞ B ＞ C ＞ D

pattern. Terms occurring earlier in the string, A and B, set the context for those occurring later in the string, such as C, while C sets the context for the next Term, D. This relationship may be diagrammed from C's point of view as:

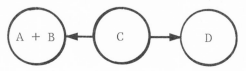

In any string with more than two Terms, those Terms between the first and the last have two-way relationships, one with the terms that precede and the other with those that follow them. This is one of those "simple, self-evident" concepts that can make all the difference in the world in understanding or not understanding. If it is not recognized, ambiguity can result.

The purpose of introducing the context-dependency feature of word order in strings in such detail is to show how meaning is retained as each Term in the string becomes the headword or first word of an index entry. The words in the string are rotated to the headword location, called the *lead position*, one at a time or grouped, as called for in the coded instructions represented by the tag called the *operator*. This rotational process is called *shunting*.

A PRECIS string of context-dependent Terms is shunted through three positions called the *lead*, the *qualifier*, and the *display*, arranged in a two line format:

The combination of *lead* and *qualifier* is called the *heading*.

By putting the string of letters representing words in vertical form and thinking of it as a string of beads, as suggested to Austin by Indian workshop participants,

when B or C start an index entry, the result physically is as if one put a finger on B or C and moved it to the left and slightly up to produce:

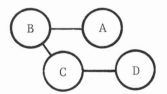 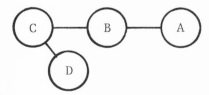

This is exactly the order of terms in the three positions, *lead, qualifier,* and *display*. The upshot is that a string that begins with A in the *lead*:

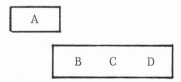

ends as a single line entry with everything in the *lead* and *qualifier* positions:

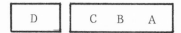

The reversal of the normal order as the various Terms in the string go, one by one, into the *lead* position is a very important feature of PRECIS and is one of the ways in which ambiguity is avoided in the process of indexing. If the string does not make the same sense in D-C-B-A order as it did in A-B-C-D order, then corrective factors have to be introduced.

This reversal and "disambiguation" feature of PRECIS is not available in other rotational indexing systems. For example, in Keyword-In-Context indexing, a title of a book, article, or report is taken as given, regardless of word order. Each significant word in turn is made a headword. The title is always given the same way as written for the context. It is assumed to be clear and to cover the contents of the work fully. In some cases it does so; in others it does not. Of course, no index can cover everything in a work. Title, abstracts, and summaries attempt to do so in varying degrees of completeness. Classification numbers try to hit the main thrust. Index entries are supposed to provide an alphabetical approach in a few selected words. PRECIS is unique in its capability for rearranging words while preserving their meaning as established by the original context.

At this point a digression will be made to explain the routine and exception-from-routine manipulation of PRECIS terms in strings. PRECIS was made for the indexer, not the indexer for PRECIS. Therefore provision has been made for:

1) excluding Terms where they are not wanted[1]
2) changing order as necessity dictates
3) adding clarifying function words as needed

Of these features that make PRECIS more flexible, only the exclusion of Terms in the process of manipulation will be covered at this point.

ROLE OPERATORS AND THEIR MANIPULATION

The standard progression of terms in a string is from *display* to *lead* to *qualifier*. The strings discussed so far have been expressed in horizontal fashion. Actually, the title-like phrase is converted to vertical order and tags called "role operators" are used as identifying markers and also as codes. These role operators are given in Figure 3 (page 62). The values for the different operators will not be discussed here. At this point it suffices to indicate that the terms in the strings are numbered from (1) to (6). These are called *main line operators*. The next group of operators are *interposed*, most generally among operators (1) to (3). The *differencing* operators are coded numerically for those used with adjectives or adjectival nouns and indicated with letters for representing other kinds of differences. The *connectives* are used mainly as function words, under prescribed circumstances. Finally, *theme interlinks* have been used when a title-like statement has two distinct themes in it. A downward-reading substitute now performs this job in some cases.

Figure 3
List of PRECIS Role Operators and Their Filing Order
This list updates the one in the *PRECIS Manual*

MAIN LINE OPERATORS

Environment of Observed System	0	Location
Observed System (Core operators)	1	Key System: Object of Transitive Action; Agent of Intransitive Action
	2	Action/Effect
	3	Agent of Intransitive Action; Aspects; Factors
Data Relating to the Observer	4	Viewpoint-as-form
Selected Instance	5	Sample population / Study region
Presentation of Data	6	Target / Form

A

INTERPOSED OPERATORS

Dependent Operators	p	Part / Property
	q	Member of Quasi-generic Group
	r	Aggregate
Concept Interlinks	s	Role Definer; Directional Property
	t	Author-attributed Association
Coordinate Concepts	f	Non-standard Coordination
	g	Standard Coordination

B

DIFFERENCING CODES

01 to 39   1st digit

	Spaced	Closed-up
Non-lead	0	1
Lead	2	3

2nd digit: Levels 1 to 9

- n   Non-lead Parenthetical Difference
- o   Lead Parenthetical Difference
- d   Date as Difference

CONNECTIVES

(Components of Linking Phrases, prefixed by $)

- v   Downward-reading Component
- w   Upward-reading Component

C

THEME INTERLINKS

- x   First Element in Coordinate Theme
- y   Second Element in Coordinate Theme
- z   Element of Common Theme

The progression in the two-line PRECIS entry is made from *display* to *lead* to *qualifier* in clockwise fashion.†

A check mark (called "tick" in the *Manual*) or an asterisk is used to indicate that a Term is wanted as a *lead*. The absence of such a mark indicates that the Term is not to be used as a *lead*. This does not mean that the Term vanishes from the string, or the index entries; it simply means that there are some words that are not needed as index entries.

THE STANDARD FORMAT

The manipulation of Terms from *display* to *lead* to *qualifier* — a clockwise rotation — is called the *Standard Format*. This format may be altered, as we shall see, by omitting Terms below the *lead*, or above the *lead*, or by using them only in the *lead*. Or substitutions may be used for situations where a different arrangement of Terms would make better sense in the *qualifier* in cases of possible ambiguity, or where a condensing or shortening of the *qualifier* would be desirable. Connectives aid in reducing ambiguity or avoid misconceptions. The basic order of operators, in turn, assures that Terms in PRECIS strings will follow a reasonable syntactic order according to preordained rules.

Examples

A few examples of indexing order should make the ordinary rotation of Terms clear. Since the tags used for operators have not yet been discussed, their content will be left blank and it is assumed that every word in the string moves automatically from the *display* to the *lead* to the *qualifier* in normal shunting order. Groups of animal names are used so that the reader can concentrate on the shunting order of the Terms and not be distracted by any semantic relationships between Terms. The Terms are given in alphabetical order in the first example and the resultant index entries noted. *Lead* terms are in bold face type. Asterisks indicate that a Term is wanted as a *lead*.

String 1:   ( )*   cat
     ( )*   chicken
     ( )*   colt
     ( )*   cow

(Example continues on page 64)

---

†The spacing is given in Appendix B. The *lead* begins at the "margin." The *display* is indented two spaces. If there are overruns, the second line of the heading (*lead* + *qualifier*) is indented 8 spaces from the margin and the second line of the *display* is indented 4 spaces from the margin. Two spaces separate the *qualifier* from the *lead*. Words in each part are separated by a single space. The word beginning each part is capitalized. Other capitalization follows normal usage.

Entries: **Cat**
　　　　　　Chicken. Colt. Cow

　　　　　　Chicken. Cat
　　　　　　Colt. Cow

　　　　　　Colt. Chicken. Cat
　　　　　　Cow

　　　　　　Cow. Colt. Chicken. Cat

Note that each of the Terms in the string became a *lead* term and then moved into the *qualifier* until there was nothing left in the *display*. The first word in each Term was capitalized and the whole Term was followed by a period. Only the first word is capitalized, unless a name is involved. This will be shown in the next string.

String 2:   ( )*   goat
　　　　　　( )   hog
　　　　　　( )*   homing pigeon
　　　　　　( )*   horse

Entries: **Goat**
　　　　　　Hog. Homing pigeon. Horse

　　　　　　Homing pigeon. Hog. Goat
　　　　　　Horse

　　　　　　Horse. Homing pigeon. Hog. Goat

In this case, the Term "hog" was not wanted as a *lead*. It was not dropped from the string, but made the rounds with it, but it never appeared in the *lead* position. The indexer decides what shall and shall not be a *lead* term, marking when Terms are wanted as *lead* and omitting to mark when they are not.

If the indexer wants a term from the string as a *lead* only, a convention (LO) is placed following the term. This causes such a term to appear in the *lead* and nowhere else. If the indexer does not want a term in the *qualifier*, it is marked (NU) – "not up." This stops its progression upwards (i.e. into the *qualifier*) from the *lead*. Similarly, if a Term is not wanted in the *display*, but is wanted in the *lead* and *qualifier*, it is marked (ND) – "not down" so that it only appears in the entries made after it has entered the *lead* position. The "lead only" and "not up" conventions are used fairly often, but the "not down" situation is relatively rare.

String 3:   ( )*   rabbit
　　　　　　( )*   rat (LO)
　　　　　　( )*   prairie dog
　　　　　　( )*   squirrel

Entries: **Rabbit**
　　　　　　Prairie dog. Squirrel

Rat.   Rabbit
Prairie dog. Squirrel

Prairie dog.   Rabbit
Squirrel

Squirrel.   Prairie dog. Rabbit

Notice that the (LO) – (lead only) – Term only appears once in the entries.

String 4:   ( )*   perch
                   ( )*   trout (NU)
                   ( )*   pike
                   ( )*   pickerel

Entries: **Perch**
              Trout. Pike. Pickerel

              Trout.   Perch
              Pike. Pickerel

              Pike.   Perch
              Pickerel

              Pickerel.   Pike. Perch

In this case, after its appearance in the *lead* position, "Trout" just disappeared. Similarly, a Term can be made to appear if for some reason it is not wanted in its normal position for the first entry.

String 5:   ( )*   deer
                   ( )*   gazelle (ND)
                   ( )*   impala
                   ( )*   moose

Entries: **Deer**
              Impala. Moose

              Gazelle.   Deer
              Impala. Moose

              Impala.   Gazelle. Deer
              Moose

              Moose.   Impala. Gazelle. Deer

In addition to these four means of varying the word order – *lead* not marked, lead only, not up, not down – there is another convention that is very convenient. This is the "substitution." Sometimes a string that reads well normally either is awkward or has a different meaning when its Terms appear in reverse order, or when a summarizing Term is desired. In this case a substitute phrase may be used.

It is coded (sub n↑) with "n" standing for how many Terms above it in the string are to be replaced. Thus (sub 4↑) would mean that the substitute is to replace four string Terms directly above the one where the (sub 4↑) occurs. The whole (sub n↑) line is ignored when reading downwards.

String 6:
     ( )* goshawks
     ( )* falcons
     ( )* harriers
  (sub 3↑)( ) hawks
     ( )* eagles
     ( )* ospreys

Entries: **Goshawks**
      Falcons. Harriers. Eagles. Ospreys

      Falcons. Goshawks
      Harriers. Eagles. Ospreys

      Harriers. Falcons. Goshawks
      Eagles. Ospreys

      Eagles. Hawks
      Ospreys

      Ospreys. Eagles. Hawks

When the Term below that designated with (sub 3↑) comes into the *lead*—in this case, "eagles"—the substitute term replaces as many terms above as indicated by the "n"—in this case, 3. With Standard Format, the (sub n↑) Term never appears in the *display*. Last, but not least, in some cases when Terms go into the *qualifier*, a function word is needed to avoid ambiguity. In a case like this a connective operator is used ($w), followed by "of, by, in, from" or whatever is needed.

String 7:
     ( )* heifers
     ( )* kids
     ( )* goats $w with
     ( )* lambs

This would give the index entries:

      Heifers
      Kids. Goats. Lambs

      Kids. Heifers
      Goats. Lambs

      Goats. Kids. Heifers
      Lambs

      Lambs. Goats with kids. Heifers

Determination of where to add a function word depends largely on the indexer's sense of the context and the possibility of ambiguity if misread. The PRECIS system provides this means of ensuring that the meaning always will be preserved in context. It supplies the connection that would make any other interpretation virtually impossible.

The strings in the last section were nonsense "sentences." Their purpose was to focus on manipulation methodology rather than on the sense of the subject matter. Normally the indexer will be concentrating on the sense of the work in hand. At times problems will come up in which it would be desirable to alter the standard order in just one aspect. Allowance for such a contingency has been built into PRECIS. The indexer is not "stuck" with an unalterable system. Figure 4 lists the special operational routines in PRECIS.

Figure 4
Special Operational Routines

These routines are used in cases where the string order required by individual role operators produces an ambiguous entry.

ROUTINE	TAG	NAME
Order-changing		
Term deleted in *qualifier*	(NU)	Not up
Term deleted in *display*	(ND)	Not down
Term in *lead* only	(LO)	Lead only
Substitutions		
Terms replaced	(sub n↓)	'n' lower Terms replaced
Terms replaced	(sub n↑)	'n' higher Terms replaced
Term deleted completely	(sub n)	'n' Terms deleted completely
Disambiguation		
Terms connected upwards	($w)	Upward-reading connective
Terms connected downwards	($v)	Downward-reading connective

MAIN LINE OPERATORS:
(0) Environment, (1) Key System, and (2) Action

A full listing of PRECIS operators was given in Figure 3 (page 62). Please note that operators numbered from zero to six are called *main line operators*. This is because they do most of the work. The others are fitted in as situations require.

The long lines, marked A,B,C are barriers between groups of operators. Barrier A indicates that operators (0), (1), (2), and (3) cannot be used after operators (4), (5), and (6). On the other hand, operators (1), (2), and (3) can be used more than once, with (1) and (2) not always in numerical order, but not one of them can ever be used after (4), (5), or (6). The *interposed operators*, as their name suggests, can readily be placed among the main line operators. *Differencing operators* have a semantic function; they are used to qualify nouns and carry their own rules and limitations, hence their placement after barrier B. Theme interlinks and the downward-reading substitute are procedural arrangements for use when two ideas are expressed in a single title-like statement. These, therefore, are placed after barrier C. The shorter barriers are for separation within the main groups. At this point, the only one that is of concern is the small barrier between operators (0) and (1). This means that the zero *must* come first and cannot be used after (1), (2), or (3) except in downward-reading substitutions.

The first three main line operators are:

Operator (0)   Represents the geographical environment or setting for the rest of the description. It is the Location involved.

Operator (1)   Represents the object of the action given or implied in the title-like phrase resulting from the subject analysis process. This is the *key system*, often referred to as "thing." It is the object of a transitive action or verb and the subject of an intransitive action or verb. Intransitive verbs have no direct object — no receiver of the action. They lack voice, being neither active nor passive.

> The rains arrived   The endangered species disappeared
>
> The train departed   The cat purred

All of these are complete intransitive verbs. Intransitive verbs needing an adverb or some other word for their completion are called linking or copulative verbs:

> The day is gloomy.
>
> Attendance was spotty.
>
> Plans are laid.
>
> The man is hungry.

For indexing purposes, adverbs can be rewritten as adjectives, although the examples here are more literary than informative to the degree needed in indexes:

> Gloomy day
>
> Spotty attendance
>
> Laid plans (as in "best laid plans")
>
> Hungry man

With intransitive verbs, since it is impossible to put the sentence in the passive voice, the subject is the key system and tagged (1). The key system in PRECIS is usually expressed as a noun, with or without more words.

Operator (2)   Represents an action itself or the effect of an action, usually expressed as a noun ("management" as the effect of "to manage") or as a verb-noun (gerund), such as "teaching."

The basic rules of PRECIS require that every string contain at least one concept introduced by operator (1) in the case of a thing, or operator (2) representing an action. All strings must start with (0), (1), or (2). The ordinal values of the numbers indicate the order in which the Terms in a string are to be used.

Examples

Operator (0)

This operator is used to introduce a place name where the relationship between the place and the concepts that follow in the string is geographical. That is, the thing or action is located in a certain spot. Place names can be used for other purposes where they represent a community involved in a political, social, or economic activity, or where a natural feature is obviously the center of attention. Then they take another role operator, (1). However, much of the time the place is merely the setting for the key system, action, and so on. Strings with place names look like this:

              d
(0)   San Francisco
(1)   airports

              d
(0)   Brazil
(1)   cathedrals

The little "d" above the place names is called a Term code. It is used as a tag to identify a geographical or political environment. The tagging includes words normally capitalized such as "Western world" or "Commonwealth countries" but not as broad a concept as "developing countries." In general, a name, as in a gazetteer or one that could be an environment, is so marked. If the geographic region is primarily the setting and not the key system, the operator (0) is used. An (0) Term may not be used as a one-line string.

Operator (1)

This operator is used for "things" when the subject consists of a single concept — physically countable things, physically non-countable things, abstract things, systems of abstract things, and systems of both physical and abstract things. The non-countable, abstract, and systems of abstract things are used in the singular form. Otherwise the plural is used. In general, this operator causes few problems. Examples are:

(1)   animals

(1)   paintings

(1)   mosquitoes

(1)   medical services

(1)   solar system

(1)   water

(1)   clouds

(1)   children

When the topic contains several syntactical roles, Terms are coded (1) if they represent the object of a transitive action or the agent of an intransitive action. This will become easier to see when some strings have been drawn up. In general, operator (1) is the most frequently used type of Term, with operator (2) following very closely behind.

Operator (2)

This operator covers all kinds of actions, as well as "phenomena" that have an action feature or component to them. As a rule, when trying to decide whether a word is an action term, putting a "to" in front of it and deriving a verb form helps to make the decision. Thus one can get "to compute" from "computation," or "to educate" from "education" or "to discuss" from "discussion." A gerund like "sailing" or "planting" is obviously an action word. There are, however, some words termed "phenomena" where the action is not quite so easy to turn into a verb. "Diseases" is such a word; or "drug therapy" or "physical analysis." Examples of "phenomena" are:

(2)   fallout†

(2)   domestic relations

(2)   baseball

(2)   local government

Sometimes two action words occur in a single statement:

(1)   children

(2)   hyperactivity

(2)   drug therapy

(1)   libraries

(2)   cataloging

(2)   evolution

---

†This kind of a word, like "input," "output," and many other neologisms, has a special meaning that is not expressed by "to fall out."

In such cases, it has been found that the second action almost always is one of three things:[2]

1) Terms indicating origin, evolution, development or some such activity on the part of the higher action term in the string

2) Terms expressing some kind of manipulation of the concepts in the earlier action: tests, experiments, measurement, research, and so forth

3) Terms expressing a change or an "interference" with the concepts higher in the string: acceleration, surgery, therapy, and such

At this point, it is necessary to introduce the rest of the Term Codes since the "d" used above is not the only one.†

TERM CODES

Four special codes are used in PRECIS for identifying different kinds of names used as index words. When the PRECIS data base is used for searching by computer, these codes serve as "fixed fields," meaning that a differentiation may be made in search requests permitting a type of name to be included or excluded from the search. Code "a" identifies topical subjects and is the most commonly used of these codes. The others, in fact, might be considered as variations from it.

In the original version of PRECIS, code "b" represented a concept called "salient focus," which, however, was never used in practice. Therefore its function has been changed, so that "b" now represents named entities that are incapable of authorship, such as buildings, monuments, paintings, bridges, and so forth.

Code "c" covers personal and corporate names. Personal names in PRECIS are given directory style (surname first). Titles of rank and other details attached to them follow the practice of the *Anglo-American Cataloguing Rules* for spacing, punctuation, and italics. Corporate bodies are tagged "c" even though the second edition of these *Rules* severely restricts their use as authors.

Code "d" represents the names of government bodies that are also geographic entities or places: countries, states, provinces, counties, cities, international organizations. Code "d" is interpreted rather broadly.

A few examples may make the function of these codes easier to grasp (*see* Figure 5, page 72). These codes serve a useful function in identifying types of entry so that the proper typographical codes, according to the *Anglo-American Cataloguing Rules* (2nd ed.), can be applied.

---

†Conventions used in this book for differentiating among different kinds of codes may be found in Appendix C.

Figure 5
Term Codes in PRECIS
Code "b" replaces an earlier, unused code for "salient focus."
[Cf. *PRECIS Manual*, p. 256]

CODE	APPLICATION	EXAMPLES
a	Any subject Term	roads cities theories cats
b	Name of something not capable of authorship	Brooklyn Bridge Mona Lisa Trafalgar Square Moonlight Sonata
c	Proper names of authors, artists, musicians, corporate bodies, government bodies—in general, names for somebody or something capable of authorship or equivalent	William Shakespeare Ludwig von Beethoven Sir Joshua Reynolds British Library Eastman Kodak Company United States. *Division of Wildlife Service* Aslib Canadian Library Association Radio Society of Great Britain American Red Cross Canada. *House of Commons* Metropolitan Museum Royal Society of Canada
d	Names of geographical places, including political entities with names that include a place component	New Haven (*CT*) Eastern Europe Strathclyde (*Scotland*) Palma (*Majorca*) Guadalajara (*Spain*)

TYPOGRAPHICAL CODES

Typographical codes are written into PRECIS strings in order to change typefonts, usually involving boldface, roman, and italic fonts. They also indicate punctuation and spacing (*see* Figure 6). If one has an entry, for example, to be used in strings, as shown below, where typefont changes are involved, this typographical code is used:

Figure 6
Typographical Codes
(*PRECIS Manual*, Sections 28.15, 33.2-33.10, 35.7, pp. 257, 330-37, 361-63.)
These codes are based on requirements of the *Anglo-American Cataloguing Rules.*

CODE	INSTRUCTIONS

$e . . . . comma, space, non-filing part in italics

$f . . . . comma, space, filing part in italics

$g . . . . no preceding punctuation, space, then roman type, or boldface if Term is in *lead*

$h . . . . period, space, filing part in italics

$i . . . . no preceding punctuation, space, filing part in italics

$j . . . . period, two spaces, then filing part in roman type

$k . . . . no preceding punctuation, space, filing part in roman type

---

(0)*   Germany $i (West)

Operator (0) in the *lead* automatically invokes boldface, while the ($i) turns "West" into italics.

Germany (*West*)

(1)*   Books on Churchill $e Sir $g Winston Spencer

produces the honorific title in italics and then returns to boldface:

Books on Churchill, *Sir* **Winston Spencer**

(2)*   World War II $i (1939-1945)

World War II (*1939-1945*)

Since the coding does not supply parentheses, these, if wanted, must be inserted in the Term in the string.

Typographical code ($f) is used in cases where personal names are accompanied by birth, death, fl. (flourished), and similar lifetime dates. In North American practice, this kind of dating is applied to all personal authors, provided it is easily obtainable at the time of cataloging. The practice has proved useful in cases of later conflict, when a new author appears with a name identical to an author already in the file.

(1)*   Davis, William Henry $f 1871-1940

Davis, William Henry, *1871-1940*

CONNECTIVES AND THEIR USE

Earlier in this chapter it was indicated that a connective could be used for overcoming ambiguity when the meaning of a Term might be ambiguous when it appeared in the qualifier. This is ($w), an upward-reading connective, upward being considered the direction from *display* to *lead* to *qualifier*. An example and its resultant entries should make this usage clear:

String: (1)*   libraries

               (2)*   catalogs $w in

               (2)*   evolution

Entries: **Libraries**
               Catalogs. Evolution

               Catalogs.   Libraries
               Evolution

               Evolution.   Catalogs in libraries

It is recommended that the connective ($w) not be overused. In most cases, the entry is perceived as ambiguous or not at the first reading — *any* entry can appear ambiguous if looked at long enough. The ($w) connective may not be used in an entry until a Term lower than the one in which it appears comes into the *lead* position. It may not begin the *qualifier*. The downward connective will be demonstrated in the next chapter.

A NOTE ON DISAMBIGUATION

"Disambiguation," which simply means "to make unambiguous," applies to the final process in string-writing. The result has to represent the subject of the document faithfully. The indexer has the responsibility of seeing that the *meaning* of the topic about which the document has been written is conveyed by the index Terms and that this meaning may not be misread or misunderstood.

The indexer's professional responsibility is involved; if the terms as expressed in the actual index entries are ambiguous or even partially ambiguous, an injustice has been done to the author of the document. The indexer has not merely failed to communicate the message, but has misrepresented it, which is far worse. The process of disambiguation, or making sure that the meaning of the author's message is preserved, is one of the most important features in PRECIS indexing.

The indexer who is limited to using words from an authorized list must try to make as close a fit as possible between what the author meant and those index terms available for use. There is a double chance for error in indexing from a list and without context. First, the individual words as used by an author may have a special twist in interpretation. This is especially true in research where new concepts are utilized and, because of lack of precise definition, have to be presented in metaphor or by reinterpretation or redefinition of old terms. The metaphor does not literally mean what it says and neither do the terms with changed meaning. The second problem relates to the first: if the indexer substitutes a term from the list, it is probably an approximation of the author's word. For an old word with a new meaning, the "nearest thing" may be another old word with another meaning. Here, the indexer is saying, in effect, that when the author writes "oranges" he means "tangerines," whereas the author actually was trying to convey the notion of "tangelos."

Furthermore, if the author does not express clearly what is meant — if the author does not write well — even the most talented indexer cannot convey meaning exactly. Perhaps the greatest single cause of controversy among intellectuals arises from the inability to express views lucidly and unambiguously. The clever indexer is the one well aware that authors make unjustified assumptions about the ability and willingness of potential readers to strive to extract the true meaning of written material. Poets are about the only people who are justified in making such an assumption.

The indexer, as interpreter, bears an all-important responsibility in helping to disseminate information. PRECIS offers a chance for exercising this responsibility with greater precision than has been possible in most systems up to the present time. Not that PRECIS is perfect, but in it there is more opportunity to be explicit.

SUMMARY

In summary, the basic order in PRECIS is in context-dependency form. Terms may be manipulated by special codes to preserve the contextual meaning. The Standard Format induces a rotation from *display* to *lead* to *qualifier*. This format occurs with main line operators (0), (1), and (2), which are numbered this way for ordinal purposes — to get the order: location, thing, action — required by the passive voice version of the title-like phrase. Every string must begin with (0), (1), or (2), and it must contain a Term prefixed by (1) or (2) representing an entity or action concept. It is possible to have a string with (1) or (2) and nothing else. No other operator may be used by itself.

The following two chapters will explain compound Term manipulation, a topic vital to the rest of the book, and four forms of dependent elements will be introduced. Then the rest of the main line operators will be presented.

PRECIS MANUAL REFERENCES

The basic order is covered in Sections 3.1-3.8 (pp. 14-18) of the *Manual*. The definitions of Sections 1.1-1.7 (pp. 7-10) should be read with care. It may be necessary to return to these definitions as new concepts and methodology are introduced.

The codes and convention for string writing appear in Sections 6.1-6.14 (pp. 40-51). This material will give the reader more information than is needed or desired at this point. Therefore, complete and immediate comprehension should not be expected. Theme interlinks will be described at a later stage.

The main line operators are discussed in several places in the *Manual*: Sections 7.1-7.2, pp. 58-59; Sections 16.1-17.9, pp. 130-38; Sections 23.1-23.7, pp. 201-206.

REFERENCES

[1] Sometimes words are wanted in print but should be passed over for filing. In the catalog code used in most libraries, for example, initial articles (The, A, Le, La, Les, Der, Die, Das, El, Los, Het, etc.) are not used for filing in catalogs; rather, the word following is the filing word. Because a computer cannot actually read and therefore has to be programmed to file or not file, in the MARC international exchange format, three backward slashes have been used as follows:

1) Data inserted between the first and second slashes is printed but not filed.

   \ A \ B \   "Print as 'A'; file as 'B' "

   \ A \\   "Print as 'A'; no filing value"

2) Data inserted between the second and third slashes are filed but not printed.

   \\ B \   "Print nothing; files as 'B' "

3) All three backward slashes must always be present. Anything before the first slash and after the third one files as printed.

4) This filing format coding is used with PRECIS except when the typographical code "e" appears.

[2] Derek Austin, *PRECIS: A Manual of Concept Analysis and Subject Indexing* (London: Council of the British National Bibliography, 1974): 137.

5
COMPOUND TERMS AND THEIR MANAGEMENT

Indexing would be simple if each word had only one distinct meaning, if each were a noun, and if there were no connections between words to affect meaning. This, of course, is not the case. Language is a social necessity for communication, and it has a very complex structure. Simple language, such as Basic English, retains the complexity. Elegant English, with its emphasis on variation in the ways of saying things and the use of imagination, also requires imagination on the part of the indexer. Meaning in spoken English is partly conveyed non-verbally. For written English, and even for the composition of title-like phrases for indexing, there are conventions and patterns to be followed.

The art of indexing begins *after* such rules are known. In this chapter, forms used for a special kind of adjectival and for similar descriptive purposes will be discussed. Compound Terms are defined as those having one or more descriptive words attached to them in some way. (The attaching medium may be another word.) One kind of descriptive words will be considered here: those that can be treated by the process of "differencing."

MECHANICS OF DIFFERENCING

Up to this point, we have seen that strings represent the title-like phrase or statement that describes the intellectual content of the item being indexed. Terms in strings are set down in a predetermined order according to role operators. These, as their name suggests, distinguish environments from key systems, key systems from actions, actions from agents, and so on. The role operation designations are tags for codes which not only identify the role of the Term in the string, but also serve as a trigger for manipulations of the Terms and the words contained in them. One example of such manipulation occurs in the process of differencing.

The operators given to this point have been Terms without subdivisions. This, however, is not the normal situation in indexing. A large proportion of index words in any index represents *classes* of things, actions, and so forth and can be grouped accordingly. For example, one may find in an index at the back of a book something like the following, usually in paragraph form with page numbers:[1]

Clock: anaphoric

astronomical

cuckoo

Habrecht

Islamic

mechanical

(List continues on page 78)

    Planetary

    Prague

    proto-clocks

    Strasbourg Cathedral

    water

These subheadings differentiate among the various *kinds* of clocks; in other words, each of these subheadings makes a *difference* in the meaning of the word "clock," each indicates a kind or class of clock. "Clock" is the *focus*; the other words are *differences*.

In PRECIS, "difference" is used in the logical sense of "differentia": "that characteristic or mark distinguishing a species from another species in the same genus" (Webster). Any word or words indicating *a kind of* main word or "focus" in a Term are treated as a difference. The purpose is to enable the indexer to use both the main Term (focus) and its modifier (difference) as headwords (index entries), while preserving the relationship between them in the process.

Differences perform a semantic function. They tend to represent a "to be" situation, specifying the subclass of a concept that is the focus. There are several kinds of differences recognized in PRECIS:

1)   Those representing subclasses in the form of
    a)   an adjective or adjectival phrase preceding the focus, e.g.,
        international networks
        stressed concrete buildings
        on-the-job training

    b)   an adjective or adjectival phrase following the focus, e.g.,
        bookstores *selling paperbacks*
        public libraries *serving children*

    c)   a prepositional phrase following the focus, e.g.,
        management *by objectives*
        games *for adults*

2)   dates, e.g.,
    1800-1899
    ca 1750

3)   place treated as an adjective for EXPORTABLE items, e.g.,
    French wines
    Hawaiian music

4)   parenthetical expressions used to indicate the names of tests and such.

"Adjectival" is used in a very broad sense. Figure 7 conveys some notion of the variety of adjectives, considered from the grammatical point of view. In general, for indexing pronominal, predicate, objective complement, and appositive do not apply.

In the process of indexing, a compound Term containing descriptive parts or other modifiers has always caused problems. When adjectives are used, should

Figure 7
Types of Adjectival Words
Taken, with modifications, from Mellie John and Paulene M. Yates,
The New Building Better English 11 [Evanston, IL: Row, Peterson, 1956].

DESCRIPTIVE (create a "picture")
types: **proper**   *French* cooking
                                  New York fashions

          common   *red* hair
                                  simple language

          participial   *broken* window
                                  growling dog

LIMITING (point out, specify)
types: **pronominal**   *this* car
                                  some rain
                                  his house

          numeral   *five* men
                                  fifth cat

          possessive   *wall's* insulation
                                  California's climate

POSITIONAL (classified according to where they are)
types: **predicate**   (completes an intransitive verb)
                                  The window is *open*

          objective complement (follows a direct object)
                                  His good manners make him *popular*.

          direct   (precedes the word modified)
                                  The actor received *generous* applause.

          appositive   (follows word modified)
                                  Trees, *tall and leafy*, bent in the wind

---

index entries be made for the adjective(s), noun, or both? In the English language very often both are required. This has led to indexes where there is no uniform practice. One may have, in the same index:[2]

Church music

Music, African

Abelian groups

Groups, Continuous

(List continues on page 80)

German drama

Mysteries and miracle plays, German

Prussian blue

Striped bass

Law, Anglo-Saxon

Part of the reasoning for inverted headings is to bring all varieties of one "species" together regardless of individual differences. At the same time, normal language puts the adjective first and many users expect an index to follow normal speech practices. In PRECIS no inverted Terms are used except certain kinds of names, which are put in directory style (Washington, George). However, it is recognized that the precise meaning of a noun (focus) may be made different (modified) by descriptive and limiting adjectives or words equivalent to adjectives. Often in indexing, the abbreviated aspect or condensing feature of the title-like phrase or sentence permits rearrangement of words into descriptive or limiting adjectives.

Levels of Differences

Differences may modify the focus directly. Such a direct difference is the first level:

toothed birds

automatic indexing

measuring instruments

Differences may also modify another difference:

serrated toothed birds

semi-automatic indexing

time measuring instruments

Such differences represent a second level, when defined in terms of their relationship to the focus. They are indirect differences. "Serrated" applies to "teeth," not to "birds"; "semi-" applies to "automatic," not to "indexing"; and "time" is used to differentiate among types of "measuring instruments."

The difference directly modifying the focus is called a "direct" or "first level" difference. The difference that indirectly modifies the focus, but directly modifies the first level difference is called a "second level" difference. The levels of difference—there may be up to nine—are numbered with respect to the focus. Therefore, a third level difference would be one that modified a second level difference that modified a first level difference, as in the example below:

elapsed-time measuring instruments

The actual writing of a Term composed of several words (focus plus one or more differences) reverses normal English word order. Thus the focus or differenced word comes first. It is followed by the various differences applied to it, in the order of their closeness to the noun or focus.

Focus	**level 1**	**level 2**	**level 3**
instruments	measuring	time	elapsed-

level 1: "measuring" ("measuring" modifies "instruments")
level 2: "time measuring" ("time" modifies "measuring")
level 3: "elapsed-time" ("elapsed" modifies "time")

It could be diagrammed thus:

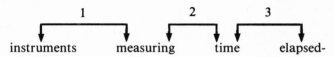

The string Term then becomes:

(1)*   instruments $ measuring $ time $ elapsed-

The "$" is a "delimiter" which is used here in the sense of an alerting code. The attached tag, to be discussed shortly, indicates what is to be done with the word directly following.

Not all differences modify each other. Sometimes there may be several, all of which modify the focus and are, therefore, first level differences. It is relatively rare in English to have levels higher than level two.

Take, for example, the differenced Term,

painted wooden ranch-style houses

This is reversed to form the string Term:

(1)*   houses $ ranch-style $ wooden $ painted

When a word, in this case "style," is not wanted as a *lead*, it may be merged or joined to a word which *is* wanted as *lead*, as with "ranch-style." This is perfectly legitimate.

Indicating Lead and Spacing of Differences

In addition to level, there are two other factors to be considered when making differences. The first is whether the difference is to be used as a *lead* or not. The second permits the word either to be used as a unit separated from words on either side of it or to be merged with the preceding word. In the above case, for example, "ranch-" will be closed up with "style" to produce "ranch-style." This closed-up process also may be used conveniently when an entry is desired under the word part of a prefixed word to make it correlate with other entries in the index:

(1)*   furniture $ upholstered $ re-

"Upholstered" would be marked for a *lead*, but the prefix would not, so that "re-upholstered furniture" would appear in the *display* when either "furniture" or "upholstered furniture" was in the *lead*.

Lead or non-*lead* and spaced or closed-up are coded as a matrix:

	Spaced	Closed-up
Non-*lead*	0	1
Lead	2	3

The codes, with the $ delimiter, are:

Non-*lead*, spaced	$0	*Lead,* spaced	$2
Non-*lead*, closed-up	$1	*Lead*, closed-up	$3

The matrix and level codes are combined into a two digit number preceded by the indicator ($). The code number for *lead*/non-*lead*, closed-up/spaced is followed directly by a second number relating the differences by level (distance: direct, indirect, very indirect) from the focus. A convenient matrix pattern for this is shown in Figure 8.

Figure 8
Matrix for Differencing

(This matrix makes it possible to perform three decisions simultaneously: *lead* or non-*lead*, level and spacing. The next additional level would code as 04, 14, 24, 34. Up to nine levels are permissible.)

Level, spacing / Lead	Level 1 Spaced	Level 2 Spaced	Level 3 Spaced	Level 1 Closed-up	Level 2 Closed-up	Level 3 Closed-up
Non-lead	01	02	03	11	12	13
Lead	21	22	23	31	32	33

The examples on the previous pages will now be coded and entries made from them for the index. The whole Term is retained in the *display* until all the parts tagged for *leads* have been used. In some cases the full Term appears as a *lead*, but in others this does not happen.

(1)* birds $21 toothed $22 serrated

(2)* indexing $21 automatic $32 semi-

(1)* instruments $21 measuring $22 time

(1)* rails $21 steel $22 welded $33 arc-

(1)* instruments $21 measuring $22 time $33 elapsed-

(1)* houses $21 ranch-style $21 wooden $21 painted

The following entries are made from these Terms:

Birds
Serrated toothed birds

Toothed birds
Serrated toothed birds

Serrated toothed birds

In this case, each word in turn became an entry. The same holds for all except the last of these differenced forms. The remaining five examples are expanded into entries as follows:

Indexing
Semi-automatic indexing

Automatic indexing
Semi-automatic indexing

Semi-automatic indexing

Instruments
Time measuring instruments

Measuring instruments
Time measuring instruments

Time measuring instruments

Rails
Arc-welded steel rails

Steel rails
Arc-welded steel rails

Welded steel rails
Arc-welded steel rails

Arc-welded steel rails

Instruments
Elapsed-time measuring instruments

(Examples continue on page 84)

Measuring instruments
Elapsed-time measuring instruments

Time measuring instruments
Elapsed-time measuring instruments

Elapsed-time measuring instruments

Houses
Painted wooden ranch-style houses

Ranch-style houses
Painted wooden ranch-style houses

Wooden houses
Painted wooden ranch-style houses

Painted houses
Painted wooden ranch-style houses

In this last case all four words never appeared in the *lead* as a unit. Where words unwanted as *leads* cannot be merged into a word-pair or word-triplet, or even larger word combination logically and grammatically, then each word must be tagged separately.

(1)*   houses $21 wooden $01 old $21 painted

Houses
Painted old wooden houses

Wooden houses
Painted old wooden houses

Painted houses
Painted old wooden houses

The indexer at all times is in full control of the form of entry, using or passing over words as the context requires.

Hyphenated and closed-up words require some care in usage. Prefixes that negate the focus (anti-, non-, un-) tend to alter the meaning so that a new or different concept is created. A prefix may be used as a *lead* if it is significant enough to call for an entry.

(2)*   grazing $31 over

Grazing
Overgrazing

Overgrazing

(2)* representation $31 under

Representation
Underrepresentation

Underrepresentation

In either of the above cases, if an entry was wanted under "overgrazing" only or "underrepresentation" only, there would be no need to difference. On the other hand, if a word is not wanted as a *lead* but it is wanted in the *display*, the code $01 is useful:

(1)* trees $01 tall

(1)* cats $01 fat

The resulting index entries are:

Trees
Tall trees

Cats
Fat cats

In all of these cases, whether the adjectival words were used in the *lead* or not, the string Term, with all its parts, would move into the *qualifier* in the same form it had in the *display*:

Hard-packed snow removal in Canada

String: (0)* Canada^d

(1)* snow $1 packed $22 hard-

(2)* removal

Entries: **Canada**
Hard-packed snow. Removal

Snow. Canada
Hard-packed snow. Removal

Hard-packed snow. Canada
Removal

Removal. Hard-packed snow. Canada

(Examples continue on page 86)

Clear cutting tall trees in California

String:

            d
(0)* California

(1)* trees $1 tall

(2)* cutting $21 clear

Entries:

California
Tall trees. Clear cutting

Trees. California
Tall trees. Clear cutting

Cutting. Tall trees. California
Clear cutting

Clear cutting. Tall trees. California

In the latter example, both options (to use or not to use) have been utilized. If the word "cutting" had not been wanted as a *lead* no asterisk would have been used after operator (2), yet the *lead* difference $21 before "clear" would produce an entry under "clear":

(2) cutting $21 clear

Clear cutting. Tall trees. California

These various options are very powerful tools for the indexer to use in conveying content and context without losing track of either one. Also, the entries are limited to the exact number required for suitable headwords.

The average direct difference (level 1) tends to be simple and the number of resultant entries may well coincide with the number of words in Terms. "Every word an index term" is no longer considered idyllic, even if limited to every substantive word. But there is a "nothing to excess" kind of beauty in a situation where this happens:

Management of academic libraries in Florida

yields the string:

            d
(0)* Florida

(1)* libraries $21 academic

(2)* management

with the index entries:

Florida
Academic libraries. Management

Libraries. Florida
Academic libraries. Management

Academic libraries. Florida
Management

Management. Academic libraries. Florida

In cases of difficulty in determining to which level a differenced word belongs, a diagram is helpful at times. The words should be in reverse of normal word order in English:

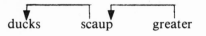

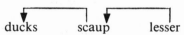

ducks   scaup   greater   ducks   scaup   lesser

(1)*   ducks $21 scaup $22 greater   (1)*   ducks $21 scaup $22 lesser

This produces:

Ducks
Greater scaup ducks

Ducks
Lesser scaup ducks

Scaup ducks
Greater scaup ducks

Scaup ducks
Lesser scaup ducks

Greater scaup ducks

Lesser scaup ducks

In an actual index, the terms would appear in alphabetical order and without the heading repeated:

Ducks
Greater scaup ducks
Lesser scaup ducks

Scaup ducks
Greater scaup ducks
Lesser scaup ducks

The word triplets would also appear in the sections of the index under *G* and *L*, respectively:

Greater scaup ducks

Lesser scaup ducks

In the case of "Canadian humorous strip cartoons," on the other hand, each word relates directly to the focus:

(Example appears on page 88)

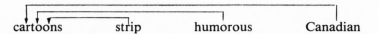

cartoons   strip   humorous   Canadian

yielding the Term:

(1)*   cartoons \$21 strip \$21 humorous \$21 Canadian

and entries:

Cartoons
Canadian humorous strip cartoons

Strip cartoons
Canadian humorous strip cartoons

Humorous cartoons
Canadian humorous strip cartoons

Canadian cartoons
Canadian humorous strip cartoons

Never are all these words used at once except in the *display*. Each word that directly modifies the focus is used with the focus sequentially. One can tell by reading down the set of entries whether all of the differences that were marked for the *lead* have been used. In a case like this, where direct difference is involved, there is a one-to-one relationship between each difference and the focus.

A more exact diagram, with everything marked, is introduced at this point for a slightly more complex Term:

(1)*   bridges \$31 foot \$01 slab \$22 concrete

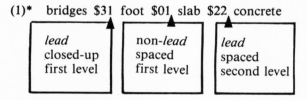

lead	non-*lead*	*lead*
closed-up	spaced	spaced
first level	first level	second level

Bridges
Concrete slab footbridges

Footbridges
Concrete slab footbridges

Concrete slab footbridges

Note that the instructions conveyed by the differencing tag (operator) indicate what is to be done with the word *following* the tag. The focus is a sort of anchor word, with everything else related to it.

An interesting kind of closed-up entry is to be found in the following commonplace subject:

Children's playrooms

(1)*   rooms $31 play $21 children's

Rooms
Children's playrooms

Playrooms
Children's playrooms

Children's rooms
Children's playrooms

As noted briefly above, when a *lead* is not wanted under the focus, but *is* wanted under the differences attached to it, the asterisk is omitted following the role operator tag, but the words that are differences, tagged $21, $22, $23 ... $29 or $31, $32, $33 ... $39, will be picked up and used because they are marked for *leads*.

Fibrous composite materials

if coded:

(1)   materials $21 composite $21 fibrous

yields entries:

Composite materials
Fibrous composite materials

Fibrous materials
Fibrous composite materials

Producing Index Entries from Compound Terms: Summary

To make entries from Compound Terms, the following rules are appropos:

1) Write down words in the Compound Term in the reverse of their natural order.
   Natural order Term = fur-lined winter coats
   Reverse order = coats, winter, fur-lined

2) Code each part to indicate:
   a) Whether it is to be a *lead* or non-*lead* word
   b) Whether it is to be spaced or closed-up with respect to the next word (preceding word in Term, following word in index entry)
   c) What *level* it is with respect to the focus
   A matrix for making all of these decisions at once, up to three levels, is shown in Figure 8 on page 82. It is possible to have more than

three levels in English, as with some kinds of chemical formulas, but rather unusual in non-technical literature.

3) When one or more parts of a Compound Term are to be used in the *lead*, the whole Compound Term is repeated in the *display* until after the last word has been led out. Then the Compound Term, in natural word order, moves into the *qualifier*, unless the indexer programs the string otherwise by using (LO) (*lead* only), (NU) (not up), or a substitution (sub n↑).

4) Compound Terms are always used in the index itself (the end-product) in natural language order. The advantage to differencing is that any part of a Compound Term may be used as a *lead* without losing the sense of the Term itself.

RULES FOR DIFFERENCING

Up to this point, we have covered the mechanics of differencing, including what differences are, how they are coded, and how to make entries from them. The rest of this chapter will be concerned with the rules and constraints involved in the process of differencing. In other words, this part will be concerned with *what* to difference rather than *how* to difference. Before proceeding, however, a word must be said about interposed operators, since these operators perform some of the most valuable kinds of context preservation in PRECIS. Some of them are very briefly introduced at this point because, under certain circumstances, they comprise the alternative to differencing. They will be considered in full detail in the next chapter.

Digression on Interposed Operators

Dependent elements	p	Part/Property
	q	Member of a quasi-generic group
	r	Aggregate
Concept interlinks	s	Role definer; Directional property
	t	Author-attributed association
Coordinate concepts	f	Coordinate concept
	g	Coordinate concept

It is almost impossible to imagine how the precision and elegance of PRECIS manipulations could be possible without these elements. Each of them defines the process in which it is involved and at the same time initiates a series of steps effecting the manipulation of the Terms tagged by the Operators. Of the seven, only dependent elements will be discussed at this point.

Dependent Elements Compared with Elements
That May Be Differenced

Dependent elements, representing a *part* or *property* of something, belong to the "to have" category as they indicate possession. These are tagged with operator (p). Dependent elements representing a sub-class or *kind* of something belong to the quasi-generic group (q). These (q) elements form a temporary class *specified by the item* being indexed. They are not a true generic class, which would be the same under all circumstances.† The dependent element (r), representing an aggregate, is a word specifically used for named groupings, such as a herd of cattle.

Of these three elements, only the first tends to cause problems in differencing. This is because in natural language Terms made up of two nouns, such as aircraft engines, brake linings and window panes, are used for "engines of aircraft," "linings of brakes," and "panes of windows." Logically, the first noun is the possessor and the second noun is a part or property of the first, rather than a kind of it.

In PRECIS these are properly represented as whole/part Terms:

    (1)*   aircraft

    (p)*   engines

        (1)*   brakes

        (p)*   linings

            (1)*   windows

            (p)*   panes

When these entities are used as adjectival nouns, however, a "to have" situation is masquarading as a "to be" one. Since mainly "to be" type of situations are differenced (with some notable exceptions to be discussed as "constraints" later in this chapter), care is needed in initial analysis.[3] In cases where a compound term consists of a part modified by its whole, as in the popular usage examples above, it must be turned around so that it appears in the string as the whole followed by its part or property. Only existential "to be" cases — kinds of things — may be differenced.

The first part of this chapter outlined the basic features necessary for differencing. This will be repeated to some extent in the rules, in the interests of having everything in one place. In PRECIS courses and in the *Manual*, the labelled rules for differencing are presented negatively ("do not ..."). Since this has the effect of indicating the rules by what is left over after subtraction, a more positive approach will be attempted here. In cases where the constraint has been the major reason for writing the rule, the constraint has been given first and then the rule.

---

†A dog is always a canine (generic class). When a dog is a pet, guardian, guide for the blind or a laboratory animal, a quasi-generic class is created.

Codification of the Rules for Differencing

General Rules

1) Differencing is used with Terms compounded of two or more words, where some or all of the words may be used as *leads*.
   a) The relationship among the words must represent a "to be" situation.
   b) The focus is a noun and the differences are words which normally are adjectival (grammar) and subclasses (logic) modifying the focus.
   c) Multiple word combinations may be used in any part of the differenced Term, provided they are logical and do not violate the constraints placed on the process of differencing (see below).

2) Differences may be adjectives, adjectival phrases, or their equivalent preceding the focus in normal word order, but reversed in order for input:

   (1)*   cats $21 shorthair $21 domestic

   (1)*   toil $21 back-breaking

   (1)*   bridges $21 suspension

   Cats
   Domestic shorthair cats

   Shorthair cats
   Domestic shorthair cats

   Domestic cats
   Domestic shorthair cats

   Toil
   Back-breaking toil

   Back-breaking toil

   Bridges
   Suspension bridges

   Suspension bridges

3) Differences may be in other forms:
   a) An adjective or adjectival phrase following the focus.

      (1)*   bookfairs *exhibiting manuscripts*

   b) A prepositional phrase following the focus.

      (2)*   horticulture *in greenhouses*

This kind of difference is called a "following difference" and has been used mainly as is until recently. It appears with a reference from the difference itself:

> **Manuscripts**
> *See also*
> **Bookfairs exhibiting manuscripts**
>
> **Greenhouses**
> *See also*
> **Horticulture in greenhouses**

Some of these rather special differences are now handled in a format not requiring the cross-reference.

4) Differences may require two kinds of spacing and *leads*. The matrix following is used for coding the first digit in differencing code, covering *lead*/non-*lead*, spaced/closed-up:

	Spaced	Closed-up
Non-*lead*	0	1
Lead	2	3

5) Differences occur in up to nine (9) levels of relatedness *with respect to the focus.* Most commonly, in English they are:

> Level 1   related directly
> Level 2   related indirectly
> Level 3   related very indirectly

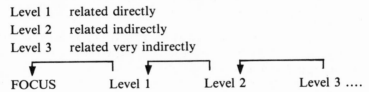

FOCUS   Level 1   Level 2   Level 3 ....

These levels form the second digit in the differencing code.

These five rules are the major ones governing the process of differencing. The remaining rules are dependent upon constraints placed on differencing. Therefore, in each case, the constraint, identified from A to F, will be presented first and then the rules.

Constraint A

> *A part or property may not be differenced by the entity or action that possesses it*, i.e. *a part or property may not be differenced by its whole.* This constraint applies under all circumstances. It is a MUST. It is a very important limitation that tends to be quite difficult for beginners to apply. One has to think very carefully about what is whole and what is part. It is helpful to remember that in differencing one is concerned with *types* of something. By changing adjectives to nouns (if possible), then considering the relationship between the adjective-turned-noun

and the focal noun, it is sometimes easier to see the *logical* relationship between the two, especially when the noun is a countable item and therefore must be used in the plural:

airplanes	engines	(NOT airplane engines)
horses	hides	(NOT horse hides)
butterflies	wings	(NOT butterfly wings)

General Rule 6.

A whole may be differenced by its part or property.

Use   (1)*   hair $21 auburn

               (1)*   engines $21 jet

               (1)*   soils $21 acid

In these three cases the property is not unlike a "kind of." Colloquial usage, as for example, "automobile engines" tends to make the part divided by its whole seem logical. To ensure that differencing is not done illegally on this type of topic, it is recommended that the novice indexer (new to PRECIS) develop a little routine to avoid being tripped up by colloquial usage. A few questions help:

—Is *airplane* a kind of *engine*? (A kind of engine would be internal combustion, jet, overhead cam, rotary, etc. Not all kinds of engines would be suitable for airplanes BUT at the same time kinds of engines are not limited to their main purpose. Airplane engines are used to power swamp buggies.)

—Is *airplane* a part or property of an *engine*? (Parts of an engine would be things like cylinders, blades, fuel pumps, etc., depending on the kind of engine.)

—Is *engine* a kind of *automobile*? (A kind of automobile would be coupe, sedan, etc. Do not be fooled by "front wheel drive"!)

—Is *engine* a part of *automobile*? *Property* of *automobile*? (Part or property would be what it is made up of or what it possesses: doors, wheels, power plant (i.e. engine), front-wheel drive, pick-up, etc.)

Careful answers to these four questions should yield information on what is "kind of" and what is "part or property of," thus separating the whole from the part. In cases where differencing is not a legitimate procedure, the interposed (p) is the operator of choice:

                (1)*   airplanes (automobiles, ships, etc.)

                (p)*   engines

                      (1)*   horses (cows, buffalos, etc.)

                      (p)*   hides

                               (1)*   butterflies (birds, bats)

                               (p)*   wings

Legal differences would be:	**Illegal ones:†**
(1)* soils $21 acid	( ) acidity $21 soil
(1)* hair $21 color	( ) color $21 hair

†From this point on, illegal examples will have the operator blank, to avoid confusion.

Here sequential usage with (p) part or property is mandatory:

(1)*   soils   ( ) acidity $21 soil

(p)*   acidity

    (1)*   cars   ( ) wheels $21 car

    (p)*   wheels

        (1)*   oceans   ( ) beds $21 ocean

        (p)*   beds

THE REMAINING CONSTRAINTS ARE DESIRABLE BUT NOT MANDATORY.

Constraint B

> *A transitive action should not be differenced by the entity upon which it is performed.*

General Rule 7.

An entity may be differenced by the name of an action that is or has been performed upon it. (In adjectival form, this is encompassed in General Rule 1b.)

        (1)*   frames $21 riveted

        (1)*   patients $21 irradiated

Under the above constraint, one would not use

        ( ) management $21 library

but instead, the sequential form is preferable:

        (1)*   libraries

        (2)*   management

Constraint C

> *A transitive action should not be differenced by the name of the agent which performs it.*
>
> (For the sake of completeness, the following rule will be stated here. It will be explained, however, in Chapter 9 and readers should ignore it at this point, unless they have gone through the book and are reviewing.)

General Rule 8.

An *agent* may be differenced by the name of the *action* for which it is intended.

        (3)*   tools $21 cutting

        (3)*   rafts $21 floating

Under the above constraint, the following should not be used:

( ) simulations $21 computer

( ) defenses $21 team platoon

Constraint D

A fixed or structural entity should not be differenced by the name of its environment.

General Rule 9.

An *exportable entity* may be differenced by the name of its environment.

(1)* wines $21 Greek

(1)* vases $21 Chinese

(1)* dances $21 Spanish

Under the constraint, one should avoid using

( ) museums $21 Italian

( ) universities $21 French

but the following are acceptable:

(0)* Italy

(1)* museums

(0)* France

(1)* universities

The indexer should also beware of false environmental names such as

reverse Polish notation

Mexican stand-off

Turkish delight

Constraint E

An intransitive action should not be differenced by the name of the entity that performs it.

General Rule 10.

An *entity* may be differenced by the name of the *intransitive action* in which it is engaged.

(1)*   birds $21 migrating

(1)*   vapors $21 disappearing

(1)*   population $21 growing

Under the above constraint, one would not use:

( ) growth $21 population

( ) migration $21 bird

( ) disappearance $21 vapor

Instead, the sequential form is acceptable:

(1)*	birds	(1)*	vapors
(2)*	migration	(2)*	disappearance
	(1)* population		
	(2)* growth		

Constraint F

   Illogical combinations should not be differenced.

   Representative examples:

                fossil fish

                synthetic gems

                counterfeit currency

                model ships

   In the first two cases, the fossils and synthetics happen to be fish and gems, respectively, but do not occur naturally in these forms. A fossil fish is not a species of fish, but a condition of any fish (within the limits of "fossil"). A synthetic gem is not precisely a gem in the sense of being a naturally-occurring jewel. Counterfeit currency denies the instance of existence: it looks like money but is not a medium of exchange because any currency not made by the government is illegal. These terms are commonly used, but the *caveats* attached to them are assumed and not stated. Normally we do not stop to consider whether they mean exactly what they say or whether they are specific and all-inclusive. The "counterfeit currency" is an especially nice example because the counterfeiter expects people to be fooled by his fake money, and the user of the word expects the reader or listener to "understand" that such currency is not actually money.

General Rule 11.

Illogical terms should be handled with cross-references, if possible.

Fish	**Ships**
See also	*See also*
Fossil fish	**Model ships**

Gems	**Criminal deception devices**
See also	*See also*
Natural gems	**Counterfeit money**
Synthetic gems	

These rules are very helpful in separating the various kinds of differences. Two more types remain to be discussed. The first, to be presented here, is a special group of limited usage: parenthetical differences.

Parenthetical Differences

Operators $n (non-*lead* parenthetical difference) and $o (*lead* parenthetical difference) are rarely used. This type of difference pinpoints the method used to define or measure the concept to which it is attached. The examples used here indicate use of operator $o. Though $n is available in principle, it is difficult to imagine a situation where a test, for example, was important enough to be put in the string, but not important enough to use as a *lead*.

Research on cognitive development of children, 1930-1939, using the Piaget Scale [4]

String:
    (1)* children
    (2)* development $21 cognitive $o Piaget Scale $d 1930-1939 $w of
    (2)* research

Entries:

Children
    Cognitive development (Piaget Scale), *1930-1939.* Research

Development. Children
    Cognitive development (Piaget Scale), *1930-1939.* Research

Cognitive development (Piaget Scale). Children
    1930-1939. Research

Piaget Scale. Cognitive development, *1930-1939.* Children
    Research

Research. Cognitive development (Piaget Scale)
    of children, *1930-1939*

Note in this example that the (Piaget Scale) stays with the subject to which it applies: "cognitive development." This example is rather nice because it has each major variety of difference, in its proper order.

Manipulation of $o-tagged operators can be complex. Parentheses have to be added or deleted as the string is turned into entries. A very simple example will show this:

Hardness of minerals on Mohs' scale

(1)*   minerals

(p)*   hardness $o Mohs' scale

Minerals
Hardness (Mohs' scale)

Hardness (Mohs' scale).   Minerals

Mohs' scale.   Hardness.   Minerals

Order of Differences

There is a suggested order when using differences in a Term of a string. It is unlikely that all will occur at once, but the possibility is there. The order is:

a)   Direct, indirect and very indirect differences
(These are set out in the reverse of their natural order.)

b)   Parenthetical differences

c)   Dates

d)   Connectives

Topical Order of Differences

In cases where the order of words in a differenced Term is not obvious, a list has been compiled. This is presented here as if all seven identifiable parts applied to a single focus, which, of course, is most unlikely. Suitable tags still have to be applied to each section:[5]

Focus	**Kinds of Differences**
Focus	/1/ Function or purpose
	/2/ Actions by or within a system
	/3/ Dynamic or driving parts
	/4/ Static or driven parts
	/5/ Materials
	/6/ Effects of past actions (incl. agents)
	/7/ Properties

(Explanation continues on page 100)

In addition, there are three more possibilities, which have come into the English language but cannot be rationalized completely:

/8/ Relative ("high technology")
/9/ Evaluative ("poor persons")
/10/ Adverbial ("very low frequency")

The order used here is that in a string Term. When read out into an entry the order would be reversed to normal English. With this type of differencing order, it is possible to handle complex descriptions such as:

Machine washable / double-knit / polyester / party / dresses
Property / Past action / Material / Function / FOCUS

Hardened / glass- / lined / storage / tanks
Past action / Material / Static parts / Purpose / FOCUS

SUMMARY

Differencing is the method of choice for handling a semantic (to be) situation found in Terms composed of a noun (focus) and its descriptive elements. A number of methods for differencing have been outlined. Within certain exceedingly important constraints, the differencing procedures are a highly effective indexing ploy for getting multiple entries with economy in string writing. The most important of the constraints is the one that says, "Do not difference a part by its whole."

Another type of semantic situation within the general syntactic process of string writing is the case of the dependent element operator (q), "member of a quasi-generic group," which defines a specific *kind* of element. The interposed dependent elements, which were only briefly mentioned at the beginning of the chapter, will be covered in detail in the next chapter.

PRECIS MANUAL REFERENCES

The topics of this chapter are covered in considerable detail in the *Manual.* It is recommended that the beginning indexer read the sections listed below and return to these and other parts of the *Manual* as problems arise during the course of indexing:

Definitions: Section 1, pp. 7-10, especially sections 1.3.2 and 1.5.
Section 7.2, p. 59.
Sections 8.1-8.17, pp. 63-73. (Compound Terms)
Sections 9.1-9.15, pp. 76-86. (Filing Order, Rules of Differencing)
Sections 10.1-10.6, pp. 87-90. (Prepositional Phrases)
Sections 12.1-12.6, pp. 94-96. (Place as Difference)
Sections 13.1-13.4, pp. 99-101. (Strategems of Differencing)

Section 23.13, pp. 210-211. (Environments of Actions)

Filing order of differences in Term: Sections 9.1-9.11, pp. 76-83.

Parenthetical differences: Sections 11.1-11.6, pp. 91-93; Algorithm 6, pp. 445-46.

Topical order: Sections 9.7-9.9, pp. 79-81.

NOTE: Differencing operators in the *Manual* are in an older format.

$h = $01 $i = $21 $k = $02 $m = $22

REFERENCES

[1]Derek de Solla Price, *Science since Babylon*, enl. ed. (New Haven, CT: Yale University Press, 1975): 210.

[2]Lois Mai Chan, " 'American Poetry' but 'Satire, American': The Direct and Inverted Forms of Subject Heading Containing National Adjectives," *Library Resources & Technical Services* 17 (1973): 330-39.

[3]See Derek Austin, *PRECIS: A Manual of Concept Analysis and Subject Indexing* (London: Council of the British National Bibliography, 1974), Sections 9.7, 9.8, and 9.12, pp. 79-80, 83. It is stated that categories of differences "which define a class in terms of its intrinsic characteristics," such as "materials," "static or driven parts and subassemblies," and "dynamic or driving parts and subassemblies," may be differenced by the names of these parts (pp. 79-80). Examples are:

> blankets, cellular, woollen
>
> sections, channelled, steel
>
> engines, steam

"Woollen" and "steel" are materials, "cellular" and "channelled" are static or driven parts, while "steam" is a dynamic or driving part. These *parts* of things (blankets, sections, engines) are also used to differentiate among classes, to separate *kinds* of blankets, sections, or engines. In such cases, the *part* may double as a *kind* for classification purposes. In a later chapter, a parallel situation in cross-referencing will be encountered.

[4]Derek Austin, Handout from PRECIS course, Dalhousie University, 1977: 4Q.

[5]Austin, *PRECIS: A Manual*, pp. 76-83.

6

OPERATIONS FOR SEQUENCE AND COORDINATION

Dependent elements, which were mentioned briefly in the preceding chapter in order to set the stage for the constraints involved in differencing, will be treated in detail in this chapter. These elements may be interposed in a string at almost any point. They serve as identification definers in three situations: where

a)   a part or property of a whole is present,

b)   a context-created sub-class is recognized, or

c)   a representative word is normally supplied for an aggregate concept.

These very useful operators are used singly or intermixed as the material being indexed may dictate.

DEPENDENT ELEMENT (p): PART/PROPERTY

The scope of the role operator (p) is given in Figure 9.[1] This is perhaps the most frequently used operator in PRECIS. It may appear as often as necessary, usually with operators (0), (1), (2), and (3). It may occur with other dependent operators (q) and (r), and it may be repeated. Some examples follow:

(1) bicycles	Whole, thing, entity
(p) frames	Part
(p) wheels	Part of frame
(p) spokes $21 plated	Part of wheel
(1) ships	Thing, entity
(2) navigation	Action
(p) chart-reading	Part of action
(0) Scot$\overset{d}{l}$and	Whole
(p) Gram$\overset{d}{p}$ian Region	Part
(p) Peterhead	Part of part
(1) glaciers	Entity
(p) moraines	Part
(1) winds	Entity
(p) velocity	Property

Figure 9
Scope of Dependent Element (p)

A two- or three-word description of the subject has been used as an indication of how the Terms are likely to occur in the material being indexed. (PRECIS Course, Dalhousie University, 1977. Handout 5A, modified slightly.) In order to show the need for careful analysis, in each case the *subject* has been written deliberately so that the whole as an adjective modifies its part.

	Dependency Type	Example	
1.	Physical parts, components, constituents and sub-assemblies of entities. *subject*: car windshields	(1)* (p)*	cars windshields
2.	Intellectual and abstract components. *subject*: airline timetables	(1)* (p)*	airline services timetables
3.	Any subject which is part of or aids in accomplishment of another action. *subject*: managerial decision-making	(2)* (p)*	management decision- making
4.	Physical or chemical properties. *subject*: soil alkalinity	(1)* (p)*	soils alkalinity
5.	Attributed properties. *subject*: children's emotions	(1)* (p)*	children emotions
6.	Inputs (considered as parts). *subject*: motorcycle fuels	(1)* (p)*	motorcycles fuels
7.	Outputs (considered as parts). *subject*: truck emissions	(1)* (p)*	trucks emissions
8.	Properties of actions. *subject*: sales expenses	(2)* (p)*	sales expenses

In general, a part or property of something is used as above. It may be used to difference a whole only when it is expressed in adjectival form to indicate a *kind* of whole:

> (2)*   growth $21 linear

Expressed as whole/property, the same concept would be used in noun form:

> (2)*   growth
> (p)*   linearity

One can almost always check a Term as part or property by supplying the word "of" to the part and reading upwards. All of these parts are represented by nouns. In certain kinds of cases, "in," "into," or "for" may be helpful, as with:

       (2)*   decision making
       (p)*   information   [for]

       (1)*   motorcycles
       (p)*   gasoline   [in]

       (2)*   physics
       (p)*   equations   [in]

       (1)*   moon
       (p)*   geological features   [of]

       (1)*   pots
       (p)*   lids   [of]

Sometimes checking the use of the (p) operator in this way may help prevent a logical error:

       (1)*   pets
       ( )*   rabbits   ["of" does not fit, but "are" or "as a
                                  kind of" does, hence the next operator
                                  (q) is called for here]

DEPENDENT ELEMENT (q):
MEMBER OF A QUASI-GENERIC GROUP

The interposed operator (q), quasi-generic element, is used in situations where a relationship is specified, but it is not a true generic one. Thus a mosquito is an insect, but it is also a pest. The category "pest" is not confined to insects. A rabbit is generically a member of the order, Lagomorpha. This is a first of all (a priori) relationship. Its secondary relationships (a posteriori) would be a pet, pest, laboratory animal, or food. For classification purposes the word "rabbit" may be required in several classes, depending upon how the creature is considered or under what circumstances rabbits are an example of the thing classed. The generic category, treating a rabbit a priori as a specific animal in the Lagomorpha order, holds for any syntactical situation and is independent of context. A rabbit is a rabbit. The a posteriori categories, called "quasi-generic" in PRECIS, are dependent on context for their meanings. For quasi-generic situations, the category must precede its member:

       (1)   pets
       (q)   rabbits

       (1)   laboratory animals
       (q)   rabbits

       (1)   gardens
       (p)   pests
       (q)   rabbits

(1)   foods
(p)   meats
(q)   rabbits

PRECIS programming requires the use of a colon (:) before the term following the operator (q) when it is in the *display*. The following string:

(1)   houses
(p)   pests
(q)   cockroaches

would produce the index entries:

Houses
    Pests: Cockroaches

Pests.   Houses
    Cockroaches

Cockroaches.   Pests. Houses

In case of doubt, the question "Which is ...?" or "Which are ...?" may help determine whether the relationship calls for the use of the quasi-generic operator (q). More formally, in PRECIS, two questions may be asked to distinguish between use of operators (p) and (q):[2]

1)   With A representing the higher term and B the lower one, could B be a part or property *of* any specific A? If so, use (p), if not, use (q).

2)   Is B a specific member of the whole category A? If so, use (q); if not, use (p).

When a situation arises in which a middle term has been left out of a title-like phrase, the indexer may have to supply the missing word:

String: (1)*   libraries
           (p)   personnel
           (q)*   paraprofessionals

In this case, a (q) immediately following "libraries" could be ambiguous, and therefore the word "personnel" has been inserted. The entries would be:

Libraries
    Personnel: Paraprofessionals

Paraprofessionals.   Personnel. Libraries

Much of the time with (q), if one inserts (mentally) the words, "which is/are," after the Term preceding the line in the string starting with operator (q), the relationship may be clarified. Also, Venn diagrams can be very helpful (*see* Figure 10, page 106).

Figure 10
Diagram to Illustrate Difference between Generic Relationships

Pure Generic Relationship (Class inclusion)

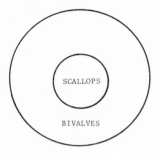

Quasi-Generic Relationship (Class overlap)

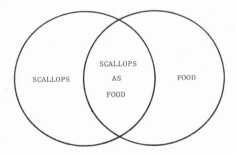

Generic relationships are commonly displayed in PRECIS in a hierarchy of cross-references like this one:

> **Bivalves**
> > *See also*
> > **Scallops**

Such a generic relationship satisfies the logical statement "all x are y" (class inclusion).

The quasi-generic relationship is a case of "some x are y" (class overlap), which is quite a different matter. Here the PRECIS string is:

> (1)*   food
> (q)*   scallops

with the entries:

Food
  Scallops

Scallops. Food

One may think of this either as "scallops as a kind of food" or "food, being scallops." The quasi-generic operator (q) represents a specific kind of entity.

When a Term coded (q) appears in the *display*, it is preceded by the Term representing the name of the class of which it has been made a member (according to context). A colon separates the class from its member in the entries.

String: (1)*   supermarkets
               (p)   stock (NU)
               (q)*   detergents
               (p)*   prices

Entries: **Supermarkets**
                 Stock: Detergents. Prices

               Detergents. Supermarkets
                 Prices

               Prices. Detergents. Supermarkets

"Stock" is added for logical reasons; without it there would be no one-to-one relationship between "detergents" and "supermarkets." The indexer must take care when using operator (q) to ensure that its relationship to the higher class is clearly spelled out. If that class is missing and for some reason cannot be supplied, operator (q) should not be used.

Last, but not least, operator (q) can be used for a *true*, not a quasi-generic relationship if ambiguity might be present:

String: (1)   birds
               (q)*   kites
               (2)*   migration

Entries: **Kites.** Birds
                 Migration

               Migration. Kites. Birds

Other homographs may be treated in this manner if necessary.

DEPENDENT ELEMENT (r): AGGREGATE

For collective words or aggregates, the operator (r) is useful. This covers specific cases such as packs, pods, networks, committees, herds, collections of some kind, and similar groupings. It is particularly helpful in indexing materials in the behavioral sciences, where the behavior of individuals must be distinguished from the behavior of the same individuals in groups.

(1)*   adolescents
(2)*   behavior

(1)*   adolescents
(r)*   gangs
(2)*   behavior

Collections of animals may have different names for their groupings:

(1)*	fish	(1)*	whales
(r)*	schools	(r)*	pods
(1)*	lions	(1)*	wolves
(r)*	prides	(r)*	packs
(1)*	sheep	(1)*	bees
(r)*	flocks	(r)*	swarms

While the dependent element (r) is not used very frequently, it can be a most convenient one. Some more examples:

(1)*   library associations

(r)*   committees $01 joint

               (1)*   libraries

               (r)*   consortia

               ^{c}
               (q)*   Research Libraries Group

(1)*   libraries

(r)*   networks

^{c}
(q)*   NELINET

The entries below are collocated as they would be in a real index:

Committees.   Library associations
   Joint committees

Consortia.   Libraries
   Research Libraries Group

Libraries
   Consortia: Research Libraries Group
   Networks: NELINET

Library associations
   Joint committees

(Example continues on next page)

NELINET. Networks. Libraries

Networks. Libraries
NELINET

Research Libraries Group. Consortia. Libraries

References: **New England Library Information Network** *See* **NELINET**
RLG *See* **Research Libraries Group**

COORDINATE CONCEPTS: OPERATOR (g)

Sometimes several separate concepts are grouped for study or explanation in terms of some common factors. These are combinations of things rather than combinations of themes. In such cases, a coordinating operator is needed to put the concepts into proper relationship with each other. For this, coordinate concepts (g) and (f) are used. These coordinate concepts are not the same as the aggregate (r). Aggregates are groupings usually involving people or animals, and may be attributed to a "herding instinct"; the groupings appear to be a result of natural selection, and, for all practical purposes occur in nature, performing a survival or social function.

Coordinate concept (g) applies to Terms that may be connected by the word "and." In general format, they may be subclasses of a given class, all on the same level (in an array), as, for example, in:

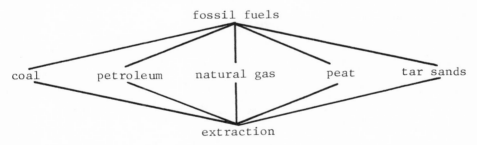

Fossil fuels are one kind of energy source, and, in turn, they are taken from the earth by some form of extraction (drilling, digging, mining). It is necessary, when dealing with Terms in this kind of a related group, to consider them as a unit or block. And the whole block must be considered in relation to the Terms above and below it.

The whole block begins with the operator (q) and ends with the final (g). The connective "($v) &" (always an ampersand) comes in the next to the last (g) element. The block, then, consists of the Term preceding the first (g), which is (q) "coal." This is followed by the entire array of (g)s. The (g)s indicate that these Terms are on a par in the array with (q) "coal." In other words, the (g)s are valued as (q)s, just as if the line read "coal & natural gas & peat & petroleum & tar sands." The action or other operators may follow or precede the "g" block, as indexing requires.

String:	(1)* energy sources	
	(q)* coal	
	(g)* natural gas	
	(g)* peat	"g" block
	(g)* petroleum $v &	
	(g)* tar sands	
	(2)* extraction	

In general, the operator (g) may be used with operators (0) to (6) and with the dependent elements (p), (q), and (r), or a combination of these.

In operation, when an element above the "g block" comes into the *lead* position, the whole block is printed as a unit in the *display*. When an element *below* the "g" block comes into the *lead*, the block is printed as a unit in the *qualifier* (provided the Standard Format is being applied). When any of the elements in the block go into the *lead* position, *all other parts of the block are suppressed*. When printing in block form, each Term tagged (g) is preceded by a comma except the last — the one following "($v) &."

Let us now proceed with the entries in the "energy sources" string:

Entries:

Energy sources
   Coal, natural gas, peat, petroleum & tar
      sands. Extraction

Coal.   Energy sources
   Extraction

Natural gas.   Energy sources
   Extraction

Peat.   Energy sources
   Extraction

Petroleum.   Energy sources
   Extraction

Tar sands.   Energy sources
   Extraction

Extraction.   Coal, natural gas, peat, petroleum &
      tar sands. Energy sources

Coordinate concepts more often occur in less lengthy strings than this. For example:

Veterinary services for birds, dogs, and horses

Strings:	(1)* birds (LO)	
	(g)* dogs (LO)	
	(g)* horses (LO)	
	(r) birds, dogs & horses	[aggregate]
	(2)* veterinary services	

Entries: **Birds**
                  Birds, dogs & horses. Veterinary services

                  Dogs
                  Birds, dogs & horses. Veterinary services

                  Horses
                  Birds, dogs & horses. Veterinary services

                  Veterinary services.   Birds, dogs & horses

This kind of string could be used in a situation where a separate class number was needed for each entry—some special usage, a classified catalog, for example. Normally, the (g) operator without the (LO)s and aggregate (r) would pertain.

The filing order of coordinate concepts can be significant. Sometimes words are normally considered in a certain order, such as "ham and eggs." There is nothing wrong with "eggs and ham," but usually the other form is followed. A preferred form is called *canonical* order. Other kinds of order are:

—time-dependent, where there is a sequence in time (infant, child, adolescent)

—alphabetical, when it is neutral as to context

If adjectives have been added, the order may have to be modified. One could have a sequence "sapphires, emeralds, synthetic rubies and diamonds." There might be a question as to whether the diamonds were natural or synthetic. In this case, an alphabetical arrangement happens to work out well: "diamonds, emeralds, sapphires and synthetic rubies," but this is not always the case. The best arrangement is the one least likely to be misinterpreted.

NON-STANDARD COORDINATION

There is a non-standard method of getting similar results without using (g) at all. This is done only under certain rather limited circumstances, as follows:[3]

1) The relationship between coordinated concepts is a *contextual creation* (created by the context), such that none of these concepts would normally occur together.

2) A *binding* term may or may not be present.

Non-standard treatment consists of creating an aggregate (r) and using it to show the relationship each time an individual Term in the collective block comes into the *lead*. The individual concepts are written one at a time *above* the aggregate and each one appears *only* in the *lead* position, never in the *qualifier* or *display*. In other words, each one is treated as a (LO) entry and the Terms as a group only appear in the aggregate (r) Term.

Joint committees of students and faculty in universities

String:		
(1)*	universities	
(p)*	students (LO)	
(p)*	faculty (LO)	
(r)	students & faculty	[aggregate]
(r)*	committees $01 joint	[binding term]

Entries:

Universities
Students & faculty. Joint committees

Students. Universities
Students & faculty. Joint committees

Faculty. Universities
Students & faculty. Joint committees

Committees. Students & faculty. Universities
Joint committees

At this point, the new operator (f) for a different treatment of coordinate concepts will be introduced and explained.

ALTERNATIVE TREATMENT OF A COORDINATE CONCEPT: OPERATOR (f)

Normally with coordinate concept (g), when one coordinate concept appears in the *lead*, the rest are suppressed. The result, in a string with a "g" block, is that each coordinate concept is led as if it were the *only* concept. For example, take the case of a document on the topic:

Physiology of frogs and toads in France

String:

               d
(0)*   France
(1)*   frogs $v & ⎤
(g)*   toads   ⎦ "g" block
(2)*   physiology

Entries:

France
Frogs & toads. Physiology

Frogs. France
Physiology

Toads. France
Physiology

Physiology. Frogs & toads. France

Sometimes each Term in a "g" block would fall into two different classes and an entry would be needed for each one (in a classified catalog). As we have seen, this has been accomplished until recently by means of a different string. The combination "frogs & toads" was used as each word came into the *lead*:

```
                        d
String:        (0)*   France
               (1)*   frogs  (LO)
               (g)*   toads  (LO)    ⎤  "g" block
               (r)    frogs & toads  ⎦
               (2)*   physiology
```

Entries: **France**
        Frogs & toads. Physiology

        Frogs. France
        Frogs & toads. Physiology

        Toads. France
        Frogs & toads. Physiology

        Physiology. Frogs & toads. France

The same result can now be obtained with a new coordinate concept operator (f). This operator identifies a member of a coordinate "f" block, but allows each element in the block to be treated separately as a *lead* while retaining the coordination of concepts in the *display*.

```
                        d
String:        (0)*   France
               (1)*   frogs  $v &    ⎤
               (f)*   toads           ⎦  "f" block
               (2)*   physiology
```

Entries: **France**
        Frogs & toads. Physiology

        Frogs. France
        Frogs & toads. Physiology

        Toads. France
        Frogs & toads. Physiology

        Physiology. Frogs & toads. France

Another example, in which each Term is differenced, shows the same thing in a more complex pattern. Here, when there are differenced Terms in the "f" block, the whole coordinated Term appears in the *display* (the whole "f" block), replacing the full differenced Term. The object is to avoid redundancy.

```
                        d
String:        (0)*   France
               (1)*   frogs $21 green  $v &   ⎤
               (f)*   toads $21 yellow          ⎦  "f" block
               (2)*   physiology
```

Entries: **France**
Green frogs & yellow toads. Physiology

Frogs.   France
Green frogs & yellow toads. Physiology

Green frogs.   France
Green frogs & yellow toads. Physiology

Toads.   France
Green frogs & yellow toads. Physiology

Yellow toads.   France
Green frogs & yellow toads. Physiology

Physiology.   Green frogs & yellow toads. France

With the (f) operator, as each Term in the "f" block comes into the *lead*, the whole "f" block is printed in the *display*. The focus and difference appear normally in the *lead*, but the full differenced Term is *not* repeated in the beginning of the display as in *normal* practice.

The net result of operator (f) is to give an entry for each of two or more subjects which may be coordinated in the document but are classified separately. The example of "frogs" and "toads" is used because it is easy to see what happens. With combinations of more widely separated classes, this method has become a necessity. An example will help demonstrate this:

Older format

String:
(1)*   small groups
(2)*   communication (LO)
(q)*   decision making (LO)
(r)   communication & decision making   [aggregate]
(2)*   record-keeping

Entries: **Small groups**
Communication & decision making. Record-keeping

Communication.   Small groups
Record-keeping

Decision making.   Small groups
Record-keeping

Record-keeping.   Communication & decision making. Small
groups

New format

String:
(1)*   small groups
(2)*   communication $v &   ⎤
(f)*   decision making   ⎦   "f" block
(2)*   record-keeping

Entries: **Small groups**
Communication & decision making. Record-keeping

Communication.   Small groups
Communication & decision making. Record-keeping

Decision making.   Small groups
Communication & decision making. Record-keeping

Record-keeping.   Communication & decision making.
Small groups

The routine for the coordinate concept (f) does not affect the existing algorithm for coordinate concept (g). Rather, it gives greater latitude and less redundancy in an "apples and oranges" situation. All of these new routines extend the indexer's skill in rendering context better, while gaining more control over classifying in separate categories and at the same time the grammatical readability is improved.

The dependent elements and coordinates may be used to produce partial strings for some of the examples from chapter 3.

USE OF DEPENDENT ELEMENTS AND COORDINATE CONCEPTS IN EARLIER EXAMPLES

With the introduction of dependent elements and coordinate concepts, string-making becomes a more flexible operation. For instance, one of the strings from chapter 3 uses coordinate concepts:

Examination of houses for physical soundness and structural stability

String: (1)*   houses
(g)*   soundness $21 physical $v &   ⎤
(g)*   stability $21 structural   ⎦   "g" block
(2)*   examination

Entries: **Houses**
Physical soundness & structural stability. Examination

Soundness.   Houses
Physical soundness. Examination

Physical soundness.   Houses
Examination

Stability.   Houses
Structural stability. Examination

Structural stability.   Houses
Examination

Examination.   Physical soundness & structural stability
Houses

A somewhat similar situation exists with the book on the work of M. C. Escher, but with coordinate concepts *and* dependent elements:

Drawings, engravings and prints by Maurits Cornelis Escher

String:
- (2)*   graphic arts $21 Dutch
- (q)*   drawings
- (g)*   engravings $v &
- (g)*   prints   c
- (p)*   Escher, Maurits Cornelis

] "g" block

Entries:

Graphic arts
Dutch graphic arts: Drawings, engravings & prints.
Escher, Maurits Cornelis

Dutch graphic arts
Drawings, engravings & prints. Escher,
Maurits Cornelis

Drawings.   Dutch graphic arts
Escher, Maurits Cornelis

Engravings.   Dutch graphic arts
Escher, Maurits Cornelis

Prints.   Dutch graphic arts
Escher, Maurits Cornelis

Escher, Maurits Cornelis.   Drawings, engravings
& prints. Dutch graphic arts

Both this string and the previous one are incomplete because each lacks a form element, to indicate that the book is intended for prospective buyers in the first case and is mainly illustrations in the second.

The "c" over Escher's name is the Term code for "class of one," for names of people and organizations capable of authorship or equivalent in arts other than writing. Names of things incapable of authorship, such as monuments, paintings, and musical compositions, are tagged "b."

The coordinate operator (g) does not produce an unambiguous set of entries when two separate *themes* occur in a single work. For this problem, a different solution has been developed, using operators called "theme interlinks" or, in special cases, a downward-reading substitution. These will be taken up in chapter 10.

Other examples used in earlier chapters would have been vastly improved by use of Compound Term procedures, and in the process, more words would have been available for use as entries. Note the doubling of the number of entries made possible by this means:

electronics industries   (1)   industries $21 electronics

folk dancing   (2)   dancing $21 folk

In addition, some of the examples of chapter 4 require dependent elements, compounding, and differencing. Only two will be given here as the remainder call for use of topics that have not yet been introduced. These two are:

Rental of offices in New York skyscrapers

String:		d
	(0)*	New York $i (N.Y.)
	(1)*	skyscrapers
	(p)*	offices
	(2)*	rentals

(The $i is used to make "N.Y." appear in italics.)

Entries: **New York** (*N. Y.*)
Skyscrapers. Offices. Rentals

Skyscrapers. New York (*N. Y.*)
Offices. Rentals

Offices. Skyscrapers. New York (*N. Y.*)
Rentals

Rentals. Offices. Skyscrapers. New York (*N. Y.*)

Although "skyscrapers" is still a common word, it has been supplanted to a considerable degree by the newer term "high rise" for tall buildings. Whether "skyscraper" should be replaced completely by "high rise" is a moot question. This will probably be the case in time; the current high rise building is much higher than the buildings for which the term "skyscraper" was coined. Either way, a cross-reference will be needed.

Bicycling on paths in Cleveland's peripheral metropolitan parks

String:		d
	(0)	Ohio $_d$
	(p)*	Cleveland
	(1)*	parks $21 metropolitan $01 peripheral
	(p)*	paths (NU)
	(2)*	bicycling

Entries: **Cleveland.** Ohio
Peripheral metropolitan parks. Paths. Bicycling

Parks. Cleveland. Ohio
Peripheral metropolitan parks. Paths. Bicycling

Metropolitan parks. Cleveland. Ohio
Peripheral metropolitan parks. Paths. Bicycling

Paths. Peripheral metropolitan parks. Cleveland. Ohio
Bicycling

Bicycling. Peripheral metropolitan parks. Cleveland. Ohio

In the above example, the choice of use or non-use of a Term in a string has been made somewhat arbitrarily to demonstrate PRECIS conventions. In an actual indexing situation, this would not happen because the material being indexed would dictate decisions. The indexer has discretionary powers to add, delete, or rearrange if necessary to bring out the sense of the material. It is the indexer's job to convey the subject content of the material as faithfully as possible. It is the system's job to make this possible.

The example used in chapter 3 for the mathematical technique of "tiling the plane" can now be written as a string. A "*See also*" reference would be used referring from "mathematics" to "geometry." As a discipline name, "geometry" would be tagged with operator (2) for the action, "study of geometry."

String: (2)* geometry
       (p) techniques
       (q)* tiling the plane

Reference: **Tessellation** *See* **Tiling the plane**

The corresponding entries are:

  Geometry
    Techniques: Tiling the plane

  Tiling the plane. Techniques. Geometry

Probably, there should also be a cross-reference:

  Planes
   See also
   Tiling the plane

In the above example and with a number of earlier ones, multiple word combinations are used. The indexer may find it difficult to determine when to use single words, when to use combinations, and when to difference. At this point, therefore, it is expedient to introduce conventions governing use of multiple word Terms.

MULTIPLE-WORD TERMS

Newcomers to PRECIS very often find the length of Terms in individual elements of a string and in entries puzzling. This is probably because they are used to different philosophies of indexing. If they are accustomed to seeing subject headings that are usually not longer than three or four words, or if they expect to find entries under almost every word, even if it requires inverted headings, they are apt to regard the length of *leads* produced by PRECIS as less than optimal. There are also problems when a topic is covered both with a multiple word entry and with a succession of entries that have been made from the kind of string elements where differencing or sequencing has been used. An apparent conflict ensues.

For a time, free association of words was widely used, as in the Uniterms example. In general, however, because of semantic problems with the free association of single words to form multiple word terms, the modern thesaurus, using the *Thesaurus of Engineering and Scientific Terms* as a prototype and now in standardized format, is preferred. Such thesauri rarely have more than four or five words in combination and the thesaurus itself is structured to show some degree of hierarchy.

The third kind of index is based on rotation of terms, usually in titles, whereby each word deemed significant is used in turn as a headword. The purpose of such indexes, notably Keyword-In-Context (KWIC), Keyword-Out-Of-Context (KWOC), and similar systems, is to index words in their context. The methodology lends itself to computerization, and a modification of it is used to produce modern concordances, covering all but the most frequently appearing words with all of their occurrences in the full text of a work.

In a way, PRECIS, where the context is related to the content of a work rather than to its title alone, stands somewhere between keyword indexing and the modern concordance. Its foundation is completely different from that of subject headings, Uniterms, KWIC or KWOC indexes, or use of thesauri terms (whether in Boolean combination or unconnected). PRECIS provides an approximation of the full text in the "title-like phrase."

One of the permitted practices in PRECIS is the use of multiple word Terms. In all cases the word pairs, triplets, and so on should be logical. In general, the following conventions apply and show in a practical manner why some of the multiple word Terms may appear as such.

A *multiple word Term* may be used

1) when a pair of words cannot be split without changing the meaning of the Term. This is the old Uniterm problem of fish food / food fish. In PRECIS, this would be expressed as a bound Term (as in thesauri): fish food; or as a following difference: food for fish. It would also include the bound term, food fish, or the sequence (preferable):

   (1) food
   (q) fish

2) when a Term is usually encountered as a unit:

   decision making

3) when writing a Term of several words. This is legitimate for the cases listed below. In each case, the reason for using a multiple word Term is that some condition has been satisfied, such as the presence of a thesaurus reference for the broader word, or for some kinds of conditions connected with differenced Terms.

   a) A thesaurus reference has been made connecting a Term to a subclass or an association:

   Turbulence
   See also
   Clear air turbulence

(Example continues on page 120)

Gems
See also
Synthetic gems

b) A lead Term consists of a focus and preceding or following difference, and only the first word is wanted as a *lead*:

Preceding: Following:
                 turbulent flow   poetry in German

c) An entry is not wanted for a focus and/or preceding differences:

edible oils

square root tables

d) An index entry is not wanted for the focus and preceding difference, but a thesaural reference is needed for the focus:

String: (1)   cars $01 Monza $21 Chevrolet

Entry: **Chevrolet cars**

Reference: **Cars**
                 See also
                 Chevrolet cars

A collective reference like this is more useful and more economical than numerous entries under "cars."

e) The focus and differences wanted as *leads* are separated by words unwanted as *leads*. This can happen more than once in a single Term:

(1)   engines $21 internal combustion

(1)*   lamps $21 mercury vapor $01 high pressure
       $21 fluorescent $21 tubular

—in the latter case the unwanted words are

vapor
high
pressure

f) The focus is the only word wanted as a *lead* in a long phrase of mainly informational character. In such cases, two lines are used, with the first marked (LO):

(1)*   post offices (LO)
(1)   post offices serving populations of less than 1,000

The unled Term will appear in the entries, but never as a *lead*.

g) An adjectival phrase follows a focus:

handicrafts using leather

In such cases, a thesaural reference is made:

Leather
See also
Handicrafts using leather

Obviously, the term "leather handicrafts" is not satisfactory!

h) An adjectival or prepositional phrase appears as a following difference:

Damage during testing

Bookstores selling greeting cards

Management by objectives

Grammatically speaking, some differences are never simple, single word adjectival types.

Finally, multiple word Terms are used

4) When too many entries would appear under a very common word, such as "analysis," "services," "systems," etc.

Systems
See also
Communication systems
Computer systems
Control systems

Computer systems
See also
Analog computer systems
Digital computer systems

In addition, the normal processing of PRECIS strings creates many multiple-word Terms as a result of use of connectives, substitutions, and special combinations introduced by operators whose function is to make such combinations.

Some of the combinations found in the *British National Bibliography* suggest that the indexer must have been at wit's end to find a viable entry. In general, however, most combinations of words have a logical foundation. Some combinations in colloquial speech and writing are grammatical or syntactical shortcuts and as such have no place in a logical-linguistic system such as PRECIS.

SUMMARY

Up to this point, the following have been covered: Main Line operators (0), (1), and (2); differencing; interposed operators consisting of dependent elements and coordinate concepts; and multiple word Terms. It is now possible to handle a good proportion of the type of index entries that are encountered, provided they do not contain highly complex relationships. Even with only this much of PRECIS, one can begin to get a feel for the system. All of these relationships are basic.

In the next chapter, the Inverted Format and operators (4), (5), and (6) will be introduced. This format and these remaining Main Line operators add to the indexer's versatility and capability in performing the job.

PRECIS MANUAL REFERENCES

Some of the topics of this chapter are covered in greater detail on pp. 83-112 of the *Manual*. It is recommended that the beginning indexer read the sections listed below and return to other parts as problems arise in the course of indexing:

Sections 9.14-9.15, Rules of Differencing, pp. 85-86.

Sections 14.1-14.14, Interposed Operators (p), (q), (r), pp. 103-112.

Sections 15.1-15.15, Coordinate Concept, pp. 113-29.

NOTE: In using the *Manual*, the differencing operators translate as follows:

$h = $01 $k = $02 $i = $21 $m = $22

REFERENCES

[1]Derek Austin, Handout from PRECIS Course, Dalhousie University, 1977: 5A. Modified slightly.

[2]Derek Austin, *PRECIS: A Manual of Concept Analysis and Subject Indexing* (London: Council of the British National Bibliography, 1974), p. 110.

[3]The description of changes in non-standard coordination and the (f) operator is based on handouts from the Subject Systems Office, Bibliographic Services Division, The British Library.

7
INVERTED FORMAT:
Concepts of Place and Time†

There are many situations in indexing where information is needed on

— data that relate to the observer

— cases where an example is used to study a subject rather than undertaking a comprehensive treatment

— presentation of data in terms of the target toward which they are directed and/or their form.

For these special cases, which appear rather frequently with books, some indication is needed to warn the user that the material is being presented in a particular way. At the same time, the Standard Format does not bring out these features, so that a more suitable format is required. This is especially true when the Term for the form, or whatever, goes into the *lead*.

INVERTED FORMAT

The Inverted Format is used with operators (4), (5), and (6). It is called "inverted" because when the Term in the string is in the *lead* position, an inversion of the Standard Format takes place. Terms that would normally go into the *qualifier* are dropped into the *display* in downward-reading string order. This inversion highlights the special cases tagged with operators (4), (5), and (6), when these are in the *lead* position.

Operator (4): Viewpoint as Form

This operator is used in situations where the material or subject under discussion may be treated from several viewpoints and it is desirable to indicate which view is being used. It is not too hard to think of examples. One may want to indicate that the work is being slanted or "biased" (in the sense of the word "bias" as used by historians) because the author belongs to a school of thought, a culture, or a group that makes it imperative for him or her to look at the world through the eyes of that group. The flat-earth proponents, for example, will have a different slant in discussing geography or voyages than those who believe the

---

†All examples from the *British National Bibliography* are marked # or indicated in the text. These examples are reproduced courtesy of Bibliographic Services Division, The British Library, London, England.

earth is round. Members of schools of thought in philosophy, such as logical positivism or acceptance of the "Received View," will write differently from members of other groups. Political, social, economic, or religious viewpoints vary greatly according to which group a writer belongs to. A Quaker, for instance, will not approach questions dealing with war from the same point of view as a military officer. Some examples from actual PRECIS entries in the *British National Bibliography* will illustrate use of the operator.[1]

— *Anthropological perspectives*

— *Philosophical perspectives*

— *Sociological perspectives*

— *Church of God viewpoints*

— *Marxist viewpoints*

— *Angola Solidarity Committee viewpoints*

When in the *display*, these Terms are always preceded by a dash and are in italics. When they come into the *lead*, the Inverted Format comes into play and the rest of the entry, *in string order*, is dropped into the *display*. Data *relating to the observer* do not go into the *qualifier*. Some examples illustrate the function of this interesting operator:

Psychological perspectives on labelling mental disorders in man

String: (1)   man
                     (2)*   mental disorders
                     (2)*   labelling
                     (4)*   psychological perspectives

Entries: **Mental disorders.**   Man
                     Labelling — *Psychological perspectives*

                     Labelling.   Mental disorders. Man
                     — *Psychological perspectives*

Inverted Format:

                     Psychological perspectives
                     Man. Mental disorders. Labelling

Note that as long as the (4) Term is in the *display*, it is italicized. When it goes into the *lead*, it is in bold face type like any other *lead* Term. In the type of indexing shown in this example, "man" may not be required as an access point, but this word is used to indicate to whom the "mental disorders" apply and it brings out the full meaning of the string elements to be preserved in context.

Two additional examples of the use of role operator (4) should aid in clarifying the usage of this operator.

Philosophical considerations of knowledge and certainty #

String:	(1)* knowledge
	(p)* certainty
	(4)* philosophical perspectives

Entries:	**Knowledge**
	Certainty — *Philosophical perspectives*

Certainty. Knowledge
— *Philosophical perspectives*

Inverted Format:

Philosophical perspectives
Knowledge. Certainty

Medical viewpoints on drug abuse

String:	(2)* drug abuse
	(4)* medical viewpoints

Entries:	**Drug abuse**
	— *Medical viewpoints*

Inverted Format:

Medical viewpoints
Drug abuse

These cases treat viewpoint *as form.* Viewpoint *as subject* is a different matter and will be treated later. The reader should remember that the type of viewpoint that calls for operator (4) is one in which a subject is treated from a certain point of view. It is as if the writer were looking at the world through rose-colored glasses. The indexer, in noting the viewpoint, is telling the user that this description will present one way of looking at a subject. Examination of the viewpoint itself, as a subject, an action, or an attitude is not the same thing and is treated differently in PRECIS.

Operator (5): Sample Population/Study Regions

In some cases, the topic of the work being indexed is limited in scope or coverage. In such cases, the indexer may wish to convey to the user the exact extent or specific limitations of the work. By using operator (5) and conventional expressions such as "study examples," "study regions," "sample populations," or some such wording, the scope can be indicated so that the reader is not deceived by an imprecise title or misdirected to an uninteresting topic or area. Unlike operator (4), operator (5) is not in itself used as a *lead*; instead, the material it specifies or points to becomes the *lead*, with the operator expression in the *qualifier*. The format for this Term consists of a dash, the operator tag, identifying words, a colon, and the actual example, all in italics (from the *British National Bibliography*):

— *Study regions: West Yorkshire (Metropolitan County). Bradford*

— *Study examples: Marriage counselling*

— *Study examples: Yequana children — Study regions: Venezuela. Bolivar State*

Two title-like phrases, strings, and entries for operator (5) follow:

Group ministry in the Episcopal Church for rural regions such as Appalachia

String:

    (0)*   rural regions

    (1)*   Episcopal Church ᶜ

    (p)*   group ministry

    (5)   study regions

    (q)*   Appalachia ᵈ

Entries:

Rural regions
Episcopal Church. Group ministry —
Study regions: Appalachia

Episcopal Church.   Rural regions
Group ministry — *Study regions: Appalachia*

Group ministry.   Episcopal Church. Rural regions
— *Study regions: Appalachia*

Inverted Format:

Appalachia. *Study regions*
Rural regions. Episcopal Church. Group ministry

Note that when the information tagged by the (5) operator goes into the *lead*, the operator expression, "study regions," goes into the *qualifier* in italics.

Norms of Maya social behaviour in Zinacantán, Mexico

String:

    (0)*   Mexico ᵈ

    (p)*   Chiapas $i (State) ᵈ

    (1)*   Maya

    (2)*   social behaviour

    (p)*   norms

    (5)   study regions

    (q)   Mexico ᵈ

    (p)*   Zinacantán ᵈ

Entries: **Mexico**
Chiapas (*State*). Maya. Social behaviour. Norms
— *Study regions: Mexico. Zinacantán*

Chiapas (*State*). Mexico
Maya. Social behaviour. Norms — *Study regions:*
Mexico. Zinacantán

Maya. Chiapas (*State*). Mexico
Social behaviour. Norms — *Study regions: Mexico*
Zinacantán

Social behaviour. Maya. Chiapas (*State*). Mexico
Norms — *Study regions: Mexico. Zinacantán*

Norms. Social behaviour. Maya. Chiapas (*State*). Mexico
— *Study regions: Mexico. Zinacantán*

Inverted Format:

Zinacantán. Mexico. *Study regions*
Mexico. Chiapas (*State*). Maya. Social
behaviour. Norms

Notice that "Mexico," which is untagged, moves into the *qualifier* as with any other normal Standard Format Term, when "Zinacantán" is in the *lead*.

The expressions, "study regions," "study examples," and such, always precede a more specific designation identified with the operator (q). This next word (or words) gives the name of the actual region, example, and so forth. The pair of Terms tagged (5) and (q) says, in effect, that the item at hand is "a special example which is...." There is a further property of operator (5) to be noted: the operator (q) denotes the specific topic. But that topic in turn may have a dependent element or elements. Any of these dependent elements, if marked for the *lead*, also induce the Inverted Format:

Location of industries in the metropolitan region of Philadelphia,
    Pennsylvania

String: (0)*   metropolitan regions

                (1)*   industries

                (2)*   location

                (5)   study regions$_d$

                (q)*   Pennsylvania$_d$

                (p)*   Philadelphia

Entries: **Metropolitan regions**
Industries. Location — *Study regions: Pennsylvania.*
Philadelphia

(Example continues on page 128)

Industries.   Metropolitan regions
Location — *Study regions: Pennsylvania. Philadelphia*

Location.   Industries. Metropolitan regions
— *Study regions: Pennsylvania. Philadelphia*

Inverted Format:

Pennsylvania.   *Study regions*
Metropolitan regions. Industries. Location — *Study regions: Pennsylvania. Philadelphia*

Inverted Format:

Philadelphia.   Pennsylvania. *Study regions*
Metropolitan regions. Industries. Location

If the items under "study regions," as above, have several dependent elements, the italicized block, starting with "study regions" and ending in "Philadelphia," is retained in the *display* until the last Term in the block comes into the *lead*. If this were not done, the entry under "Pennsylvania" would not have left any inkling that the metropolitan region being studied was in the vicinity of Philadelphia. This is one of the finer points of PRECIS that gives the system an unexpected degree of elegance for such special meanings.

Operator (6): Target/Form

This operator is probably the most widely used of the three calling for Inverted Format. It covers both the "target" at which a document is aimed and the "form" of material it contains. Targets are usually given with the word "for" as a non-*lead* direct difference. A listing from the *British National Bibliography* illustrates the scope of this operator.

Target: (6)   Irish students $01 for

            (6)   British businessmen $01 for

            (6)   slow learning adolescents $01 for

            (6)   motoring $01 for

            (6)   design $01 for

            (6)   business enterprise $01 for

Form divisions are almost unlimited:

(6)	guidebooks	(6)	early works
(6)	case studies	(6)	conference proceedings
(6)	collections	(6)	illustrations
(6)	codes of conduct	(6)	critical studies
(6)	readings	(6)	amateurs' manuals
(6)	yearbooks	(6)	proposals
(6)	teaching kits	(6)	texts with commentaries
(6)	directories	(6)	recipes
(6)	reports, surveys	(6)	lists
(6)	feasibility studies	(6)	practical information

(6) biographies	(6) standards
(6) scripts	(6) exercises, worked examples
(6) personal observations	

Whether Target comes before Form or Form before Target is left to the discretion of the indexer. The indexer uses whichever order makes better sense in its context. If in doubt, Form goes before Target.

Sources of information about social services for handicapped persons in Canada

String:
                             d
          (0)* Canada
          (1)* social services
          (p)* information sources
          (6)* handicapped persons $01 for
          (6) directories

Entries:

Canada
   Social services. Information sources — *For handicapped persons — Directories*

Social services. Canada
   Information sources — *For handicapped persons — Directories*

Information sources. Social services. Canada
   — For handicapped persons — Directories

Inverted Format:

Handicapped persons
   Canada. Social services. Information sources — *For handicapped persons — Directories*

Note that when the Target is in the *lead*, the word "for" is deleted. The Target statement is retained in the final entry, however, for textual clarity.

In making the actual index, a number of similar entries may be brought together under a single heading. Where there are multiple entries, the heading is suppressed after the first usage so that a neat indentation is obtained. The examples below are taken from the *British National Bibliography*:

Inflation. Finance. Great Britain
   Control. Policies of government. Pay limit
   Control. Policies of government. Pay limit — *Communist Party of Great Britain viewpoints*

Motoring
   England. Canals — *Guidebooks — For motoring*
   Kent — *Guidebooks — For motoring*
   North-east England — *Guidebooks — For motoring*
   Salop — *Guidebooks — For motoring*

Christian life
  — *Daily readings*
  — *For East African students* — *Secondary school texts*
  — *Lectures, speeches*
  — *Personal observations*
Love of enemies. Psychological aspects
Meditation
Meditation groups. Organisation — *Manuals*
Mysticism
Prayer
Prayer — *Prayer books*
Transactional analysis

In the actual index, as may be seen from the "Christian life" example above, form divisions, targets, viewpoints, and study examples are listed before the other items. This is because a dash files before a letter or number. Some examples:

Term with form division only:

Daily readings about the Christian life #

String: (1)*   Christian life
                 (6)   daily readings

Entries: **Christian life**
                   — *Daily readings*

Manuals for organisation of meditation groups on Christian life #

String: (1)*   Christian life
                 (p)*   meditation groups
                 (2)*   organisation
                 (6)   manuals

Entries: **Christian life**
                 Meditation groups. Organisation — *Manuals*

                 Meditation groups.   Christian life
                 Organisation — *Manuals*

                 Organisation.   Meditation groups. Christian life
                   — *Manuals*

With PRECIS, the indexer has to give some thought to collocation. Indexers working with an authority file do not have this problem because the authority file is designed to take care of such things. The PRECIS indexer would have to look at the entries in the previously finished index and decide how to work out the new string so that the new entry would add to the index rather than complicate it. For example, if the topic being indexed was "early Christian life," a thesaural reference would have to be made from "Christian life":

Christian life
See also
Early Christian life

unless the Term were differenced:

(1)*   Christian life $21 early

Entry under "early Christian life" alone, without differencing or with no way of relating it to existing entries under "Christian life" would be a disservice to the user who might want both but not be aware of the two kinds of entries.

Role Operators (4), (5), and (6) in Combination

Operators (4), (5), and (6) are often found in combination, as may be seen from the following examples taken from the *British National Bibliography*:

Society
Role of science — *Philosophical perspectives* — *Polish texts*

Monopolies.   Great Britain
Efficiency — *Aims of Industry viewpoints* — *Case studies*

United States
Metropolitan regions. Social planning. Leadership — *Sociological perspectives* — *Study regions: Atlantic coast states* — *Reports, surveys* — *For social agencies*

Finally, to make quite clear where the Inverted Format is used and where it is not, an example will be given in both the Inverted and the Standard Format.

Standard Format

Waterfalls from hanging valleys in Yosemite National Park

String: (0)*   California d b
(p)*   Yosemite National Park
(1)*   valleys $21 hanging
(p)*   waterfalls

Entries: **California**
Yosemite National Park. Hanging valleys. Waterfalls

Yosemite National Park.   California
Hanging valleys. Waterfalls

(Example continues on page 132)

Valleys.   Yosemite National Park. California
Hanging valleys. Waterfalls

Hanging valleys.   Yosemite National Park. California
Waterfalls

Waterfalls.   Hanging valleys. Yosemite National
Park. California

Inverted Format

*Bridal Veil Falls, an example of a waterfall from a hanging valley in
Yosemite National Park*

String:
$$\overset{d}{(0)^*}\quad \text{California}$$

$$\overset{b}{(p)^*}\quad \text{Yosemite National Park}$$

(1)*   valleys $21 hanging

(p)*   waterfalls

(5)   study examples

$$\overset{b}{(q)^*}\quad \text{Bridal Veil Falls}$$

Entries:
California
Yosemite National Park. Hanging valleys. Waterfalls
— *Study examples: Bridal Veil Falls*

Yosemite National Park.   California
Hanging valleys. Waterfalls — *Study examples:
Bridal Veil Falls*

Valleys.   Yosemite National Park. California
Hanging valleys. Waterfalls — *Study examples:
Bridal Veil Falls*

Hanging valleys.   Yosemite National Park. California
Waterfalls — *Study examples: Bridal Veil Falls*

Waterfalls.   Hanging valleys. Yosemite National Park.
California
— *Study examples: Bridal Veil Falls*

Inverted Format

Bridal Veil Falls.   *Study examples*
California. Yosemite National Park. Hanging valleys.
Waterfalls

Inverting the order when the viewpoint, sample, or form is needed as a *lead*
has the advantage of a special physical layout for emphasis. As is the case in using
indentations to show hierarchies in a classification schedule, so also may the

judicious use of space in printing lend emphasis and even provide some degree of classification in the order of words in a group of entries.

At this point, more of the sample topics in chapter 4 may be indexed.

Computers as an example of marketing in Japanese electronic industries

String:
                             d
- (0)*   Japan
- (1)*   industries $21 electronics
- (2)*   marketing
- (5)   study examples
- (q)*   computers

Entries:

Japan
    Electronics industries. Marketing — *Study examples:*
      Computers

Industries. Japan
    Electronics industries. Marketing — *Study examples:*
      Computers

Electronics industries. Japan
    Marketing — *Study examples: Computers*

Marketing. Electronics industries. Japan
    — *Study examples: Computers*

Inverted Format:

Computers. *Study examples*
Japan. Electronics industries. Marketing

Photography of folk dancing in Kentucky using the Virginia Reel as an example

String:
                             d
- (0)*   Kentucky
- (2)*   dancing $21 folk
- (2)*   photography
- (5)   study examples
- (q)*   Virginia Reel

Entries:

Kentucky
    Folk dancing. Photography — *Study examples:*
      Virginia Reel

Dancing. Kentucky
    Folk dancing. Photography — *Study examples:*
      Virginia Reel

Folk dancing. Kentucky
    Photography — *Study examples: Virginia Reel*

Photography. Folk dancing. Kentucky
    — *Study examples: Virginia Reel*

Inverted Format:

Virginia Reel. *Study examples*
Kentucky. Folk dancing. Photography

The book on how to buy a house, partially completed in the last chapter, can now be completed by adding another string Term:

(6)*   prospective buyers $01 for

This would add "For prospective buyers" in italics and preceded by a dash, at the end of each entry shown in chapter 6 plus an inverted format entry under "Prospective buyers." When a Target item is not used as a *lead*, the string Term does not have to be differenced, but can be written out:

(6)   for prospective buyers

Little shortcuts like this and other use of multiple word Terms can save time, whether the index is made by hand or by computer.

Viewpoint as form (operator 4), Sample population/Study regions (operator 5) and Target/Form (operator 6) are very convenient role operators in conveying information about the material to the user. They add details of the context of the subject and its format. The latter is particularly helpful for the user who may only want a certain kind of information for specific needs.

Dropping the (4), (5), or (6) Terms
from the *Display*

Where there are (4), (5), or (6) operators in a string, a different set of instructions is employed:[4]

If the last Term in the *lead* is not also the last in the string, it is repeated in the display.

Tables of physical constants for engineering

String: (2)*   physics
                 (p)*   constants
                 (6)*   engineering $01 for
                 (6)*   tables

Entries: **Physics**
                 Constants — *For engineering* — *Tables*

                 Constants.   Physics
                 — *For engineering* — *Tables*

                 Engineering
                 Physics. Constants — *For engineering* — *Tables*

                 Tables
                 Physics. Constants — *For engineering*

"Tables" was the last Term in the string. When it came into the *lead*, "— *Tables*" could be dropped from the *display*. "*For engineering*," however, was never the last Term in the string, so it had to be repeated in the *display*.

An example from the *British National Bibliography:*

Manuals on flower arrangement for cultivated flowering plants

String:
                  (1)*   flowering plants
                  (2)*   cultivation
                  (6)   manuals
                  (6)*   flower arrangement $01 for

Entries:
    Flowering plants
      Cultivation — *Manuals* — *For flower arrangement*

    Cultivation.   Flowering plants
      — *Manuals* — *For flower arrangement*

    Flower arrangement
      Flowering plants. Cultivation — *Manuals* — *For
      flower arrangement*

Note that "— *For flower arrangement*" has been repeated in this final entry because the "for" never appears in the entry and therefore the phrase "for flower arrangement," not being complete, does not qualify as a duplicate for the entry. This kind of entry occurs somewhat rarely.

CHINESE PLATE SYNDROME

The Chinese Plate Syndrome describes a situation in which the indexer receives a work such as "The History of Chinese Plates in the Ming Dynasty" and is given such a plate to index.[5] The sequence in real time is that the plate was made before a book was written about it. A similar sequence occurs when an indexer is called upon to index both a literary work and a critical study of it. The case in point is well handled with form divisions, such as

Texts for the work itself,

Anthologies for collected works,

Critical studies for criticism.

This assumes that general works are involved. With classics or other specific works, and this includes art and music, treatment as a class-of-one may be required in addition:

Critical studies of Winslow Homer's painting, "The Herring Net"

String:

                           (1)*   paintings $21 American
                                        c
                           (p)*   Homer, Winslow $f 1836-1910

(sub 2†) (1)   Homer, Winslow $f 1836-1910
                                    b
                           (p)*   Herring net $e The
                           (6)*   critical studies

Entries:

Paintings
   American paintings. Homer, Winslow, *1836-1910*
   Herring net, *The* — *Critical studies*

American paintings
   Homer, Winslow, *1836-1910*. Herring net, *The*
   — *Critical studies*

Homer, Winslow, *1836-1910*. American paintings
Herring net, *The* — *Critical studies*

Herring net, *The*. Homer, Winslow, *1836-1910*
— *Critical studies*

Critical studies
   American paintings. Homer, Winslow, *1836-1910*. Herring
   net, *The*

    The substitute was to get rid of the generic Term when the name of the painting came into the *lead*. "The Herring net" was inverted to make it file under "herring" and not "the." As a convention, the article, "the," is italicized. Clearly, anyone looking specifically for this picture should know who painted it.

    There is another facet to this syndrome: the indexer will run into books or other intellectual works "re-packaged" into alternate physical formats. Lewis Carroll's *Alice in Wonderland* may appear as a book, a play, a motion picture with actors or a cartoon, a sound recording, on microfilm or microfiche, or as a video recording. All of these forms except the play require some "early warning device" (medium designator) to inform the potential user that special equipment is needed. Therefore, more form divisions are imperative:

motion picture

sound recording

microfilm

microfiche

video recording

The need for such treatment is caused by the later-in-time nature of the alternative means of access, a result of the changed format of the intellectual work.

    Among other things, one of the operators requiring the Inverted Format, operator (5), may include place names. This is another area in which place names occur in PRECIS. We have already mentioned place as an environment (operator 0) and place as a difference for an exportable entity:

(1)*   wines $21 Italian

In addition, under certain circumstances, place may also be used as the key system. Thus, there are four areas where place can be used.

PLACE AS KEY SYSTEM

Place as key system is used in cases where the name of a geographical entity precedes one of the following terms:[6]

Balance of payments

Civics

Colonial administration

Constitution

Economic conditions

Economic relations

Emigration

Environment planning

Exploration

Exports

Foreign relations

Foreign trade

Geographical features

Government

Immigration (but not Immigrants)

Imports

Industrialization

Law

Local government

Political events

Politics

Population

Relations

Settlement

Social change

(List continues on page 138)

    Social conditions

    Social customs

    Social life

    Social planning

    Social reform

    Urban development

    Wars (including Civil Wars, Revolution)

Basically, these Terms relate primarily to economics, political science, law, and sociology. An example will illustrate usage as a political entity.

Politics in Canada from the Liberal Party point of view

String:
           d
        (1)* Canada
        (2)* politics
        (4)* Liberal Party viewpoints

Entries:
        Canada
        Politics — *Liberal Party viewpoints*

        Politics. Canada
        — *Liberal Party viewpoints*

Inverted Format:

        Liberal Party viewpoints
        Canada. Politics

Place can be used as a key system when it is the sole item in a string:

           d
        (1)* Mexico

In addition, it can be used as the key system for a geographical entity in context with a natural physical feature or phenomenon, provided that name does *not* imply use by man:

           d
        (1)* Mexico
        (p)* mountains

Other usages are:

social
           d
        (1)* Mexico
        (2)* social change

legal
           d
        (1)* Mexico
        (2)* law

economic
           d
        (1)* Mexico
        (2)* foreign trade

In some cases where place is the key system, operators (4), (5), or especially (6) may apply. One such case is with laws, statutes and other legal material (from the *British National Bibliography*):

		d
String:	(1)*	Great Britain
	(p)*	law
	(p)*	statutes
	(2)*	repeal
	(6)	statutes

Entries:

Great Britain
Law. Statutes. Repeal — *Statutes*

Law. Great Britain
Statutes. Repeal — *Statutes*

Statutes. Law. Great Britain
Repeal — *Statutes*

Repeal. Statutes. Law. Great Britain
— *Statutes*

This is a case of statutes (form) whose content consists of statutes (part of law) passed to repeal existing statutes. Form divisions for laws include those that are commonly found in legal citation practice.[7] In a case, such as the one above, part of the legal system is made up of statutes. The legal system itself is part of the social/political entity, "Great Britain." The entity takes precedence, so that "law" is coded as a subsystem.

Operator (6) is also used with place as key system when the topic concerns treaties:

Treaties between United States & Canada

Treaties between United Nations & European Economic Community

"— *Treaties*" may be used alone. No "the" is placed before "United States," "United Nations," or "European Economic Community." Many indexers will have to make a special effort to remember to omit this article.

At this point, an example using place as the key system and all three types of operators calling for the Inverted Format is of interest:

Leadership in social planning for metropolitan regions of the United States, based on a survey of the New England states; report for social agencies

		d
String:	(1)*	United States
	(p)*	metropolitan regions
	(2)*	social planning
	(p)*	leadership

(String continues on page 140)

String (cont'd)

    (4)*   sociological perspectives

    (5)   study regions

             d
    (q)*   New England states

    (6)   reports, surveys

    (6)*   social agencies $01 for

Entries:

United States
Metropolitan regions. Social planning. Leadership
— *Sociological perspectives* — *Study regions:*
New England states — *Reports, surveys* — *For*
social agencies

Metropolitan regions. United States
Social planning. Leadership — *Sociological per-*
spectives — *Study regions: New England states* —
Reports, surveys — *For social agencies*

Social planning. Metropolitan regions. United States
Leadership — *Sociological perspectives* — *Study*
regions: New England states — *Reports, surveys*
— *For social agencies*

Leadership. Social planning. Metropolitan regions. United
States
— *Sociological perspectives* — *Study regions: New*
England states — *Reports, surveys* — *For social*
agencies

Inverted Format:

Sociological perspectives
United States. Metropolitan regions. Social planning.
Leadership — *Sociological perspectives* — *Study*
regions: New England states — *Reports, surveys*
— *For social agencies*

Inverted Format:

New England states. *Study regions*
United States. Metropolitan regions. Social planning.
Leadership — *Sociological perspectives* — *Study*
regions: New England states — *Reports, surveys*
— *For social agencies*

Inverted Format:

> **Social agencies**
> United States. Metropolitan regions. Social planning.
> Leadership — *Sociological perspectives* — *Study*
> *regions: New England states* — *Reports, surveys*
> — *For social agencies*

In each case of the Inverted Format, where more than one operator is used, the whole series [two or more operators (4), (5), or (6), or any combination thereof] is reproduced in the *display*, unless the Term in the *lead* is the whole of the final Term in the string. If the Term in the *lead* is the final Term in the string, the Term is dropped from the *display*.

While *place*, under varying circumstances, can be treated as a geographical location, a difference, and a key system, in contrast, *time* is most commonly used as a difference.

TIME: DATE AS DIFFERENCE — OPERATOR $d

The basic differences and their rules were introduced in chapter 5. The difference for time, $d, is used rather frequently, but never as a *lead*. A date introduced by $d comes after all other differences except connectives. It normally is at the end of a Term and as low in the string as the subject permits. A few examples:

(1)   horses $21 Arabian $d 1900-1975

(2)   accidents $d 1975

(2)   poverty relief $d 1870-1950

(3)   social aspects $d 1960-1976

(q)   Svidine, ᶜNicholas $d ca. 1914 - ca. 1970

(1)   broadcasting services $21 commercial $d to 1976

Dates are normally expressed as a span of years rather than the less specific "20th century" or "Merovingian Period." Where connectives are present, they follow the date:

(2)*   combined operations $d 1942 $v by $w in

When a date is not wanted as a difference, it is included in the Term:

(p)*   Breeding of ᵇDogs Act 1973

(6)   forecasts for 1973-1980

The routine for dates as Terms are shunted as follows:

1)   Dates in the display stay at the end of the Term to which they are attached.

2) When the Term goes into the *lead,* the dates stay below, in the *display,* as its first part.

3) As the Term moves from the *lead* to the *qualifier,* the dates rejoin the Term, as its last part.

4) The date is always printed in italics, wherever it is.

A few examples with dates should assist in making their function clear. A combination of place as the key system and time is quite commonly used:

Social conditions in Brazil from 1964 to 1979

String:
                                 d
                         (1)*   Brazil
                         (2)*   social conditions $d 1964-1979

Entries:
                         Brazil
                         Social conditions, *1964-1979*

                         Social conditions.   Brazil
                         1964-1979

An example with place as environment:

Preservation of houses (built 1675-99) in Salem

String:
                                   d
                         (0)   Massachusetts

                                   d
                       (p)*   Salem

                       (1)*   houses $d 1675-1699

                       (2)*   preservation

Entries:
                       Salem.   Massachusetts
                       Houses, *1675-1699.* Preservation

                       Houses.   Salem. Massachusetts
                       1675-1699, Preservation

                       Preservation.   Houses, *1675-1699.* Salem. Massachusetts

There are limitations to the use of date as a difference. In British cataloging, birth and death dates for individuals are added to their names only when essential to distinguish between two otherwise identical names, and not as standard practice. In PRECIS, such dates used to distinguish between two names are not regarded as differences and so they are introduced by the typography code ($f). In general, dates are intended for use in places where only a restricted time period is needed, such as part of a lifespan or part of the time span of an event or just for the event:

World War II $d 1944

c
Faulkner, William $d 1922-1924

In the first case, only one year of the war is covered and the second covers the period in Faulkner's life when he was postmaster in Oxford, Mississippi.

When a full lifetime is covered — or the date of a battle or some event, a full reign or term of office, and so on — the dates are treated as a *Typographical* code, ($f), meaning "filing part in italics, preceded by a comma." The dates, words, or whatever, following the ($f) stay with the Term to which they are attached. Thus, the lifespan dates attached to "William Faulkner," 1897-1962, will stay with the name as a *lead*, whereas the differenced $d dates would remain in the *display* and move to the *qualifier* as the name does, but would never appear in the *lead*.

William Faulkner, Mississippi postmaster

String:
                d
          (0)   Mississippi

                d
          (p)* Oxford

          (1)* postmasters

                       c
          (q)* Faulkner, William $d 1922-1924

Entries:
          Oxford. Mississippi
             Postmasters: Faulkner, William, *1922-1924*

          Postmasters. Oxford. Mississippi
             Faulkner, William, *1922-1924*

          Faulkner, William. Postmasters. Oxford. Mississippi
             1922-1924

William Faulkner, American writer

String:
          (1)* writers $21 American

                       c
          (q)* Faulkner, William $f 1897-1962

Entries:
          Writers
             American writers: Faulkner, William, *1897-1962*

          American writers
             Faulkner, William, *1897-1962*

          Faulkner, William, *1897-1962.* American writers

The practice of using partial timespan $d when a difference is required and full lifespan ($f) when the time should go along with the name of the person or event is also applied to subjects:

Davis, William Henry $f 1871-1940

Davis, William Henry $d 1901-1927

World War II $f 1939-1945

World War II $d 1942-1944

At this point, the Escher book (example used in chapter 3) finally can be completed, using the typographical ($f) dates for the artist.

String:	(2)* graphic arts $21 Dutch
	(q)* drawings
	(g)* engravings $v &
	(g)* prints c
	(p)* Escher, Maurits Cornelis $f 1898-1972
	(6) Illustrations

Entries:

Graphic arts
Dutch graphic arts: Drawings, engravings & prints.
Escher, Maurits Cornelis, *1898-1972 — Illustrations*

Dutch graphic arts
Drawings, engravings & prints.   Escher, Maurits
Cornelis, *1898-1972 — Illustrations*

Drawings.   Dutch graphic arts
Escher, Maurits Cornelis, *1898-1972 — Illustrations*

Engravings.   Dutch graphic arts
Escher, Maurits Cornelis, *1898-1972 — Illustrations*

Prints.   Dutch graphic arts
Escher, Maurits Cornelis, *1898-1972 — Illustrations*

Escher, Maurits Cornelis, *1898-1972*.   Drawings, engravings
& prints. Dutch graphic arts
— Illustrations

Dates as differences were a problem under the older method of handling a series of *lead* only (LO) Terms in a string. The date as difference was attached to each Term, which resulted in redundancy:

Tales
1800-1899. Tales & legends, *1800-1899*

This problem was solved by omitting the date on a Term with (LO) attached to it. The string, therefore, changed:

String:	(1)* tales (LO)
	(g)* legends (LO)
	(r) tales & legends $d *1800-1899*

Entries: **Tales**
             Tales & legends, *1800-1899*

             Legends
             Tales & legends, *1800-1899*

One remaining consideration in making PRECIS strings and entries is that concerning parentheses which may be needed in the process.

NORMAL PARENTHETICAL USAGE

Normally, expressions in parentheses are written right into Terms with the parentheses included. These then come out in the entries the same way. No differencing is required other than the normal delimiter-identified ones. Some examples should make this clearer [the ($i) means "italics without preceding punctuation"]:

De facto government in Russia in 1918
                     d
String: (1)*   Russia
             (p)*   government $i (de facto) $d 1918

Entries: **Russia**
             Government (*de facto*), *1918*

             Government (*de facto*).   Russia
             1918

Report on comparability of grading standards of the English G.C.E.
(A level) mathematics examinations in secondary schools #
                     d
String: (0)*   England
             (1)*   secondary schools
             (p)   curriculum subjects
             (q)*   mathematics
             (2)*   examinations $21 G.C.E. (A level)
             (p)*   grading standards
             (p)*   comparability
             (6)   reports, surveys

Entries: **England**
             Secondary schools. Curriculum subjects: Mathematics.
             G.C.E. (A level) examinations. Grading standards.
             Comparability — *Reports, surveys*

             Secondary schools.   England
             Curriculum subjects: Mathematics. G.C.E. (A level)
             examinations. Grading standards. Comparability
             — *Reports, surveys*

(Entries continue on page 146)

Entries (cont'd)

Mathematics.   Curriculum subjects. Secondary
   schools. England
G.C.E. (A level) examinations. Grading standards.
Comparability — *Reports, surveys*

Examinations.   Mathematics. Curriculum subjects. Sec-
   ondary schools. England
G.C.E. (A level) examinations. Grading standards.
Comparability — *Reports, surveys*

G.C.E. (A level) examinations.   Mathematics. Curriculum
   subjects. Secondary schools. England
Grading standards. Comparability — *Reports, surveys*

Grading standards.   G.C.E. (A level) examinations.
   Mathematics. Curriculum subjects. Secondary
   schools. England
Comparability — *Reports, surveys*

Comparability.   Grading standards. G.C.E. (A level)
   examinations. Mathematics. Curriculum subjects.
   Secondary schools. England
— *Reports, surveys*

Incidentally, this example is a very good illustration of the use of special spacing
in the qualifier when a long string is involved. It is also a lengthy example of the
Standard Format.

When a word in parentheses is explaining or defining or otherwise qualifying
a *name*, it is put in italics in conformity with the *Anglo-American Cataloguing
Rules*.[8] Some examples:

New York (*State*)

New York (*N.Y.*)

Ireland

Epping Forest (*District*)

Triton (*Ship*)

Unbroken (*Submarine*)

Church of England (*Diocese of Lincoln*)

The string for such entries has a special printing instruction ($i) before the word
in parentheses, indicating that the word is to be italicized:

Proposals for social planning in Manhattan (New York Borough)

String: (1)*   New York (*N.Y.*)

                     d

                     d

            (p)*   Manhattan $i (New York, *N.Y.*)

            (2)*   social planning

            (6)   proposals

Entries: **New York**
                Manhattan (*New York, N. Y.*). Social planning
                — *Proposals*

                Manhattan (*New York, N. Y.*)
                Social planning — *Proposals*

                Social planning. Manhattan (*New York, N. Y.*)
                — *Proposals*

Most of the remaining examples from chapter 3 require Inverted Format. The strings and entries for these appear in appendix B.

SUMMARY

In this chapter, three more of the seven Main Line operators were explored and illustrated: (4) Viewpoint-as-form, (5) Sample populations/Study regions, and (6) Target/Form. The Standard and Inverted Formats have now been covered. In addition, use of place as the key system and the time differencing operator $d were outlined. Normal parenthetical treatment was described briefly.

The next major operational procedure and the last of the three formats in PRECIS is the Predicate Transformation. This is used when a combination of action and agent occurs, and also in some other situations. Use with an agent will be the subject of the next chapter.

PRECIS MANUAL REFERENCES

Operator (4): Sections 25.1-25.5, pp. 220-23.

Operator (5): Sections 23.8-23.11, pp. 206-211.

Operator (6): Sections 24.1-24.8, pp. 212-17.

Algorithm 17: pp. 470-72 is a convenient summary of the operations involved with (4), (5), and (6).

The Inverted Format is outlined in Section 23.12, pp. 209-210.

Operator (d): Section 12.7-12.10, pp. 96-98.

Place as a subject or as a difference (used adjectivally): Sections 12.1-12.6, pp. 94-96.

Algorithm 7: for date as difference, p. 447, is helpful.

This is the first time that use of Algorithms has been suggested. These carry the user through a step-by-step process from string to entry. They are most convenient for consultation when one is not quite sure what to do next.

Dropping (4), (5), (6) Terms from the *display*: Sections 23.1-23.12, pp. 203-210; Sections 24.1-24.8, pp. 212-17; Sections 25.1-25.5, pp. 220-23; Algorithm 17, pp. 470-72.

Chinese Plate Syndrome: Section 27.9, pp. 241-43.

REFERENCES

[1]These examples, as well as similar ones used in this chapter were taken from the 1975 issue of the *British National Bibliography*.

[2]Derek Austin, Handout from PRECIS Course, Dalhousie University, 1977: 8B.

[3]This admonition is in accordance with the second edition of the *Anglo-American Cataloguing Rules* (Chicago: American Library Association, 1978).

[4]Derek Austin, *PRECIS: A Manual of Concept Analysis and Subject Indexing* (London: Council of the British National Bibliography, 1974), pp. 206-210, 212-17, 220-23; Algorithm 17: 470-72. The algorithm also allows for a situation where a (4), (5), or (6) operator is followed by a dependent operator. This appears to be limited to (5) in practice.

[5]Austin, *PRECIS: A Manual*, pp. 241-43. (Obviously the indexer was bonded.)

[6]Austin, PRECIS Handout, p. 24.

[7]This may be in part a leftover from earlier cataloging codes wherein the cataloger indicated whether the entry was a law, a statute, an ordinance, etc. Current citation practice is permitted for uniform titles. Cf. *Anglo-American Cataloguing Rules*, 2nd ed. (Chicago: American Library Association, 1978), Rule 25.15, pp. 455-56.

[8]Under the *Anglo-American Cataloguing Rules*, 2nd ed., Chapter 23, the geographic subheadings are (N.Y.) instead of (City) and Manhattan (New York, N.Y.) instead of (New York Borough). Cf. *AACR2 Institute Handbook; the Library of Congress Interpretation and Application of the Anglo-American Cataloguing Rules, 2nd Edition* (Chicago: American Library Association, 1980), pp. 112-24.

8
THE CONCEPT OF THE AGENT:
Predicate Transformation

The permutations and combinations for indexing Terms introduced so far have been applicable to a number of situations that have caused problems in other indexing systems such as subject headings or Keyword-In-Context. The operator and format to be introduced here add considerable elegance to indexing procedures. They make it possible to handle a number of situations where awkwardness could easily inhibit understanding, even where the context has been preserved faithfully.

OPERATOR (3): AGENT

In the process of indexing, we have noted that the indexer first makes an analysis of the content of the material, starting with the action and the object of the action. This object becomes the key system. Parts or properties are added; the environment is supplied, if essential to the index; various differencing Terms may be needed, and operators for viewpoint, study samples or target, and/or form. In all of this, so far an agent has not been included.

Sometimes there is clearly an agent performing the action. The indexer is always wise, in looking for an agent, to ask "Who or what performed this action?" If an agent can be identified, it is tagged with operator (3).

The agent may not be involved in an action, but at the same time is clearly acting in an agentive role. A few examples will illustrate this usage:

Conference proceedings on BASIC computer programming language

String: (1)*   digital computer systems

                (3)*   programming languages

                (q)*   BASIC ^{b} language

                (6)   conference proceedings

Entries: **Digital computer systems**
       Programming languages: BASIC language — *Confer-*
           ence proceedings

       Programming languages.   Digital computer systems
           BASIC language — *Conference proceedings*

       BASIC language.   Programming language. Digital compu-
           ter systems
           — *Conference proceedings*

Cross-reference:

Beginners All-purpose Symbolic Instruction Code *See*
BASIC language

Swedish language reading books on the legend of Theseus

String: (1)*   Swedish language

                  (3)   reading books

                  (p)   special subjects

                  (q)*   legends $21 Ancient Greek

                  (p)*   Theseus
                         c

Entries: **Swedish language**
                  Reading books. Special subjects: Ancient Greek legends.
                  Theseus

                  Legends.   Special subjects. Reading books. Swedish
                            language
                  Ancient Greek legends. Theseus

                  Ancient Greek legends.   Special subjects. Reading books.
                            Swedish language.
                  Theseus

                  Theseus.   Ancient Greek legends. Special subjects.
                            Reading books. Swedish language

Standards for technical information manuals for glass products

String: (1)*   glass products
                  (3)*   technical information
                  (q)*   manuals
                  (6)   standards

Entries: **Glass products**
                  Technical information: Manuals — *Standards*

                  Technical information.   Glass products
                  Manuals — *Standards*

                  Manuals.   Technical information. Glass products
                  — *Standards*

Critical analysis of journal literature, in the form of review articles and book reviews included in journals

String:
    (1)*   journal literature
    (3)*   critical analyses \$w of
    (q)* review articles \$v &   ⎤ "f" block
    (f)* book reviews   ⎦
    (2)   inclusion in journals

Entries:
Journal literature
    Critical analyses: Review articles & book reviews.
    Inclusion in journals

Critical analyses.   Journal literature
    Review articles & book reviews. Inclusion in journals

Review articles.   Critical analyses of journal literature
    Review articles & book reviews. Inclusion in journals

Book reviews.   Critical analyses of journal literature
    Review articles & book reviews. Inclusion in journals

This kind of string is relatively common. The examples so far have had the (1)(3) combination at the beginning of the string. This, however, is not a requirement. A good number of strings look like the next ones:

Probate inventories of personal property in the Flatbush section of Brooklyn (N.Y.) 1855-1899 (text)

String:
                  d
    (0)* Brooklyn \$i (N.Y.)

                  d
    (p)* Flatbush section

    (1)* personal property

    (3)* inventories \$21 probate \$d 1855-1899

    (6)   texts

Entries:
Brooklyn (*N.Y.*)
    Flatbush section. Personal property. Probate
    inventories, *1855-1899 — Texts*

Flatbush section.   Brooklyn (*N.Y.*)
    Personal property. Probate inventories, *1855-1899*
    — Texts

Personal property.   Flatbush section. Brooklyn (*N.Y.*)
    Probate inventories, *1855-1899 — Texts*

(Entries continue on page 152)

> **Inventories.**   Personal property. Flatbush section.
> Brooklyn (*N.Y.*)
> Probate inventories, *1855-1899 — Texts*
>
> **Probate inventories.**   Personal property. Flatbush
> section. Brooklyn (*N.Y.*)
> *1855-1899 — Texts*

Insect pests of Pacific Northwest shrubs

String:

(0)   United $\overset{d}{\text{States}}$

(p)*   Pacific $\overset{d}{\text{Northwest}}$

(1)*   shrubs

(3)*   pests $w of

(q)*   insects

Entries:

Pacific Northwest.   United States
Shrubs. Pests: Insects

Shrubs.   Pacific Northwest. United States
Pests: Insects

Pests.   Shrubs. Pacific Northwest. United States
Insects

Insects.   Pests of shrubs. Pacific Northwest. United States

In this example, the name of the agent, "insects" implies a whole range of activities — chewing, sucking, nesting, scale producing, and such — so many that the general effect of an insect as a pest can be made without specifying a particular activity. In such a case, the action is omitted and the Standard Format ensues.

All of these items have two things in common: there is no action Term tagged (2) and yet all have an agent. Where there is no action, the Standard Format pertains. Where there is an action, where a (2) Term precedes the agent (3), a different situation exists. The agent is involved in a transitive action (an action described with a transitive verb). It is also possible that the agent may be an aspect or factor (social aspect, deciding factor, for example). At this point, only the agent with an action will be considered.

PREDICATE TRANSFORMATION

The name of an agent, preceded by an action Term, invokes the third Format developed for PRECIS — the Predicate Transformation. This is best explained with a rather simple example:

the cat pursued the mouse

The action is "pursuing" or "pursuit." The object of the action, "pursuit," is "mouse." With "mouse" as the key system, the agent of the action is "cat." With this sentence in the passive voice and written in telegraphic form, the tentative title-like phrase is:

Mouse, pursuit, cat

This, however, still does not render the topic unambiguous. Two connectives, ($v) reading downward and ($w) reading upward, each with a suitable function word ("by," "for," "in," "of," etc.), are added to the action word. With the Predicate Transformation, these connectives are mandatory:

(2)*   pursuit $v by $w of

Upward in this case literally means reading up the string from operator (3) to operator (2) to the line before operator (2). If there are further ($w) connectives attached to the string element above the Term, these also are collected. The whole lot is dropped into the *display*. Any string elements remaining above the parts interconnected by the ($w)s, go into the *qualifier*. Earlier, we used "upward" to mean shunting from the *display* to the *lead* to the *qualifier*. In either case, the function word accompanying the connective ($w) may not begin the *qualifier*.

One more operation is needed. Since "mouse" is a countable thing, the singular is replaced by the plural, "mice," and a cross-reference is made:

Mouse *See* **Mice**

The disambiguating operators ($v) and ($w) are added to our telegraphic statement when it is turned into a string:

(1)*   mice
(2)*   pursuit $v by $w of
(3)*   cats

Since mice and cats are countable, they are used in the plural. The first two entries are:

Mice
Pursuit by cats

Pursuit.   Mice
By cats

So far, it is clear which is chasing which. The operator (3), *following* an operator (2), brings into play the Predicate Transformation when the Term coded (3) is in the *lead*.

This is a literal transformation of the normal reading order of the string. When the Predicate Transformation is used—in cases where operator (3) is preceded by operator (2)—the words in the Term tagged (3) are placed in the *lead* position. Then the string is read upward, starting with the word in the operator (2) Term, skipping over the ($v) word. The action word itself, plus the function word attached to it with ($w)

pursuit of

are completed with the Term immediately above to form the clause,

Pursuit of mice

If there is another ($w), its function word and the Term that it connects are added to the others. When there are no more ($w) connections, the whole is dropped into the *display*.

Cats
Pursuit of mice

A string may be read upwards as long as there are connectives ($w) attached to action Terms. For example, one might have the entry:

Extermination of pests of livestock by farmers in Ohio

		d		
String:	(0)*	Ohio		
	(1)*	livestock		
	(3)*	pests	$w of	
	(2)*	extermination	$v by	$w of
	(3)*	farmers		

Entries: **Ohio**
Livestock. Pests. Extermination by farmers

Livestock. Ohio
Pests. Extermination by farmers

Pests. Livestock. Ohio
Extermination by farmers

Extermination. Pests of livestock. Ohio
By farmers

Farmers. Ohio
Extermination of pests of livestock

It is recommended that the key system and agent occurring in a string like this be combined into a phrase for the *qualifier* when the action Term comes into the *lead*. Note that "Ohio" remains in the *qualifier* when the rest of the Terms are pulled down into the *display* by upward-reading connectives.

Incidentally, there is a mnemonic device for differentiating among the connectives. Consider the midpoint of the v as the head of an arrow pointing downward, and midpoint of the w as the head of an arrow pointing upward:

w   ↓
| v

It is, of course, the words attached to the ($v) or ($w) that actually connect one Term to another.

Anything not connected with ($w)s would go into the *qualifier*, as in the following example:

Eradication of Japanese beetles with milky spore in New York State

		d		
String:	(0)*	New York $i (State)		
	(1)*	beetles $21 Japanese		
	(2)*	eradication	$v with	$w of
	(3)*	milky spore		

Entries: **New York** (*State*)
                Japanese beetles. Eradication with milky spore

                Beetles. New York (*State*)
                Japanese beetles. Eradication with milky spore

                Japanese beetles. New York (*State*)
                Eradication with milky spore

                Eradication. Japanese beetles. New York (*State*)
                With milky spore

                Milky spore. New York (*State*)
                Eradication of Japanese beetles

The final entry is the result of transforming the predicate so that "eradication," which was attached to "milky spore," is attached to "Japanese beetles" when "milky spore" is in the *lead*.

With operator (3) and the Predicate Transformation, it is now possible to write the strings for the first three examples in chapter 4. In order to show context dependency, these were written:

California >   sea otters >   protection >   wardens

Canada >   caribou >   hunting >   Indians

Kenya >   elephants >   observation >   tourists

The title-like phrases, strings, and entries for these run as follows:

Protection of California sea otters by wardens

                        d
String: (0)*   California
                (1)*   sea otters
                (2)*   protection $v by $w of
                (3)*   wardens

Entries: **California**
                Sea otters. Protection by wardens

                Sea otters. California
                Protection by wardens

                Protection. Sea otters. California
                By wardens

                Wardens. California
                Protection of sea otters

In this case, there would be a cross-reference:

Otters
See also
Sea otters

This is necessitated because of the generic relationship. It is desirable to have an indication in the index of all the kinds of otters that may be represented in the data base. The user looking for sea otters may start with "otters" as the most general possibility. Since there are so many different ways of indexing, the wary user does not always expect to find an entry under the specific word in mind, and, instead, may look under the entry where he or she *thinks* the indexer *would have put it*. The experienced indexer gives a fighting chance either way.

Caribou hunting in Canada by Indians

String:
                d
(0)*   Canada
(1)*   caribou
(2)*   hunting $v by $w of
(3)*   Indians

Entries:
Canada
Caribou. Hunting by Indians

Caribou. Canada
Hunting by Indians

Hunting. Caribou. Canada
By Indians

Indians. Canada
Hunting of caribou

Cross-reference:

Rangifer *See* **Caribou**

Observation of elephants by tourists in Kenya

String:
                d
(0)*   Kenya
(1)*   elephants
(2)*   observation $v by $w of
(3)*   tourists

Entries:
Kenya
Elephants. Observation by tourists

Elephants. Kenya
Observation by tourists

Observation. Elephants. Kenya
By tourists

Tourists. Kenya
Observation of elephants

Cross-reference:

Loxodonta *See* **Elephants**

The use of operator (3) in relatively simple cases like these is not especially complex. In case of difficulty, it may help to think of a sentence in grammatical terms, as subject and predicate. The action is equivalent to the verb that starts the predicate. It and the *objects* of the action, *if connected to the action terms* with the ($w) connective(s), form the full predicate. Normally a sentence in the active voice goes SUBJECT - VERB - OBJECT. Verb and object, with any attached words or phrases, are the predicate where transitive verbs are involved. With intransitive verbs, it is the verb plus the phrase (or equivalent) indicating an indirect object, if there is one. In PRECIS, the reader will remember, the sentence representing the topic is turned into a phrase in the passive voice: OBJECT -VERB - SUBJECT. Therefore in the PRECIS string, the predicate comes earlier than the subject. All of this rather involved discussion approximates the reasoning behind the Predicate Transformation Format. The "transformation" is to restore the normal order: Subject (agent) - Verb - Object.

One of the fundamentals in PRECIS is definition of a key system as the *object* of the transitive action and the *agent* of an intransitive one. Since the predicate in an intransitive action is the verb and there is no object, the Predicate Transformation is not used because there is nothing to transform. The intransitive actions illustrated in chapter 4 may be written as strings:

(1)*	rains	(1)*	endangered species
(2)*	arrival	(2)*	disappearance
(1)*	trains	(1)*	cats
(2)*	departure	(2)*	purring

The Standard Format yields entries under each Term and satisfies the logic of context dependency.

Two Terms are the minimal length for a string calling for the Predicate Transformation, although differencing does make more entries than two:

Moon-bounce communication by amateur radio operators†

String: (2)* communication $21 moon-bounce $v by
               (3)* radio operators $21 amateur

Entries: **Communication**
               Moon-bounce communication by amateur radio operators

(Entries continue on page 158)

---

†Moon-bounce, also called "earth-moon-earth (E.M.E.)" communication, means bouncing a signal off the moon and back to earth. Satellites perform the same function in communication.

Entries (cont'd)

Moon-bounce communication
By amateur radio operators

Radio operators
Amateur radio operators. Moon-bounce communication

Amateur radio operators
Moon-bounce communication

Theoretically one can have a string calling for the Predicate Transformation with only two words and a connective, but such are not too common:

String: (2)*   murder $v by
         (3)*   terrorists

Entries: **Murder**
         By terrorists

         Terrorists
         Murder

Where the agent has dependent parts, these, too, must be considered in the *display* before the transformation may be made:

Income tax calculation by tax consultants H & R Block (Firm)

String: (1)*   taxes $21 income

         (2)*   calculation $v by $w of

         (3)*   tax consultants

                c
         (q)*   H & R Block $i (Firm)

Entries: **Taxes**
         Income taxes. Calculation by tax consultants:
         H & R Block (*Firm*)

         Income taxes
         Calculation by tax consultants: H & R Block (*Firm*)

         Calculation. Income taxes
         By tax consultants: H & R Block (*Firm*)

         Tax consultants
         H & R Block (*Firm*). Calculation of income taxes

         H & R Block (*Firm*). Tax consultants
         Calculation of income taxes

Cross-reference:

> **Consultants**
> *See also*
> **Tax consultants**

Once more the Term code "c" above the name, in this case "H & R Block (Firm)," identifies a "class-of-one," capable of authorship.

This last example is particularly interesting because the last two lines of the string are encoded to mean "H & R Block (Firm) who are tax consultants," with the quasi-generic operator (q) performing the "who are" function. [The addition for (*Firm*) comes from the *Anglo-American Cataloguing Rules*.] When the dependent element (q) goes into the *lead*, the Term upon which it is dependent is put into the *qualifier*, thus retaining the one-to-one relationship between the two Terms. The Predicate Transformation takes place when the dependent element is in the *lead* just as it does when the agent itself is in the *lead* position. From the last entry it may be seen that there is no doubt as to what H & R Block do or who they are.

The same principle of retaining the relationships between Terms that are interdependent like this is also used with the operator that defines the role of one Term vis-a-vis another. This operator will be discussed in the next chapter. Before undertaking this, several examples will be given to show the workings of operator (3) and the Predicate Transformation.

Examples

Presidential control of the executive branch of the United States government

String:
        d
(1)*   United States
(p)*   government
(p)*   executive branch $w of
(2)   control $v by $w of
(3)*   president

Entries:

United States
   Government. Executive branch. Control by president

Government. United States
   Executive branch. Control by president

Executive branch. Government. United States
   Control by president

President. United States
   Control of executive branch of government

The following example comes from the 1975 issue of the *British National Bibliography*:

State Insurance issued by the Export Credits Guarantee Department of the British government against risks in exporting

String:

(2)*   exporting

(p)*   risks $w in

(2)*   state insurance $v by $w against

                    c

(3)*   Great Britain $h Export Credits Guarantee Department

Entries:

Exporting
Risks. State insurance by Great Britain.
Export Credits Guarantee Department

Risks.   Exporting
State insurance by Great Britain. *Export Credits Guarantee Department*

State insurance.   Risks in exporting
By Great Britain. *Export Credits Guarantee Department*

Great Britain.   *Export Credits Guarantee Department*
State insurance against risks in exporting

Cross-reference:

Insurance
See also
State insurance

In this last entry, note that the "($w) in" took effect when "risks" went into the *qualifier* as well as when the read-up process took place with the Predicate Transformation. As mentioned in an earlier chapter, this is a possibility when ambiguity might arise in terms going into the *qualifier* position. It is one of the options allowed the indexer to increase the possibilities for preserving precise meaning.

Exploitation by Mexican industries of natural gas and petroleum deposits in the coastal waters of the Gulf of Mexico

String:

                           d

(0)*   Gulf of Mexico

(p)*   coastal waters

(1)*   natural gas deposits $v & ⎤ "g" block

(g)*   petroleum deposits   ⎦

(2)*   exploitation $v by $w of

(sub 5↑) (2)   exploitation of natural gas & petroleum deposits
        in Gulf of Mexico coastal waters

(3)*   Mexican industries

Entries:

Gulf of Mexico
Coastal waters. Natural gas deposits & petroleum
deposits. Exploitation by Mexican industries

Coastal waters. Gulf of Mexico
Natural gas deposits & petroleum deposits. Exploitation
by Mexican industries

Natural gas deposits. Coastal waters. Gulf of Mexico
Exploitation by Mexican industries

Petroleum deposits. Coastal waters. Gulf of Mexico
Exploitation by Mexican industries

Exploitation. Natural gas deposits & petroleum deposits.
Coastal waters. Gulf of Mexico
By Mexican industries

Mexican industries
Exploitation of natural gas & petroleum deposits in
Gulf of Mexico coastal waters

Note that in the entry under "exploitation" the block represented by (1) and (g) in the string has appeared intact in the *qualifier*. When the Predicate Transformation came into play, a substitute phrase was used. This was clearer and less complex operationally than working backward step by step, and, of course, more economical.

Routine for Predicate Transformation

In summing up the operational features of the Predicate Transformation, the following routine should be helpful. Beginners may wish to follow it until they feel certain in its use.

1) Is there an operator (2) followed by an operator (3)? The Predicate Transformation requires both. If both are present, proceed. If not, use Standard Format.

2) Follow Standard Format until operator (3) is in the *lead*.

3) With the words tagged by operator (3) in the *lead* position, any Terms attached to (3) such as (p), (q), or (r) remain in the *display*.

4) The next Term above (3) also goes into the *display*, *after* the Terms tagged (p), (q), or (r).

5) If the next Term above (now in the *display*) is connected to the word above *it* by ($w) and a function word, write the function word in the *display* followed by a word above it, making a phrase.

6) Continue upwards until the trail of connecting ($w)s comes to an end.

7) The whole sequence of Terms connected by ($w)s should be in the *display* as a unit.

8) Anything still left in the string, any remaining Terms above the lot that went into the *display*, now goes into the *qualifier* in Standard Format order.

9) A dependent element (p, q, r) Term *below* the agent (3) Term may be tagged as a *lead*. If so, when it goes into the *lead* position, the next Terms above, up to and including the agent (3), are put into the *qualifier*. (See tax consultant example on page 158.)

10) Terms identified by operator (2), with any upward connections (as in steps 4 to 6 above), are dropped into the *display*.

11) Any remaining Terms above, not connected to the action Term (2) by connectives ($w)s, are added to the *qualifier*.

12) Remaining downward Terms stay in the *display*, unless tagged.

These instructions are based on a "worst possible case" situation and rarely will they all be implemented. It is an understatement to say that this sequence is easier to do than to explain.

Before ending this chapter, a further clarification of Term and Typographical Codes will be useful. These useful codes serve double purposes in many instances. They call attention to special kinds of entries and they also are printing instructions.

FURTHER DETAILS ON TERM AND TYPOGRAPHICAL CODES

In earlier chapters, Term codes have been introduced (*see* table on page 72). These codes are very useful, first for identifying certain kinds of entries, such as geographical or political names; names of persons or corporate bodies who, as individuals, represent "one of a kind" and may be authors, artists, musicians, or others acting in some similar creative capacity; names of things incapable of such creativity; and a very general "a" code that covers everything else. Secondly, all of these codes may be differenced. Examples of each of these cases will give an indication of the values of these interesting codes:

Term Code "a": (1)* bookstores
               (p)   stock
               (q)* books on Churchill $e Sir $g Winston
                      Spencer $21 illustrated
               (2)* advertizing

Term code "a" is the most common and applies to everything not taking "b," "c," or "d." It is not added to Terms in the string, but does appear in the manipulation code (to be discussed in chapter 12). In the above string, the Terms "bookstores," "stock," "books on ... illustrated," and "advertising" are all coded "a." The Term as a whole, not its content, determines which Term Code to use.

Entries: **Bookstores**
Stock: Illustrated books on Churchill, *Sir* Winston
Spencer. Advertizing

Books on Churchill, *Sir* Winston Spencer.   Stock.
Bookstores
Illustrated books on Churchill, *Sir* Winston Spencer.
Advertizing

Illustrated books on Churchill, *Sir* Winston Spencer.   Stock.
Bookstores
Advertizing

Advertizing.   Illustrated books on Churchill, *Sir*
Winston Spencer. Stock. Bookstores

In this case, not only was the (q)-Term differenced, but it also had in it a name requiring special typographical treatment (italics for *Sir*).

For the first few years of PRECIS, the codes for differencing were in lower case letter form, so that in a case like this, where the typographical code was in the same kind of letters, both codes could not be used at once. Therefore, an extra line had to be added to the string with the adjective tagged as "part." The numerical differencing removed the necessity for such a line.

Term Code "d":   **old**
$$d$$
(1)*   Asia (LO)
(p)*   South-east Asia
(p)*   politics

current
$$d$$
(1)*   Asia $21 South-east
(p)*   politics

Entries: **Asia**
South-east Asia. Politics

South-east Asia
Politics

Politics.   South-east Asia

String: (0)*   Dakota $i (State) $21 North
(1)*   roads

Entries: **Dakota (*State*)**
North Dakota (*State*). Roads

North Dakota (*State*)
Roads

Roads.   North Dakota (*State*)

The placement of a word like "state" is important. If it had been after the word "North," it would have been attached to the word "North" with the odd wording:

( )*   Dakota $21 North (State)

North (State) Dakota

Term Code "c":   (1)*   fiction in English

c
(p)*   Austen, Jane

c
(g)*   Bronte, Charlotte $v &

c
(g)*   Bronte, Emily

Entries: **Fiction in English**
Austen, Jane; Bronte, Charlotte & Bronte, Emily

Austen, Jane.   Fiction in English

Bronte, Charlotte.   Fiction in English

Bronte, Emily.   Fiction in English

Term Code "c" stands for "class of one" and is used for names capable of being authors, painters, composers, etc. Each person is such an entity; therefore, each of the Brontes is tagged separately with a "c." Fiction in English," the key system, does not fit any other category and therefore belongs in Term Code "a."

In the case of three authors like this, a semicolon is inserted after the first one for purposes of clarity. In the normal "g" block a comma would have been used, but with personal names the "c" signals first that a "class of one" is present and second, that a semicolon must appear after the first name. Presumably, with four names two semicolons would be needed.† The Term "fiction in English" (or other language) is used in the *British National Bibliography* rather than "British fiction," "American fiction," "Canadian fiction," and such. Where a differentiation on a nationalistic basis is needed, the Term "American writers," "Canadian writers," etc. is added. This example also applies to an item in which the other coordinate operator appears, the "f" block, and for Term Code "b" (name incapable of authorship).

An example of a Term Code "b" will be given next, and then several examples of "b" and "c" combined. In the first case a blank substitution eliminates the first two string elements because they are not needed in the index entries.

---

†The *Anglo-American Cataloguing Rules* and the *International Standard Bibliographic Description* call for "et al." after the first name when more than three names appear.

Term Code "b":   (0)*   Southern ^dEngland

                  (1)*   railway services

(sub 2↑) (1)

                  (q)* ^bLondon and South Western Railway

                  (g)* ^bLondon, Brighton and South Coast Railway $v &

                  (g)* ^bLondon, Chatham and Dover Railway

Entries: **Southern England**
             Railway services: London and South Western Railway;
                London, Brighton and South Coast Railway & London,
                Chatham and Dover Railway

         Railway services.   Southern England
             London and South Western Railway; London, Brighton
                and South Coast Railway & London, Chatham and
                Dover Railway

         London and South Western Railway

         London, Brighton and South Coast Railway

         London, Chatham and Dover Railway

In examples like this, where there are so many commas, the value of the semicolon after the first Term is obvious. The blank substitution very conveniently got rid of the first two Terms. Presumably, anyone looking under the exact name would be doing a different kind of searching from a user who started with "Southern England" or "railway services." Here is another place where PRECIS can tailor its index to fit the various kinds of users who will be employing it.

    In a "c," class-of-one personal name, the name has to be placed in context to indicate to whom it belongs. We have seen this above with "fiction in English" where the authors were included as a property or part of the genre. In the examples below, a variant format is illustrated, indicating *what kind of* (q) writer, poet, painter, the artist is. Either system may be used in an index, but *not both*.

String: (1)* American writers

                (q)* Faulkner, ^cWilliam $f 1897-1962

Entries: **American writers**
             Faulkner, William, *1897-1962*

         Faulkner, William, *1897-1962.* American writers

Notice that with Typographical Code ($f), the lifespan dates go along with the name, whereas a $d differenced date would have remained in the *display*.

In this book, the operator (p) identifying a writer, painter, musician or other artist as part of the genre will be used, because there are individuals who contribute to more than one art form and identifying an artist as a member of a profession, when there are several, could be confusing. The following example illustrates a case of both Term codes "b" and "c" in a single string.

Three paintings by Winslow Homer: "After the hurricane, Bahamas,"
"Stowing sail, Bahamas," and "North Woods Club, Adirondacks"

String: (1)*   paintings $21 American

                 (p)*   Homer, Winslow $f 1836-1910

                 (5)   study examples
                              b
                 (q)*   After the hurricane, Bahamas
                              b
                 (g)*   Stowing sail, Bahamas $v &   "g" block
                              b
                 (g)*   North Woods Club, Adirondacks

Entries: **Paintings**
                 American paintings. Homer, Winslow, *1836-1910* —
                      Study examples: After the hurricane, Bahamas;
                      Stowing sail, Bahamas & North Woods Club,
                      Adirondacks

                 American paintings
                 Homer, Winslow, 1836-1910 — Study examples: After the
                      hurricane, Bahamas; Stowing sail, Bahamas & North
                      Woods Club, Adirondacks

                 Homer, Winslow, *1836-1910*.   American paintings
                      — *Study examples: After the hurricane, Bahamas;*
                      Stowing sail, Bahamas & North Woods Club,
                      Adirondacks

                 After the hurricane, Bahamas.   *Study examples*
                 American paintings. Homer, Winslow, *1836-1910*

                 Stowing sail, Bahamas.   *Study examples*
                 American paintings. Homer, Winslow, *1836-1910*

                 North Woods Club, Adirondacks.   *Study examples*
                 American paintings. Homer, Winslow, *1836-1910*

In a case of several items in a series following operator (5) *Study examples* (or equivalent), each Term in a (q)(g)(g) or "g" block appears in the *lead*. When this happens, the statement of the whole block (as in the first two entries) is not given in the *display*. This is standard procedure for a "g" block and should not be confused with the situation in the last chapter where there were multiple (4), (5), and (6) operators. The special rules for the "f" block also apply when the content is Terms with Term codes "b" and "c."

SUMMARY

The Predicate Transformation Format increases intelligibility of entries. It tells what the agent was doing. It ensures that one-to-one relationships are maintained between concepts, even though they are separated in the string for grammatical or syntactical reasons. It enables a special kind of entry to be made so that the Term for agent will collocate with simpler forms resulting from the Standard and Inverted Formats.

At the same time, special systems for Term codes and Typographical codes have been developed so that varying needs of different kinds of Terms could be satisfied.

The Predicate Transformation Format is also used in its essentials when the role definer operator (s) is present. This interesting operator will be explained in chapter 9.

PRECIS MANUAL REFERENCES

Operator (3): Sections 17.10-17.14, pp. 138-41.

Predicate Transformation: Sections 18.1-18.11, pp. 143-51.

Algorithm 14: pp. 458-61.

Italicized qualifying words for names are found in Algorithm 9, p. 449. An incomplete listing is in Section 28.15, pp. 256-57.

Term and Typographical Codes were based on a communication from the Subject Systems Office, Bibliographical Services Division of the British Library.

Examples from the British National Bibliography reproduced courtesy of the Bibliographic Services Division, The British Library, London, England.

9
AGENTS AND ROLES

The introduction of the notion of an agent into indexing has revealed a greater degree of complexity in the syntactic and semantic relationships among index words than had been recognized. Linguists and designers of faceted classification schemes are well aware of the agentive role, but indexers using authority files or thesauri as sources of indexing words or phrases, as well as those who use keyword-in-context systems, are accustomed to considering individual words by themselves as entry points. Keyword-In-Context, as a rule, supplies the context only as given in titles. If the title is not descriptive of the content, then information is lost. The authority list or thesaurus has relationships, either overt or hidden, ready-made and does not ordinarily go further, as for example, would be the case in formally relating words to each other in terms of their context. PRECIS is one of a very few systems where words are deliberately kept in full context from the very beginning. In PRECIS, assumptions normally unstated are included in the title-like phrase or in the thesaurus of relationships.

In the process of developing PRECIS, it was discovered that the agent required some elaboration of its "agentiveness." That is, additional context had to be supplied to clarify the relationships in which the agent was involved. For this, the operator (s) for role definer was introduced. It was also necessary in some cases to indicate that the agent Term was not directly connected with the action that immediately preceded it in the string. For this the Blank Field Insert was added.

CONCEPT INTERLINK: OPERATOR (s) — ROLE DEFINER, DIRECTIONAL PROPERTY

The role definer operator has two main purposes: first, to introduce a phrase that explains the role of an agent when this is not clear from the content alone, and second, to indicate the direction of an agent's activity. For the latter, rather than the term "role," a number of other terms are available:

influence of *or* on

implication of *or* for

effects of *or* on

applications of *or* for

use of *or* by *or* for *or* in

participation of *or* in

The role definer (s) Term is always followed by operator (3) and it must contain connectives ($v) and ($w).

There are three types of situations where these terms are needed:

1) where the indexer is confronted with a case involving an *unusual role.* The normal role is the one where the relationship between the agent and action is direct and obvious.

2) where an *indirect agent* is operating

3) where an *indirect action* is present

In the last two cases, the role of the *indirect agent* or the *indirect action* may not be immediately apparent.

The Unusual Role

Most cases of an *unusual* role can be expressed with one of two words: "role" or "participation."

(s)   role $v of $w in

(s)   participation $v of $w in

For example:

The role of hurricanes in erosion of rocks

String: (1)*   rocks
                 (2)*   erosion $w of
                 (s)   role $v of $w in
                 (3)*   hurricanes

The normal factors contributing to rock erosion are winds, water, wind plus sand, rain with or without wind, vegetation, snow, ice, and so forth. Hurricanes, tornados, flash floods, tidal waves and similar occurrences are less likely to be considered in studying such erosion because their wearing action does not take place so steadily and regularly. These, therefore, have an unusual role in erosion of rocks.

Entries: **Rocks**
                 Erosion. Role of hurricanes

                 Erosion.   Rocks
                 Role of hurricanes

                 Hurricanes
                 Role in erosion of rocks

Since the (s) role indicator was not tagged for entry, this string followed the normal Predicate Transformation pattern. If the (s) had been tagged for *lead*, there would have been one more entry similar to the type of entry used when a dependent element follows the agent.

Role.   Hurricanes
In erosion of rocks

What happens here is that with (s) tagged for entry, the (s) term, in this case "role," is put into the *lead* position. Then, since this is never the last element in a string, the word immediately below, in this case "hurricanes," is picked up and put into the *qualifier*, without its connective word [because ($w) words may never begin the *qualifier*]. When "hurricanes" has been removed to the *qualifier*, then the string is read upwards in Predicate Transformation fashion, gathering in all ($w) connected Terms, and the whole phrase thus made is dumped into the *display*, starting with the ($w) word, "in." The *display* may begin with a preposition tagged ($v) or ($w), but the *qualifier* cannot begin with a preposition.

Two of the examples given in chapter 4 can now be finished:

Formation of ice on Lake Erie by low temperature

String:
                                                       d
                                   (0)*   Great Lakes
                                                         d
                                   (p)*   Lake Erie

                                   (1)*   ice

                                   (2)*   formation $w of

                                   (s)   role $v of $w in

                                   (3)*   temperature $01 low

Entries:
                                   Great Lakes
                                      Lake Erie. Ice. Formation. Role of low temperature

                                   Lake Erie.   Great Lakes
                                      Ice. Formation. Role of low temperature

                                   Ice.   Lake Erie. Great Lakes
                                      Formation. Role of low temperature

                                   Formation.   Ice. Lake Erie. Great Lakes
                                      Role of low temperature

                                   Temperature.   Lake Erie. Great Lakes
                                      Low temperature. Role in formation of ice

Role of the San Andreas Fault in causing earthquakes in California

String:
                                                         d
                                   (0)*   California

                                   (1)*   earthquakes

                                   (2)*   causation $w of

(String continues on next page)

(s)   role $v of $w in
                b
(3)*   San Andreas Fault

Entries: **California**
             Earthquakes. Causation. Role of San Andreas Fault

             Earthquakes. California
             Causation. Role of San Andreas Fault

             Causation. Earthquakes. California
             Role of San Andreas Fault.

             San Andreas Fault. California
             Role in causation of earthquakes

In both of these cases, it is obvious that "low temperature" and "San Andreas Fault" by themselves are not direct agents. Neither by itself produces ice or earthquakes.

The medical distinction between remote and proximate causes is helpful in understanding cases like this. Remote causes are factors *outside* the human body, such as pathogenic microorganisms, changes in temperature, polluted air, and such. Proximate causes are those *within* the body, such as exhaustion, predisposition, lowered resistance, and so forth. It requires the combination of both factors to produce illness. In general, a remote cause is something required for the effect to exist at all.

In the above examples, the remote cause is climate in the first case and the movement of giant plates floating across the surface of the earth in the second. A proximate cause is a localized triggering factor, in these cases, first, the low temperature necessary for producing ice and, second, the jerky motions of the plate edges where they meet and slide past each other, producing earthquakes. Notice that in the Lake Erie ice example, since no entry was wanted in the *lead* under "low," the whole Term appears in the *display* preceding the results of the operation of the Predicate Transformation.

Before discussing the directional properties associated with the role definer operator, it may be noted that this category of operator permits a solution to the kind of complex statement where the object of an action must be clearly identified for intelligible entries to be produced. The order of individual elements of a string, with operator (s), role definer, as *lead* is given in the first diagram in Figure 11 (page 172). It is particularly troublesome to have a "3" block present (rather than plain agent). When role definer (s) is led, the agent goes to the *qualifier*. But if the agent has a dependent element, this element goes first in the *qualifier*, followed by the agent itself. This is shown in the second diagram. The third covers the case where the dependent element in the "3" block is in the *lead*.

If the role definer Term is differenced, the normal pattern is followed. First, the focus appears as a *lead*, with the whole differenced Term beginning the phrase in the *display*. Then the difference + focus is in the *lead* and the *display* begins with the preposition represented by ($w):

             Accountability. Industries
             Public accountability for pollution

             Public accountability. Industries
             For pollution

Figure 11
Diagrams Giving Order of Individual Terms in Complex Cases
with both Agent and Role Definer Operators

DIAGRAM 1. ROLE DEFINER (s) in <u>lead</u>

| <u>lead</u>

ROLE DEFINER
word | <u>qualifier</u>

DEPENDENT ELEMENT to Agent. AGENT. Any leftover
HIGHER TERMS |

| <u>display</u>

($w) connective + ACTION TERM + ($w) word + NEXT TERM above . . .

Any TERMS <u>below</u> the "3" block |

DIAGRAM 2. AGENT in <u>lead</u>, "s" block present

| <u>lead</u>

AGENT | <u>qualifier</u>

TERMS not connected upward from ACTION |

| <u>display</u>

DEPENDENT ELEMENT OF AGENT. ROLE DEFINER word + ($w) word +

ACTION TERM + ($w) word + NEXT TERM above . . . Any TERMS

<u>below</u> the "3" block |

DIAGRAM 3. DEPENDENT ELEMENT of AGENT in <u>lead</u>, "s" block present

| <u>lead</u>

DEPENDENT ELEMENT OF AGENT | <u>qualifier</u>

AGENT. Any leftover HIGHER TERMS |

| <u>display</u>

ROLE DEFINER (s) + ($w) word + TERM to which it is connected . . .

Any TERMS <u>below</u> the "3" block |

Another example in illustration is helpful at this point, even though the (s) element in the string is not needed as a *lead*:

Report of cost-benefit analysis of the role of information sources in technology in Great Britain

String:
                                d
	(0)*	Great Britain
	(2)*	technology
	(s)	role $v of $w in
	(3)*	information sources
(sub 3↑)	(2)	role of information sources in technology
	(2)*	cost-benefit analysis
	(6)	reports, surveys

Entries:

Great Britain
    Technology. Role of information sources. Cost-benefit analysis — *Reports, surveys*

Technology.   Great Britain
    Role of information sources. Cost-benefit analysis — *Reports, surveys*

Information sources.   Great Britain
    Role in technology. Cost-benefit analysis — *Reports, surveys*

Cost-benefit analysis.   Role of information sources in technology. Great Britain — *Reports, surveys*

This is a relatively complex statement in which "role of information sources in technology" had to be substituted in order to clarify the *object* of the action "cost-benefit analysis."

Directional Properties

Operator (s) has two functions: to define a role and to indicate a specific directional property. For example, "attitudes" may be a dependent property, as when one is studying the attitudes in general of a person or group, or it can be an attitude directed specifically toward one group, person, or thing. In the latter case, the operator (s) is appropos. An example:

Attitudes of lumbermen toward dogwood trees

This kind of title-like phrase has to be analyzed carefully as there is an implicit meaning present. Lumbermen regard dogwood trees as weeds in their forests. Hence their attitudes are not toward the tree as such—they may have them in their own gardens—but toward the tree in a forest where it is not suitable for timber.

String: (1)*   forests
                   (p)*   weeds
                   (q)*   trees $21 dogwood
       (sub 3↑)   (1)   dogwood trees as forest weeds
                   (s)   attitudes $v of $w toward
                   (3)*   lumbermen

Entries: **Forests**
                   Weeds: Dogwood trees. Attitudes of lumbermen

                   Weeds.   Forests
                   Dogwood trees. Attitudes of lumbermen

                   Trees.   Weeds. Forests
                   Dogwood trees. Attitudes of lumbermen

                   Dogwood trees.   Weeds. Forests
                   Attitudes of lumbermen

                   Lumbermen
                   Attitudes toward dogwood trees as forest weeds

Returning to the discussion of situations calling for use of the role defining operator (s), there are two more situations where clarification may be advisable. The first is the case of the *indirect agent* and the other of the *indirect action*. Both are used fairly frequently.

The Indirect Agent

The *indirect agent* usually appears in places where something is being applied to or used on something else:

                   (s)   applications $v of $w in

                   (s)   use $v of $w in

*Applications of mathematical models in research on information
       retrieval*

String: (1)*   information retrieval
                   (2)*   research $w in
                   (s)   applications $v of $w in
                   (3)*   models $21 mathematical

Entries: **Information retrieval**
                   Research. Applications of mathematical models

                   Research.   Information retrieval
                   Applications of mathematical models

                   Models
                   Mathematical models. Applications in research in
                      information retrieval

Mathematical models
Applications in research in information retrieval

When the agentive operator (3) is differenced, or has a dependent element, the Predicate Transformation is affected thereby. Where the agent is differenced, there are as many entries as the differencing requires, and these are presented one at a time.

Use of disposable hypodermic needles for sterile injections of insulin

String:
    (1)*   insulin
    (2)*   injections $21 sterile $w of
    (s)   use $v of $w for
    (3)*   hypodermic needles $21 disposable

Entries:
    Insulin
       Sterile injections. Use of disposable hypodermic
         needles

    Injections.   Insulin
       Sterile injections. Use of disposable hypodermic
         needles

    Sterile injections.   Insulin
       Use of disposable hypodermic needles

    Hypodermic needles
       Disposable hypodermic needles. Use for sterile
         injections of insulin

    Disposable hypodermic needles
       Use for sterile injections of insulin

The Indirect Action

With indirect actions, two distinctive types of agents may be identified. If the agent is living (in a broad sense), the (s) role definer is usually:

    (s)   influence $v of $w on

In the social sciences, "implications" may prove to be a more satisfactory word than "influence." If the agent is non-living, then generally "effects of" is more satisfactory. This is not always the case, however, as will be seen in the first example below:

Influence of television programs on violence in crime

String:
    (1)*   crimes
    (2)*   violence $w in
    (s)   influence $v of $w on

(String continues on page 176)

(2)*   television programs

Entries: **Crimes**
Violence. Influence of television programs

Violence. Crimes
Influence of television programs

Television programs
Influence on violence in crimes

Effects of winter ice, 1977-1978, upon spring floods, 1978

String: (1)*   spring floods $d 1978
(s)*   effects $v of $w on
(3)*   winter ice $d 1977-1978

Entries: **Spring floods**
1978. Effects of winter ice, *1977-1978*

Effects. Winter ice, *1977-1978*
On spring floods, *1978*

Winter ice
1977-1978. Effects on spring floods, *1978*

In practice, there probably would not have been an entry under "effects," but for illustrative purposes, this hypothetical example suffices.

Effects of floods on plant growth in rice fields

String: (1)*   rice fields
(p)*   plants
(2)*   growth
(sub 2↑) (2)   plant growth
(s)   effects $v of $w on
(3)*   floods

Entries: **Rice fields**
Plants. Growth. Effects of floods

Plants. Rice fields
Growth. Effects of floods

Growth. Plants. Rice fields
Effects of floods

Floods. Rice fields
Effects on plant growth

Sometimes the (s) Term is wanted in the *lead*. In such cases, the Term below, tagged (3), goes into the *qualifier* before reading upwards. Consider the title-like phrase:

Responsibility of airlines for safe delivery of passengers and
baggage

String:

	(1)*	air transportation
	(p)*	passengers $v &
	(g)*	baggage
	(2)*	safe delivery
(sub 4↑)	(2)	safe delivery of passengers & baggage
	(s)*	responsibility $v of $w for
	(3)*	airlines

Entries:

Air transportation
    Passengers & baggage. Safe delivery. Responsibility
        of airlines

Passengers.   Air transportation
    Safe delivery. Responsibility of airlines

Baggage.   Air transportation
    Safe delivery. Responsibility of airlines

Safe delivery.   Passengers & baggage. Air transportation
    Responsibility of airlines

Responsibility.   Airlines
    For safe delivery of passengers & baggage

Airlines
    Responsibility for safe delivery of passengers &
        baggage

Cross-reference: **Transportation**
            See also
            Air transportation

Substitutions often are convenient in situations calling for the use of role definer operators, especially where a combination of elements is more lucid than would be the case with ordinary rotation. The next example comes from the 1975 *British National Bibliography*:

Effects of attitudes on human behaviour

String:

	(1)*	man
	(2)*	behaviour
(sub 1↑)	(2)	human behaviour
	(s)	effects $v of $w on
	(d)*	attitudes

Entries: **Man**
                Behaviour. Effects of attitudes

                Behaviour. Man
                Effects of attitudes

                Attitudes. Man
                Effects of human behaviour

There is some blurring of lines between living and non-living agents in cases of indirect action. Throughout PRECIS when there is doubt, the indexer should rely on his or her intuitive understanding of the English language. If a result does not sound reasonable and no alternative can be found in the *Manual*, the linguistic approach may be used. It has been found in developing PRECIS that the English language is not quite as illogical as it appears. In many cases, where a modification has been made because the original index entries did not "sound right," later the modification has turned out to be acceptable on grammatical and syntactical grounds. The indexer, therefore, should make a note of problems and queries because solutions and answers may be found with greater experience in using the system.

DIFFERENCE BETWEEN PREDICATE TRANSFORMATION WITH AGENT AND WITH ROLE DEFINER

Beginning indexers sometimes have trouble discerning what to do when both role definer (s) and the agent (3) are wanted as *leads*. In such a case, the string is read normally and entries made until one comes to the (s). The tagged-for-*lead* (s) is handled with the Predicate Transformation. However, before using this operational format, the indexer looks downward, finds the Term tagged (3) and puts it up into the *qualifier*. Then the string is read up as far as ($w) connectives will permit and the whole sequence dropped into the *display*. Any Terms still remaining higher in the string and *not* connected from lower Terms via a ($w) go into the *qualifier* to the right of the (3) Term. An example of this is taken from the *British National Bibliography*:

> *Participation by the public in structure plans for environment planning in Great Britain*

String: d
                  (1)* Great Britain
                  (2)* environment planning
                  (p)* structure plans
                  (2)   plan making
      (sub 3↑) (2)   structure planning
                  (s)* participation $v of $w in
                  (3)* public

Entries: **Great Britain**
                Environment planning. Structure plans. Plan making.
                Participation of public

Environment planning. Great Britain
Structure plans. Plan making. Participation
of public

Structure plans. Environment planning. Great Britain
Plan making. Participation of public

Predicate Transformation with (s):
Participation. Public. Great Britain
In structure planning

Predicate Transformation with (3):
Public. Great Britain
Participation in structure planning

Notice where the word "public" went when the (s) Term, "participation," came into the *lead*. The substitution of "structure planning" for the three preceding Terms simplified the wording of the entry when (s) and (3) came into the *lead*. Only "Great Britain" was left unconnected when the string was read up. The Predicate Transformation, when the agent (3) was in the *lead*, proceeded to read upward as far as it could go, ending at "structure planning," the substitution Term. Tagging of (s) for the *lead* is relatively rare. Most of the time the indexer does not want entries under such words as "role," "effect," "influence," and such.

In using operator (3), the indexer should always consider whether the agent's role is *direct* or *indirect*. This is best done by asking, "Is the agent the sole subject performing the action or are there intermediate steps to be considered?" At the same time, it is important to remember that ambiguity can be read into anything if one is persistent. As a rule, first impressions are reliable in PRECIS, provided one is reasonably familiar with the system.

Consider the following title-like phrases:

Repairs of cars by skilled mechanics

Depending on the context, this could be treated as if the agent were a direct one:

String: (1)*   cars
                (2)*   repairs $v by $w of
                (3)*   skilled mechanics

Entries: **Cars**
                Repairs by skilled mechanics

                Repairs. Cars
                By skilled mechanics

                Skilled mechanics
                Repairs of cars

Since the verb is transitive, the agent may be considered as acting *directly*. However, from another context, one might be concerned with:

Use of wrenches in repairing cars

String:	(1)* cars
	(2)* repairs $w of
	(s) use $v of $w in
	(3)* wrenches

Entries: **Cars**
Repairs. Use of wrenches

Repairs. Cars
Use of wrenches

Wrenches
Use in repairs of cars

In this case, an unstated assumption, understood by the indexer and user alike, has been made. The wrench is used by a person, which makes it an indirect *agent* since it is the *person* who repairs the car.

Yet another title-like phrase, assuming a third type of context, describes an indirect *action*:

Effects of inflation on car repairs

String:	(1)* cars
	(2)* repairs $w of
	(s) effects $v of $w on
	(3)* inflation

Entries: **Cars**
Repairs. Effects of inflation

Repairs. Cars
Effects of inflation

Inflation
Effects on repairs of cars

The assumption in this latter case is that the unstated additional agent, "prices," increased by inflation, is what causes drivers to have second thoughts about repairing their cars.

Once again these various possibilities illustrate the techniques available to the indexer in pinpointing meaning. In the latter case, however, the leap from inflation to effects on the repairing or non-repairing of cars is a non-sequitur. The unstated assumption is less obvious than in the previous case and therefore more open to misinterpretation and to creation of errors as Terms are manipulated.

At this point, with the agent (3) introduced and role definer (s) clarified, it is possible to explain several options in differencing which require one or both of them. Differencing Constraint C (a transitive action may not be differenced by the agent which performs it) and/or Rule 8 (an agent may be differenced by the name of the action for which it is intended) may be used where one has a topic such as "Digital computer problem solving." In this kind of case, one may not use:

( )   problem solving $21 digital computer

Instead, it is possible to use role definer (s) in the string:

(2)*   problem solving
(s)   applications $v of $w in
(3)*   digital computer systems

Sometimes, using Rule 8, agents may be differenced by names of actions:

(3)*   machines $21 washing

(3)*   devices $21 timing

This rule is helpful in indirect agent problems.

There are other means for clarification when indirect agents are present. Use of a method called the "Blank Field Insert" has been very convenient.

THE BLANK FIELD INSERT

Where "the agent named in the string is *not the system which is* directly and obviously responsible for the action which appears as the next higher term,"[1] one does not want the Predicate Transformation to occur because this would give an erroneous and illogical result. It would, in fact, be obvious to the user that the named and tagged agent was not actually the agent for the action given. In the case earlier, the agent "inflation" obviously acted upon a human being, who was affected by the rise in prices caused by inflation and decided not to get the car repaired. In the next case, it was a human being who applied the digital computer system to the problem.

In order to stop the Predicate Transformation from taking place and creating a false relationship in such cases, a Blank Field Insert is used to disrupt the regular pattern initiated by the (2)(3) sequence. This consists of the operator (2) placed in the string with a blank where the Term tagged by (2) would normally be. An example:

Rules for cataloging audiovisual materials

Trial string: (1)*   audiovisual materials
                  (2)*   cataloging $v by $w of
                  (3)*   rules

While users probably would understand this, the rules obviously do not catalog the materials. Employing an added line to the string:

(s)   use $v of $w in

would have been helpful, since the rules are an indirect agent. The direct agent is the librarian, who uses the rules as a guide to cataloging the audiovisual materials.

The issue here lies in commonplace use of language. In communicating, we tend to make assumptions and take shortcuts because usually it is not necessary to spell out every link in our chains of thought; the redundancy would bore us to extinction, not to mention our auditors. Habits of speech and thought tend to become abbreviated and telegraphic (if not telepathic). This sort of thing is not desirable for indexing with attention to context. Either all of the steps have to be put in or some standardized way must be devised to indicate an omission. The Blank Field Insert is a device that does just this.

Using the Blank Field Insert in the above string makes two things happen: the sequence from indirect agent to action is interrupted, and the Predicate Transformation, which is made on the assumption of a direct connection between the agent and the action, is aborted:

String: (1)* audiovisual materials
 (2)* cataloging $w of
 (2)
 (3)* rules

Entries: **Audiovisual materials**
 Cataloging. Rules

 Cataloging. Audiovisual materials
 Rules

 Rules. Cataloging of audiovisual materials

The invalid entry under "rules" in the trial string would have produced a false relationship with regard to subordination:

Rules
Cataloging of audiovisual materials

To understand this difference clearly, it is necessary to go back to the basics of PRECIS: The terms in the *qualifier* represent the wider context of the *lead*, while those in the *display* represent its narrower context. The Predicate Transformation literally transforms subject and object, but the subject (agent) has to be directly related to the object through the action. In over 500 examples chosen at random from the BNB files, very few cases of the (1)(2)(3) sequence could be found which did not require a blank field. In most cases, the agent was *not* directly related to the action, but rather to an unlisted or assumed action. All of the examples below except the last are taken from the *British National Bibliography*:

Construction of models of communication #

String: (2)* communication
 (2)
 (3)* models
 (2) construction

\# Reproduced courtesy of the Bibliographic Services Division, The British Library, London, England.

Entries: **Communication**
                  Models. Construction

                  Models. Communication
                  Construction

Social aspects of cybernetics #

String: (2)*   cybernetics
                  (2)
                  (3)*   social aspects

Entries: **Cybernetics**
                  Social aspects

                  Social aspects. Cybernetics

Sequential tests in medical therapy #

String: (2)   medicine
                  (p)*   therapy
                  (2)
                  (3)*   sequential tests

Entries: **Therapy.** Medicine
                  Sequential tests

                  Sequential tests. Therapy. Medicine

N-haloamides: reagents in qualitative analysis of organic compounds

String: (1)*   organic compounds
                  (2)*   qualitative analysis $w of
                  (2)
                  (3)*   reagents
                  (q)*   N-haloamides

Entries: **Organic compounds**
                  Qualitative analysis. Reagents: N-haloamides

                  Qualitative analysis. Organic compounds
                  Reagents: N-haloamides

                  Reagents. Qualitative analysis of organic compounds
                  N-haloamides

                  N-haloamides. Reagents. Qualitative analysis of
                        organic compounds

Reproduced courtesy of the Bibliographic Services Division, The British Library, London, England.

Logical Explanation of the Need for
the Blank Field Insert

There is a serious problem in logical relationship between agents and actions. The passive voice sequence:

key system	—	action	—	agent
(grammatical object)		(verb)		(grammatical subject)

is not representative of normal English in an unexpectedly large number of cases. Deeper analysis has to be used to ascertain what the actual logical sequences are.

Three of the previous four cases may be analyzed by asking a set of questions and using the answers to fill in the missing parts. The questions are:

What was the action?

Who/what performed the action?

With what means?

On what?

Applying these, the following strings were produced. The added operators are indicated in square brackets:

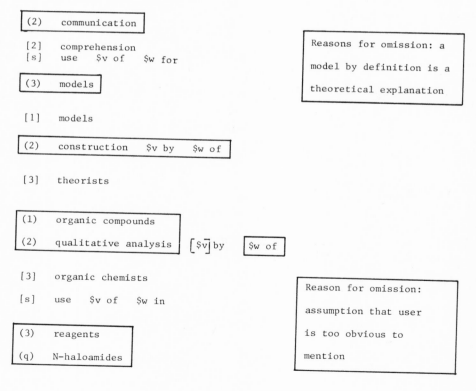

```
┌─────────────────────────────┐
│ (2)    medicine             │
│                             │
│ (p)    therapy              │
└─────────────────────────────┘

 [2]    progress

 [s]    use   $v of    $w in

┌─────────────────────────────┐
│ (3)    sequential tests     │
└─────────────────────────────┘
```

```
┌─────────────────────────────────┐
│ Reason for omission:            │
│                                 │
│ assumption that reason          │
│                                 │
│ for using test is               │
│                                 │
│ obvious                         │
└─────────────────────────────────┘
```

Of course, as written above *all of these strings are illegal.* They are used here only to point out what is missing and why the Blank Field Insert is useful.

The remaining example,

> (2)   cybernetics
> (3)   social aspects

represents a situation where there is a two-way interaction between the concept represented by the higher Term and the concept represented by the word modifying "aspects," in this case "social."[2] What does "social aspects of cybernetics" mean? Is it "the effects of cybernetics on society" or "the effects of society on cybernetics"? It means both. So there are two strings implied here:

> (2)*   society   (2)*   cybernetics
> (s)   effects $v of $w on   (s)   effects $v of $w on
> (3)*   cybernetics   (3)*   society

yielding:

Society
  Effects of cybernetics

Cybernetics
  Effects on society

Cybernetics
  Effects of society

Society
  Effects on cybernetics

In common parlance, the two-way interactions have been reduced to a simple, ambiguous, summary/substitute "social aspects." The net result is adequate English, but difficult for the careful indexer.

Any other kinds of "aspects" are subject to this kind of analysis so that one could have, for example:

> (2)   cybernetics
> (2)
> (3)   educational aspects

> (2)   cybernetics
> (2)
> (3)   political aspects

(Example continues on page 186)

(2)   cybernetics
(2)
(3)   mathematical aspects

In all of these cases, the omission makes more sense for indexing purposes than the inclusion, which inserts things that "everybody knows," or redundancies. Thus there is a practical logic to PRECIS that can be explained in terms of ordinary language usage.[3] The reasoning may not be explicitly stated in the strings, but the user of the index who is familiar with the language will have little trouble in making the necessary inferences and assumptions, *provided the Predicate Transformation has been bypassed in favor of Standard Format.* The Blank Field Insert is particularly valuable in dealing with topics where some kind of aspect is involved in an agentive role, but that aspect is clearly open to two-way interpretation of its actions. The word "factors" is treated in similar fashion.

THE BLANK SUBSTITUTION INSERT

A similar but somewhat simpler strategem called the "Blank Substitution Insert" has been designed to perform a very useful purpose. Suppose a string makes good sense reading downward, but as parts of it move into the *qualifier* they either become redundant or unnecessary. By use of the Blank Substitution Insert (substitution of blanks for one or more terms), unwanted Terms can be made to disappear after they have served their purpose. Examples of this should make the action clear:

Guidebooks to castles in Scotland: Stirling Castle

String: d
                  (0)*   Scotland

                       d
                  (p)*   Stirling

                  (1)*   castles

(sub 3↑) (1)

                  (q)*   Stirling Castle

                  (6)   guidebooks

Entries: **Scotland**
                  Stirling. Castles: Stirling Castle — *Guidebooks*

                  Stirling. Scotland
                  Castles: Stirling Castle — *Guidebooks*

                  Castles. Stirling. Scotland
                  Stirling Castle — *Guidebooks*

Stirling Castle
— *Guidebooks*

*Government publications in the collections of university libraries in
Illinois: University of Chicago. Regenstein Library*

String:
          (0)*   Illinois $i (State)

          (p)*   Chicago

          (1)   universities

          (p)*   libraries

(sub 4↑) (1)

          (q)*   University of Chicago $h Regenstein Library

          (p)   collections

          (q)*   government publications

Entries:
        Illinois (*State*)
           Chicago. Universities. Libraries: University of
           Chicago. *Regenstein Library*. Collections:
           Government publications

        Chicago.   Illinois (*State*)
           Universities. Libraries: University of Chicago.
           Regenstein Library. Collections: Government
           publications

        Libraries.   Chicago. Illinois (*State*)
           University of Chicago. *Regenstein Library*.
           Collections: Government publications

        University of Chicago.   *Regenstein Library*
           Collections: Government publications

        Government publications.   Collections. University
           of Chicago. *Regenstein Library*

    The convenience of the Typographical Code ($h) appears here. This tag puts down a period after the name of the system (University of Chicago) followed by the name of its subsystem in italics.

    Another case for the Blank Substitution Insert occurs when there is a class-of-one involved:

(String appears on page 188)

		d	
String:	(0)*		France
	(1)*		bicycles
	(2)*		racing
(sub 3↑)	(2)		b
	(3)*		Tour de France

Entries: **France**
Bicycles. Racing. Tour de France

Bicycles.   France
Racing. Tour de France

Racing.   Bicycles. France
Tour de France

Tour de France

The context-establishing Terms in such a case should not remain in the *qualifier* when the class-of-one, which is the name of a bicycle race, is in the *lead*. Any user of the index who knows enough to look under "Tour de France" does not need to be told its context.

Finally, examples containing both the Blank Field Insert *and* the Blank Substitution Insert provide a fitting end to this chapter:

Production of UK MARC records for machine-readable cataloging of documents

String:	(1)*	documents
	(2)*	cataloging $w of
	(2)	
	(3)*	machine-readable files
(sub 4↑)	(1)	b
	(q)*	MARC records $21 UK
	(2)	production

Entries: **Documents**
Cataloging. Machine-readable files: UK MARC records.
Production

Cataloging.   Documents
Machine-readable files: UK MARC records. Production

Machine-readable files.   Cataloging of documents
UK MARC records. Production

MARC records
UK MARC records. Production

UK MARC records
Production

The following case includes the Blank Field Insert, the Blank Substitution Insert, Term, and Typographical Codes in a single string:

Legal aspects of the entry of the Republic of Ireland into the
    European Economic Community

                                        b

String: (1)*   European Economic Community
                (2)   entry $v of $w into
                (3)*   Ireland $i (Republic)
   (sub 3↑) (2)   entry of Ireland $i (Republic) $g into
                          European Economic Community
                (2)
                (3)*   legal aspects

Entries: **European Economic Community**
                Entry of Ireland (*Republic*). Legal aspects

                Ireland (*Republic*)
                Entry into European Economic Community. Legal
                aspects

                Legal aspects.   Entry of Ireland (*Republic*) into
                European Economic Community

The middle Term, "Ireland (Republic)," invokes the Predicate Transformation. The Blank Field Insert prevents a second such Transformation from taking place and permits the substitution to go into the *qualifier*, thus modifying "aspects." The word "aspects" implies a two-way interaction of some kind between the system named higher in the string, "Ireland (*Republic*)," and the word preceding "aspects," which is "legal." "Legal aspects of Ireland (*Republic*)" is not a logical statement. It is the legal aspects of the *entry* of Ireland into the Community that is involved, but repeating the word "entry" would be redundant. The mind "understands" what the upward-reading substitution makes explicit.

SUMMARY

The complexities resulting from the introduction of agents into indexing practice have necessitated techniques for ensuring that meaning would not be lost in the process of retaining content. This led to consideration of agents and roles. The addition of the role definer (s) and identification of four areas where it applied has been a clarifying step. Further recognition of jumps in logic in standard language usage — the difference between surface structure and the underlying deep structure — resulted in the addition of the Blank Field Insert to retain the one-to-one relationships between Terms. This rectified the omission of intermediate steps. The missing links upset the logic of the Predicate Transformation (called for by the action-following agent) and required reversion to the Standard Format. Recognition of the two-way nature of "aspects" and "factors" in agentive behavior was logically resolved in a similar manner. The Blank Substitution Insert tidied up the method of removal of unwanted Terms in the *qualifier*.

At this point, all the significant parts of PRECIS operations except those dealing with interactive situations have been described. The next chapter will correct this omission.

PRECIS MANUAL REFERENCES

System, action and agent: Sections 19.1-19.16, pp. 156-69.

Operator (s): Sections 20.1-20.12, pp. 171-81, and Sections 26.1-26.9, pp. 224-33.

The Blank Field Insert: Sections 18.12-18.14, pp. 151-53.

The Blank Substitution Insert: Sections 22.2, 22.6, pp. 190-91, 195-97.

Aspects: Sections 17.14, 18.12-18.14, pp. 141, 151-53.

Rules for differencing: Rule 4: p. 86.

Algorithms for operator (s): No. 15, pp. 462-66.

REFERENCES

[1]Derek Austin, *PRECIS: A Manual of Concept Analysis and Subject Indexing* (London: Council of the British National Bibliography, 1974): 151.

[2]Austin, *PRECIS: A Manual*, pp. 141, 151-53.

[3]An example of the variation in "what everybody knows" may be seen by comparing the names given to characters and places, as well as conversational constructions, in the English and French versions of the cartoon "Asterix and Obelix" by Goscinny and Uderzo (Neuilly-sur-Seine: Dargaud Editeur; London: Hodder & Stoughton). Since this is available in some twenty languages, the comparison between others is probably equally valid.

10

MULTIPLE THEMES AND OTHER COMPLEXITIES

There are times in indexing when two subjects are encountered in a single title-like phrase. Operators (f) and (g) are used when a simple coordination is involved, but sometimes more complex relationships are present. With two themes occurring at once, the indexer can solve the problem by writing two separate strings. But if the two themes are closely intertwined, a single string solution is preferable. This requires means of combining common and unique Terms in such a way that the two concepts involved may be separated and yet their relations retained. Special indexing operators called "theme interlinks" have been devised in PRECIS for this process. Current practice has added downward-reading substitutes especially for situations where the relationship between the themes is a reciprocal one. Several of these complexities will be discussed in this chapter.

THEME INTERLINKS

Theme interlinks come in three categories:

(x) = first element of a coordinate theme

(y) = other elements of a coordinate theme

(z) = elements common to both themes

The (z) tag is also used for all elements in ordinary strings which do not have varying themes. The (x), (y), and (z) elements are written into a theme interlink string, in addition to the regular elements, for purposes of identification. Since the (z) tag is common to all elements of an ordinary string, it is only written in the manipulation code for the computer (to be discussed in chapter 13).

Since the (x), (y), and (z) operators are written in addition to the other operators, it is easy to notice a theme interlink string, because it has a double row of tags representing the operators. These make it possible to identify two themes so that the syntax order in each theme is preserved, while the overall relationship is not lost in the process.

When two (or even three) themes occur, the first begins with the operator (x) and continues with operators (y) so long as separation of this theme from the other theme(s) is needed. The presence of a second theme is indicated by a second (x), followed by as many (y) operators as may be needed for the second theme. Terms coded (z) are common to both themes. They may not, however, be used in the middle of either individual theme sequence. A string may begin or end with a (z) operator. If a common Term is needed in the middle of the sequence in either theme, it has to be repeated in each one. This is done to keep the themes separate. Any number of (z) operators may be used at the beginning or end of the whole string, but normally one to three appear to suffice.

The easiest way to handle a work with two themes is to begin by writing a separate string for each one and then to look for common elements. In some cases there may be nothing that can be used as a common element. In any situation where it is exceptionally difficult to write a normal string, it is advisable to take a second look — for a second theme. Very often this will turn out to be present, but hidden, in a seemingly intractable problem.

One Subject, Two Themes

A work may present a subject such as:

Sports and measured strength of 14 year old girls who are students

Obviously there are two themes involved:

1) measuring the strength of 14 year old girls who are students

2) sports as an activity of 14 year old girls who are students

These themes can be written as two strings, one for each theme:

Theme 1:	(1)*	students
	(q)*	girls, 14 years
	(p)*	strength $01 physical
	(1)*	measurement

Theme 2:	(1)*	students
	(q)*	girls, 14 years
	(2)	activities
	(q)*	sports

Putting the two together into a single string connected by theme interlinks would produce the following:

(z)(1)*	students
(z)(q)*	girls, 14 years
(x)(p)*	strength $01 physical
(y)(2)*	measurement
(x)(2)	activities
(y)(q)*	sports

Entries:

Students
Girls, 14 years. Physical strength. Measurement

Girls, 14 years. Students
Physical strength. Measurement

Strength. Girls, 14 years. Students
Physical strength. Measurement

Measurement. Physical strength. Girls, 14 years. Students

Students
Girls, 14 years. Activities: Sports

Girls, 14 years. Students
Activities: Sports

Sports. Activities. Girls, 14 years. Students

In this type of entry, one proceeds from (z) to the second (z), then to the first (x) and the (y)s that follow it. When a second (x) is reached, the first two (z)s are again used and then the second (x) and the (y)s following it.

A few more examples should help in making clear the operation of theme interlinks, and the different kinds of relationships involved.

Parallel Themes

Feasibility studies of applications of computers to reference question analysis and to formulation of search strategies for answering reference questions[1]

Theme 1: reference questions, analysis, applications of computer systems, feasibility studies

Theme 2: reference questions, answering, formulation of search strategies, applications of computer systems, feasibility studies

Both themes deal with applications of computers to the problem of answering reference questions. The first theme concerns analysis of the questions; the second involves devising a search strategy. Presumably there is a time sequence in that there is an implication that the analysis will help make the search strategy. Notice the repetition in terminology:

String:		
	(z)(1)*	questions $21 reference
	(x)(2)*	analysis $w of
	(y)(s)	applications $v of $w in
	(y)(3)*	computer systems
	(x)(2)	answering $w of
	(y)(p)*	search strategies
(sub 3↑)	(y)(1)	search strategies for answering reference inquiries
	(y)(2)	formulation $w of
	(y)(s)	applications $v of $w in
	(y)(3)*	computer systems
	(z)(6)	feasibility studies

This string has several interesting elements that should be noted before the entries are shown. First of all, the second string's beginning Term, marked with an (x), is actually the second Term in that theme, the first being the (z) Term shared with the first theme. The (x)'s connective ($w) looks as if it applied to the last Term in the first theme. Since the whole gist of the string is in answering reference questions, the two themes are parallel developments of the same subject, one from the point of view of *analyzing* the question in preparation for answering it and the other from the point of view of answering it by means of a *search strategy* based on the analysis. In each case a computer system is used. The separation of the common Term, (z)(1)*   questions $21 reference

from the second theme can be confusing unless one remembers to look for it. The final element in the string is also a common element, but this is more difficult to overlook. The Terms tagged by (s) and (3) are in both themes, but cannot be tagged (z) because they are in the middle of the string. Therefore they have to be repeated.

The entries for this string follow:

Entries: **Questions**
                Reference questions. Analysis. Applications of
                computer systems — *Feasibility studies*

                Reference questions
                Analysis. Applications of computer systems
                — *Feasibility studies*

                Analysis.   Reference questions
                Application of computer systems — *Feasibility studies*

                Computer systems
                Applications in analysis of reference questions
                — *Feasibility studies*

                Questions
                Reference questions. Answering. Search strategies.
                Formulation. Applications of computer systems
                — *Feasibility studies*

                Reference questions
                Answering. Search strategies. Formulation.
                Applications of computer systems —
                Feasibility studies

                Search strategies.   Answering of reference questions
                Formulation. Applications of computer systems
                — *Feasibility studies*

                Computer systems
                Applications in formulation of search strategies
                for answering reference inquiries —
                Feasibility studies

The problems of this string were compounded by the fact that the Terms in the string, for the second theme in particular, represent surface structure in the English language. The deep structure connects the two themes just as much as the common subject, "reference questions." The analysis in the first theme is the basis, in the second theme, for structuring the search strategy to answer the question. And the necessity for analyzing the reference question and structuring a search strategy was to get answers. The agent or tool was the computer, used indirectly both in analysis and for searching. Furthermore, all this is assuming that the question has been negotiated with the person who produced it and actually is the one to be asked in order to get the desired answer.

There is an additional kind of situation in which the theme interlink solution is useful. This occurs in some kinds of two-way interactions.

Interactive Type

Theme interlinks solve the kind of problem where emigration from one country is immigration into another:

Emigration from Scotland to the United States, 1776-1914

String:

        (x)(1)* Scotland^d

        (y)(2)* emigration $d 1776-1914 $v to

        (y)(3)   United States

        (x)(1)* United States^d

        (y)(2)* immigration $d 1776-1914 $v from

        (y)(3)   Scotland^d

Entries:

        Scotland
           Emigration, *1776-1914* to United States

        Emigration.   Scotland
           1776-1914 to United States

        United States
           Immigration, *1776-1914* from Scotland

        Immigration.   United States
           1776-1914 from Scotland

A similar problem occurs with imports/exports.

Complex Syntax

Sometimes theme interlinks are used because of complex syntactical relationships, rather than for the presence of two themes. An example follows:

Proceedings of a conference on the effects of food additives on human allergies

The indexer would probably begin with a single string:

      Man / allergies / effects $v of $w on / food additives

and then realize that "food additives" was a complex agent, requiring "whole-part" treatment. Beginning with "food additives" would be just as indecisive:

food / additives / effects $v on $w of / human allergies

From this, the indexer would realize that two themes were involved, and would work out two strings:

String 1:   (1)   man
             (p)   allergies
             (2)   effects of food additives

String 2:   (1)   food
             (p)   additives
             (2)   effects on human allergies

A special procedure exists in PRECIS for combining themes that are inter-linked into one longer string. Each theme starts with (x) and uses (y)s as long as the theme lasts. The second theme starts again with (x) and carries on through the (y)s. Anything common to both themes, in this case "Conference proceedings," is tagged (z) and is applied to each entry from each theme:

String: (x)(1)*   man
           (y)(p)*   allergies
           (y)(2)   effects of food additives
           (x)(1)*   food
           (y)(p)*   additives
           (y)(2)   effects on human allergies
           (z)(6)   conference proceedings

Entries: **Man**
            Allergies. Effects of food additives — *Conference proceedings*

            Allergies.   Man
            Effects of food additives — *Conference proceedings*

            Food
            Additives. Effects on human allergies — *Conference proceedings*

            Additives.   Food
            Effects on human allergies — *Conference proceedings*

Theme interlinks are extremely useful devices for handling situations where two ideas are presented simultaneously or so intertwined that they cannot and should not be treated separately.

Complex Interrelationships

Theme interlinks sometimes solve a complex interrelationship, such as the following:

	d
(z)(0)	United States
(x)(1)*	atmosphere
(y)(2)*	pollution $v by
(y)(3)	combustion of aircraft fuels
(x)(1)*	aircraft
(x)(p)*	fuels
(y)(2)*	combustion
(y)(2)	pollution of atmosphere
(z)(6)	reports, surveys

Entries:

Atmosphere.   United States
Pollution by combustion of aircraft fuels — *Reports, surveys*

Pollution.   Atmosphere. United States
By combustion of aircraft fuels — *Reports, surveys*

Aircraft.   United States
Fuels. Combustion. Pollution of atmosphere — *Reports, surveys*

Fuels.   Aircraft. United States
Combustion. Pollution of atmosphere — *Reports, surveys*

Combustion.   Fuels. Aircraft. United States
Pollution of atmosphere — *Reports, surveys*

In this case, "United States" has not been led because it is an environment for the rest of the string components. The second theme is necessary because the agent is a complex concept. When it is led, it has had to be broken up into three parts, each with its own role operator:

aircraft   = the basic concept

fuels   = a part of it; vital to making the aircraft go

combustion   = the action; what happens to the fuel in the aircraft

The second action, "pollution," is both an action of the whole concept

combustion-of-fuels-in-aircraft

and a *product* of the earlier action, "combustion."

With PRECIS, indexing does not have to be a one-word-at-a-time process. This is somewhat difficult for indexers who are accustomed to the indexing theory underlying both modern thesauri and Keyword-In-Context (KWIC) or Keyword-Out-Of-Context (KWOC) indexing.

Modern thesauri go back to Mortimer Taube's Uniterms. When single unit-terms tended to cause an unacceptable amount of ambiguity, they were replaced in strategic places with "bound terms" of two or more words, which were regarded as permanently tied together in a given order. In KWIC or KWOC indexing, each *significant* word in a term is used as a headword, accompanied by the whole phrase that serves as its context (or as much of it as can be printed as a single line of text).

In PRECIS, however, the indexer *selects* the significant words and is not bound by the title in this selection process. In fact, use of the title is very strongly discouraged, since titles are notoriously poor vehicles for conveying content. The selected words, plus any missing ones needed for logical context, are analyzed as indicated in chapter 3 and put into string order. Unlike terms in a thesaurus or in a subject heading list, not only is it possible to have entirely unique word combinations in the output from the string, but these may be used once or frequently, depending on the context. In other words, no Term, whether it contains one word or twenty, is cast in bronze in an authoritative printed list, because there is no such list. Later PRECIS entries may duplicate earlier ones, but it is not mandatory that they do so. In fact, this would be discouraged unless precisely the same topic was encountered more than once.

This freedom for the indexer also has its price. Attention does have to be paid to the matter of collocation of index entries. With an authority list, whether subject headings or thesaurus, collocation is automatic because the *list* makes it so. The PRECIS indexer does have to think about how *this* Term will fit in with similar Terms. Some of the algorithms and special processes have been written with the needs of this collocation problem very much in mind. The PRECIS thesaurus, to be discussed in chapter 14, supplies a supporting framework which, among other things, helps in the collocation.

The main part of the *British National Bibliography* is printed in order according to the Dewey Decimal Classification. Since it is a classified catalog, entries for works where two different classes of concepts are being dealt with simultaneously require two different class numbers. Where two themes class in different places, there will be one class number for each theme. Thus, even if the index failed to put like materials together via index entries, the classification would do so via class numbers, providing a sort of fail-safe system. The vast majority of North American catalogs and bibliographies are not made this way.

A special routine has been developed to treat some kinds of complex subjects with a method other than using theme interlinks. While this does not provide multiple classes for the problem discussed above, it does make a more logical sequence, or an equally logical one, compared with theme interlinks.

DOWNWARD-READING SUBSTITUTION (DRS)[2]

In previous chapters, a convenient substitution routine has been described for use when reading the string upward, as in the case of operators requiring the Predicate Transformation or when using Standard Format and reading upward into the *qualifier*. As we have seen, phrases, shortened Terms, or even blanks can be substituted for existing Terms when it is desirable to have shorter or grammatically improved English or when Terms can be eliminated without loss of information.

It had been postulated for some time that a similar downward-reading substitution routine would be equally helpful in some situations, particularly some of the ones covered by Theme Interlinks (x) and (y). Such a routine has been developed and will be added at the *British National Bibliography* when re-programming for the forthcoming MERLIN system is done.

Conditions for which the downward-reading substitution is suitable are those in which the complexity of the agent has been so great that theme interlinks had to be employed even though two distinct themes were not necessarily involved. The substitute block itself consists of a specified number of Terms following the Term to which the substitution indicator (sub n↓) is attached. The "n," as in the upward-reading substitution, stands for the number of Terms to be replaced below it, *when the string is read downward*. This process can also be utilized for other complex situations.

The Case of the Dependent Term

Sometimes an agent is wanted both for a phrase and as a *lead* for each word in cases where the Term cannot be given in colloquial form without violating differencing Constraint A (a part may not be differenced by its whole). Consider the first approximation of a string for:

Use of electron beams in radiotherapy

Tentative string:

(2)*	radiotherapy
(s)	use $v of $w in
(3)*	electrons
(r)*	beams

The first entry would be

Radiotherapy
Use of electrons. Beams

This is awkward. And so is "electrons in beams" or "beams of electrons," neither of which would get entries under both words. The colloquial "electron beams" cannot be differenced, and yet an entry is desired under "beams." What remains? Further examination of the string above reveals that there is actually a dual and reciprocal action:

1) electron beams used for radiotherapy

2) radiotherapy using electron beams

So the first approximation fails and has to be replaced with the theme interlink approach. With the theme interlink approach we can get entries under "electrons" and "beams" and at the same time make use of the colloquial (and more readable) "electron beams." This is done by writing a pair of title-like phrases in telegraphic style for each of the reciprocal relationships:

electron beams — use in radiotherapy

radiotherapy — use of electron beams

The solution produces the first theme:

(x)(1)*   electrons
(y)(r)*   beams
(y)(s)   use $v in $w of
(y)(3)*   radiotherapy

followed by its mirror-image:

(x)(2)*   radiotherapy
(y)(s)   use $v of $w in
(y)(3)*   electron beams

This second approximation "saves the appearances" but still is lengthy and somewhat awkward. We have used a two-theme approach to solve a complex one-theme problem. Until recently, this was the best that could be done, but now, with the introduction of the downward-reading substitution, a better solution is possible.

The downward-reading substitution makes it possible to use a string with one theme:

String: (2)*   radiotherapy
                 (s)   use $v of $w in
      (sub 2↓)   (3)   electron beams
                 (1)*   electrons   ⎤
                 (r)*   beams   ⎦ substitute block

To make the first entry, the new string is read downward through the Term tagged by the substitution indicator, (sub 2↓)(3), yielding:

Radiotherapy
Use of electron beams

The entries for the string, with the downward-reading substitution, are:

Radiotherapy
Use of electron beams

Electrons
Beams. Use in radiotherapy

Beams.   Electrons
Use in radiotherapy

Notice that when the agent, below the downward-reading substitution comes into the *lead*, the substitute Term is ignored in reading upward, just as, with an upward-reading substitution, the Term with the substitution was overlooked when reading downward in a string.

The upward-reading substitution (sub n↑) is ignored when reading the string *downward*; the downward-reading substitution (sub n↓) is ignored when reading the string *upward*. In either case, the tags for the operators perform their normal functions called for by the Format. In Standard Format, Terms are read upward from *lead* to *qualifier* unless otherwise indicated. Predicate Transformation takes place with operators (s) and (3), unless these are not marked as *leads*. With Inverted Format, the string is read down and into the *display* in normal Term order, including the substitution Term, but excluding the substitution block. The (4), (5), or (6) operators are picked up as the rules for these three operators may dictate.

With the Term in the substitute block as *lead*, Terms in the block below the *lead* come first in the *display*, followed by the phrase created by the Predicate Transformation. This happens whether Terms in the block below the *lead* are or are not dependent upon it (the *lead*) or otherwise attached to it. In other words, the downward-reading substitution and the upward-reading substitution are basically identical operations, but one works when reading down and the other works when reading up, as their names suggest.

The tag attached to the downward-reading substitution is the one normally given to the role operator according to its *logical role* in the string. In the case above, the logical role was agent (3). The individual Terms below the downward-reading substitution get the role operators that normally would have been assigned to them in a second (x) and (y) theme.

The Case of the Upward and Downward Substitutions

It sometimes happens that both upward-reading and downward-reading substitutions are needed in the same string. This may be done. In fact, if needed such substitutions may be used more than once. The following case represents one such situation.

Implications of Wittgenstein's theories of philosophy of religion for religious belief

String:
	(2)*	religion
	(p)*	belief
(sub 2↑)	(2)	religious belief
	(s)	implications $v of $w for
(sub 3↓)	(3)	theories of philosophy of religion of
		Wittgenstein, Ludwig
	(1)*	philosophy of religion
	(s)	theories $v of $w of ⎤ substitute block
	(3)*	Wittgenstein, Ludwig ⎦

The results obtained by these substitutions are essentially those formerly obtained with two themes (or, once in a long time, even three). Quite frequently, one theme or the other had a long substitute phrase similar to the downward-reading substitution in this case. Sometimes both had such substitutions. The advantage to using the downward-reading procedure, if it can be applied, is economy and less complexity than with the theme interlinks.

The entries from the above string are:

Religion
Belief. Implications of theories of philosophy of
religion of Wittgenstein, Ludwig

Belief. Religion
Implications of theories of philosophy of religion
of Wittgenstein, Ludwig.

Philosophy of religion
Theories of Wittgenstein, Ludwig. Implications for
religious belief

Wittgenstein, Ludwig
Theories of philosophy of religion. Implications for
religious belief

The routine used in this example is especially valuable where there are complex concepts on both sides of a "gated" Term. A Term is called "gated" when connectives ($v) and ($w) are used. These connectives may be thought of as gates because one opens one way (downward) and the other opens the opposite way (upward). One kind of gate, as we have seen, may be used alone for disambiguation or both may be used together, as with operator (s). In the string above, both (s) Terms are gated, but the first has substitutions on each side of it, while the second has the familiar form of gating (required with operator "s"). The Term in the substitution itself is used when reading downward from the first two *leads*. Once these are completed, the Terms in the substitute *block* appear in the entries for the first time. From this point, the downward-reading substitution, for all practical purposes, vanishes. The string is then read as if the DRS did not exist. But the upward-reading substitution now is "seen" for the first time. (It was ignored in reading down the string.) When, at last, "Wittgenstein" is in the *lead*, two Predicate Transformations apply, one after the other. Beginning with "theories," the string is read up, picking up both (s) Terms and resulting in "Theories of philosophy of religion. Implications for religious belief." Note in this case that there does not have to be a connective between the Terms "philosophy of religion" in the substitute block and "implications for" higher in the string. Heretofore, when there was no connective, the statement for the *display* ended. What remained, if anything, went into the *qualifier*. With this kind of substitution, however, the rule is:

—Finish up the substitute block first,

—then deal with the role definer (s) Term and the upward-reading substitution;

—both go into the *display*.

A Term for the *qualifier* would have to be higher yet in the string and one not replaced by the upward-reading substitute.

The Case of the Role Definer Tagged as *Lead*

The example following has the role definer operator (s) tagged for a *lead*. Normally when this happens, the (s) is followed by the agent (3). The (3) block, which is operator (3) and any dependents, goes into the *qualifier* in the reverse of normal order; that is, with the dependent element first. The situation here is similar.

Toxic effects of pollution of environment on human behavior

String:		(1)*	man
		(2)*	behavior
(sub 2↑)	(2)	human behavior
		(s)*	toxic effects $v of $w on
(sub 2↓)	(3)	pollution of environment
		(1)*	environment
		(2)*	pollution

(1)* environment
(2)* pollution   ] substitute block

Entries:

Man
Behavior. Toxic effects of pollution of environment

Behavior.   Man
Toxic effects of pollution of environment

Toxic effects.   Pollution.   Environment
On human behavior

Environment
Pollution. Toxic effects on human behavior

Pollution.   Environment
Toxic effects on human behavior

What happens when (s) is in the *lead* is slightly tricky. After "Toxic effects" has been placed in the *lead*, the normal procedure is to go to the *bottom* of the (3) block—that is, the Terms dependent upon the agent (3)—and read the block up into the qualifier. With the downward-reading substitution, the substitute block is treated in the same way as the "3" block below a normal (s). The bottom in this case is "pollution" and the next to bottom Term is "environment." These are read up into the *qualifier* in the reverse of their string order. At the same time, the (3) Term itself is ignored because a downward-reading substitution is passed over when reading upward into the *qualifier*, or, in fact, in reading upward in any situation. The algorithm for dealing with (s) as *lead* followed by a (3) block has been altered slightly to make it applicable in cases of the downward-reading substitution.

One of the features of the theme interlink routine has been the ability to use operator (0) environment once in each theme. Normally this operator can be used once and only once in a string. Since, however, the downward-reading substitution involves an interactive situation and this may require re-use of operator (0), the original (0) is retained for those entries in the string that come after the downward-reading substitution.

The Case of the Retained Environment

Effects of government financial assistance for agricultural industries on foreign trade in agricultural products in Western bloc countries

String:

	(0)*	Western bloc countries
	(2)*	foreign trade $v in $w of
	(3)*	agricultural products
(sub 2↑)	(2)	foreign trade in agricultural products
	(s)	effects $v of $w on
(sub 3↓)	(3)	government financial assistance for agricultural industries
	(1)*	agricultural industries
	(2)*	financial assistance $v by $w for
	(3)*	governments

substitute block

By now the reader should have noticed that these single strings have repetitive operator sequencing, that is the order (1)(2)(3) is repeated in the string. Operators (2) and (3) have been repeated before, but (0) has not and (1) only under circumstances to be discussed in the next chapter.

Entries: **Western bloc countries**
   Foreign trade in agricultural products. Effects of
   government financial assistance for agricultural
   industries

Foreign trade.   Western bloc countries
   In agricultural products. Effects of government financial
   assistance for agricultural industries

Agricultural products
   Foreign trade of Western bloc countries. Effects of
   government financial assistance for agricultural
   industries

Agricultural industries.   Western bloc countries
   Financial assistance by governments. Effects on
   foreign trade in agricultural products

Financial assistance.   Agricultural industries. Western
   bloc countries
   By governments. Effects on foreign trade in
   agricultural products

Governments.   Western bloc countries
   Financial assistance for agricultural industries.
   Effects on foreign trade in agricultural products

The first line of the *display* in the third entry represents the Predicate Transformation. With "agricultural products" in the *lead*, the string up to that point is read upward and then dropped into the *display*. "Effects of" and the downward-reading substitute come next. The lower Terms (in the substitute block) for which the (3)-tagged Term substitutes are omitted.

When making entries under the *lead* Terms *within* the downward-reading substitution block, the Terms in the block,

> (1)*   agricultural industries
> (2)*   financial assistance $v by $w for
> (3)*   governments

are dealt with first. Then the gated Term,

> (s)   effects $v of $w on

plus any higher Term connected to it, are added to the *display*:

> (sub 2↑) (2)   foreign trade in agricultural products

Finally, any Term below the "substitute" block completes the *display*. In this case, there were no Terms below the *display*, but the next example remedies that lack.

The Case of the Extended String: *Lead*-Only Terms at the Beginning and Terms Below the Downward-Reading Substitute at the End

Virtually any condition that occurs in PRECIS may happen where there are complex relationships involved. The operators and the routines associated with them are not new, but the context is.

Implications for natural gas & petroleum production of variations in pressure of strata — an evaluation

The string for this topic is a long one. The division point at which the second string would have begun in a Theme Interlink case is easily recognized as the key system (1) coming after the agent (3). The final action Term, which comes below the substitution block and an upward-reading substitute for all nine earlier Terms, calls for Standard Format.

```
String:          (1)*   natural gas (LO)
                 (1)*   petroleum (LO)
                 (r)    natural gas & petroleum
                 (2)    production   $w of
                 (s)    implications   $v of   $w for
      (sub 3↓) (3)      variations in pressure of strata
                 (1)*   strata        ⎤
                 (p)*   pressure      ⎥ substitute block
                 (2)*   variations    ⎦
      (sub 9↑) (2)      implications of variations in pressure of strata
                            for production of natural gas & petroleum
                 (2)*   evaluation
```

Entries:

Natural gas
    Natural gas & petroleum. Production. Implications of
    variations in pressure of strata. Evaluation

Petroleum
    Natural gas & petroleum. Production. Implications of
    variations in pressure of strata. Evaluation

Strata
    Pressure. Variations. Implications for production of
    natural gas & petroleum. Evaluation

Pressure.   Strata
    Variations. Implications for production of natural
    gas & petroleum. Evaluation

Variations.   Pressure. Strata
    Implications for production of natural gas & petroleum.
    Evaluation

Evaluation.   Implications of variations in pressure of
    strata for production of natural gas & petroleum

It was necesary to make the upward-reading substitution in the next to last line of the string because the final Term "evaluation" referred to the whole of the subject-matter included in the string.

The first example in this section concerned an indirect agent. The other four covered various kinds of indirect actions. It should be emphasized that the *kind* of role definer is not necessarily the reason for using the downward-reading substitution. The number of distinct themes determines that.

APPLICATION OF THE DOWNWARD-READING SUBSTITUTIONS TO EARLIER EXAMPLES OF THEME INTERLINKS

The common factor in all examples of the downward-reading substitution is that they all involve an interactive situation, usually with operator (s) role definer, but occasionally with the operator (t) which will be introduced in the next chapter. The downward-reading substitution usually replaces the agent (3), and the substitute block usually begins with a key system (1), but this is not mandatory. All of the earlier examples of theme interlinks have two themes except a) proceedings of a conference on the effects of food additives on human allergies (treated without the role definer), and b) pollution of the atmosphere by combustion of aircraft fuels (also handled without using a role definer).

Problems a) and b) are similar to the mirror-image and "toxic effects" types found in the discussion of the downward-reading substitutes.

String: (1)*   man
                 (p)*   allergies
        (sub 2↑) (1)   human allergies
                 (s)   effects $v of $w on
        (sub 2↓) (3)   food additives
                 (1)*   food   ⎤
                 (p)*   additives   ⎦ substitute block
                 (6)   conference proceedings

Entries: **Man**
                 Allergies. Effects of food additives — *Conference proceedings*

                 Allergies. Man
                 Effects of food allergies — *Conference proceedings*

                 Food
                 Additives. Effects on human allergies — *Conference proceedings*

                 Additives.   Food
                 Effects on human allergies — *Conference proceedings*

As a matter of convenience, and in order to show the entries without too much extraneous material, the second conversion will be given without the geographical location or form division.

String: (1)*   atmosphere
                 (2)*   pollution
        (sub 2↑) (2)   pollution of atmosphere
                 (s)*   effects $v of $w on
        (sub 3↓) (3)   combustion of aircraft fuels
                 (1)*   aircraft   ⎤
                 (p)*   fuels   ⎥ substitute block
                 (2)*   combustion   ⎦

Entries: **Atmosphere**
                 Pollution. Effects of combustion of aircraft fuels

                 Pollution.   Atmosphere
                 Effects of combustion of aircraft fuels

                 Effects.   Combustion. Fuels. Aircraft
                 On pollution of atmosphere

                 Aircraft
                 Fuels. Combustion. Effects on pollution of atmosphere

                 Fuels.   Aircraft
                 Combustion. Effects on pollution of atmosphere

                 Combustion.   Fuels. Aircraft
                 Effects on pollution of atmosphere

This kind of substitution is a welcome solution to a collection of rather difficult problems. It allows a greater degree of flexibility in making relationships clear.

SUMMARY

The relatively complex sets of interrelationships that call for either theme interlinks or use of a downward-reading substitution have been discussed. Theme interlinks are applied where two or even three themes appear in one title-like statement. In other words, two things are happening at once in the same context. This situation was covered by a special technique which permitted each theme to be identified and yet also allowed it to be considered as a whole.

In leaving theme interlinks and downward substitutions, it suffices to say that these are extremely useful devices for handling situations where there are two themes or a theme of great complexity. There are somewhat similar instances with *author-attributed* connections or associations, special two-way interlinks, and various kinds of directional properties, to which we turn next.

PRECIS MANUAL REFERENCES

Theme Interlinks: Sections 6.15-6.20, 22.7-22.9, 27.1-27.5, pp. 51-55, 197-200, 234-38; Algorithm 18, 473-74.

REFERENCES

[1]This example (theme interlink solution) is taken from Derek Austin and Veronica Verdier, *String Indexing: PRECIS. Introduction and Indexing* (London, Ontario: University of Western Ontario, School of Library and Information Science, 1977). The indexing was performed on a corpus of articles taken from the *Journal of the American Society for Information Science,* vol. 25. This particular item is identified as JASIS 25:139. An unusually large number of theme interlinks occurred among the things indexed, probably a result of the type of material.

[2]Examples of the downward-reading substitution are taken from a communication from the Subject Systems Office, Bibliographic Services Division, British Library.

11
INTERACTIVE SITUATIONS

The concept interlink discussed earlier — operator (s), role definer — was used to indicate the unusual role, the indirect agent, and the indirect action. The activities of a direct agent, acting directly upon the object and in a well-recognized role can often be harder to illustrate. Much of bibliographic material being indexed reflects effects and influences or equivalent relationships. Another type of relationship has to be used in cases where the author of the work being indexed did something to the organization of its content. In such cases, there may be a reciprocal action between two subjects or topics, either as a one-way action or as a two-way action. For satisfactory indexing, both of these situations must be shown.

CONCEPT INTERLINK:
OPERATOR (t) — AUTHOR-ATTRIBUTED ASSOCIATION

An author-attributed association, indicated with the operator (t), is used in situations where there has been a comparison, or an explanation from a certain angle or viewpoint to the exclusion of other angles or viewpoints or where some specific relationship was introduced by the author of the work being indexed. (This should not be confused with "bias" as the historian sees it. All that is meant here is that the author made some connection between two apparently independent concepts.) Several forms are involved, depending upon how many actions or interactions are present.

One-Way Interaction

Islam as interpreted by Marxism

String: (1)* Islam
        (t) $v interpreted by $w interpreting
        (3)* Marxism

In this case, the key system is "Islam." The author has selected Marxist interpretations of it. The relationship, in this case requiring one Term when reading down and the other when reading up, connects the two. Note that with the operator (t), no *word* has to precede the connectives, ($v) and ($w). In this gated situation, the concept interlinking Term is written in italics and is followed immediately by the agent.

Entries: **Islam**
        interpreted by Marxism

       Marxism
        interpreting Islam

The author-attributed association represents an act of mental association of two concepts to form a single unit of thought. These concepts, of course, would not be totally different but related closely enough to enable an author to make the association. Another one-way action would occur in a case where the author has made an explanation of something by some other system, group philosophy, and so on.

Continuance of titles of nobility explained by primogeniture

String:
- (1)* titles of nobility
- (2)* continuance $w of
- (t) $v explained by $w explaining
- (2)* primogeniture

Entries:

Titles of nobility
Continuance *explained by* primogeniture

Continuance. Titles of nobility
explained by primogeniture

Primogeniture
explaining continuance of titles of nobility

The Term below the (t), when in the *lead* position, invokes the Predicate Transformation. In this case, the upward connection from "continuance" left nothing to go into the qualifier. One-way actions like this are less common than two-way actions.

Author-Attributed Two-Way Actions

Two-way or interactions make use of the concept interlink (t) and words such as:

related to

compared with

Obviously when relating or comparing "A" to "B," one is also comparing or relating "B" to "A."

Comparison of Monte Carlo Roulette with Las Vegas Roulette

String:
- (1)* Monte Carlo roulette
- (t)   compared with
- (1)* Las Vegas roulette

An order has been introduced here which has not been presented previously. Here is a situation where there are two key systems, which is normally forbidden, unless one is restricted to *lead* only (LO). With a (t) operator, an interlink is made between each system. This is truly a reciprocal situation.

Entries: **Monte Carlo roulette**
                    compared with Las Vegas roulette

                    Las Vegas roulette
                    compared with Monte Carlo roulette

In both of these cases, the (t)-defined connection is made and the connected Term appears directly after it in the *display*. In contrast to the first examples, the action goes two-ways. The reading, in the string above the (t) Term, is downward. When the lower Term is in the *lead*, reading is upward and the resultant phrase is dropped into the *display*.

The (t) author-attributed association has never been used as *lead*. Operator (t) may have connectives without a word before them. Both upward-reading and downward-reading substitutes may be used with (t) to replace Terms for smoother reading and greater clarity, if needed.

The Terms representing the concepts thus associated cannot have dependent elements. Also, a single concept with two associated dependent elements may be such that there can be an author-attributed association between the dependent elements. In such cases, both dependent elements should relate directly to the higher Term. A general diagram for this situation is:

```
 ┌─►( )    [referent]
 └─(p)     part or property
   (t)     concept interlink
 └──(p)    part or property
```

The relationship between reflexes and agility in the domestic cat

String: (1)*   cats $01 domestic
                    (p)*   agility
                    (t)   related to
                    (p)*   reflexes

Entries: **Cats**
                    Domestic cats. Agility *related to* reflexes

                    Agility.   Domestic cats
                    related to reflexes

                    Reflexes.   Domestic cats
                    related to agility

Retrieval in automatic indexing: recall related to precision

String: (2)*   automatic indexing

```
      ┌─►(p)*   retrieval
      └─(q)*    recall
        (t)     related to
      └──(q)*   precision
```

Entries: **Automatic indexing**
             Retrieval: Recall *related to* precision

             Retrieval.   Automatic indexing
             Recall *related to* precision

             Recall.   Retrieval. Automatic indexing
             related to precision

             Precision.   Retrieval. Automatic indexing
             related to recall

In a case like this, great care has to be taken during the analysis process to ensure that both dependent Terms do indeed relate directly to the higher Term upon which they are both supposed to be dependent.

A (t) Term is not used as a *lead*. This is characteristic. The word defining the kind of relationship is always in italics. Operator (t) words may have connectives without a word before them. An upward-reading substitute can be used to replace higher Terms for smoother reading and greater accuracy, as in the case below:

> *Retrieval performance in automatic indexing compared with
>   search strategy*

String: (2)*   automatic indexing
              (p)*   retrieval
              (p)*   performance
   (sub 2↑) (p)   retrieval performance
              (t)   related to
              (2)   search strategy

Both compared Terms relate to "automatic indexing." To get entries under both "performance" and "retrieval," two lines had to be used, but the comparison was made with the substitution.

Entries: **Automatic indexing**
             Retrieval. Performance *related to* search strategy

             Retrieval.   Automatic indexing
             Performance *related to* search strategy

             Performance.   Retrieval. Automatic indexing
             related to search strategy

             Search strategy.   Automatic indexing
             related to retrieval performance

A number of variations in the elements before and after the (t) are possible, but dependent elements must have some close relationship with a common higher Term. Examples of various types are given below.

Information theory related to linguistics

String: (1)*   information theory
(t)   related to
(2)*   linguistics

Entries: **Information theory**
related to linguistics

Linguistics
related to information theory

Readings on the relationship between children's acquisition of language skills and children's adjustment

String: (1)*   children
(p)*   language skills
(2)*   acquisition $w of
(t)   related to
(2)*   adjustment
(6)   readings

Entries: **Children**
Language skills. Acquisition *related to*
adjustment — *Readings*

Language skills.   children
Acquisition *related to* adjustment — *Readings*

Acquisition.   Language skills. Children
related to adjustment — *Readings*

Adjustment.   Children
related to acquisition of language skills — *Readings*

Organisms' control systems explained by information theory

String: (1)*   organisms
(p)*   control systems $w in
(t) $v explained by $w explaining
(3)*   information theory

Entries: **Organisms**
Control systems *explained by* information theory

Control systems.   Organisms
explained by information theory

Information theory
explaining control systems in organisms

Development of organisms explained by information theory

String:
    (1)*   organisms
    (2)*   development $w of
    (t) $v explained by $w explaining
    (2)*   information theory

Entries:
    Organisms
    Development *explained by* information theory

    Development. Organisms
    explained by information theory

    Information theory
    explaining development of organisms

Most of the substitutions used so far have been the type needed to improve terminology when reading upward, either into the *qualifier* or with the Predicate Transformation. We have also noted that blanks can be used to dispense with Terms no longer needed for context.

Author-Attributed Association:
Downward-Reading Substitutions

The main types of author-attributed associations may be found in Figure 12. In general, when there are no dependent Terms related to each other and subsumed under a higher Term, the basic patterns are shown in the chart. The interlinks may represent one- or two-way actions. The (t) Term must have an upper and a lower Term, whether or not the action between these Terms is one- or two-way. Operator (t) itself is rarely if ever used as a *lead*. Most of the time it contains words that might be called "connectors" and, as such, are almost never used as leads. If (t) is used with dependent elements, these must relate to a higher Term. The words tagged with the (t) must bind the Terms directly above and below into an interrelationship that is a conceptual unit. The last requirement means simply that the relationships must make sense. For example, the statement "God compared with bricks" would be most unlikely as a concept.

The downward-reading substitution may be used with an author-attributed association. Two examples are given below.[1]

Achievement motivation of women related to their role in society

String:
    (1)*   women
    (2)*   motivation $21 achievement $w of
    (t)   related to
(sub 3↓) (2)   role of women in society
    (1)*   society
    (s)   role $v of $w in   ⎤ substitute block
    (3)*   women   ⎦

Figure 12
Major Types of Author-Attributed Associations

Interlinks may represent one- or two-way actions. Dependent elements may be used if necessary in the Term above the (t) Term, or both above and below this Term, provided both dependent Terms refer to a common higher Term.

READ DOWN		T Y P E S			READ DOWN
i	ii	iii	iv	v	Content
(1)	(1)	(1)	(2)	(3)	entity, action or agent
(t)	(t)	(t)	(t)	(t)	concept interlink
(1)	(2)	(3)	(2)	(3)	entity, action or agent

Entries:

Women
 Achievement motivation *related to* role of women
  in society

Motivation. Women
 Achievement motivation *related to* role of women
  in society

Achievement motivation. Women
 related to role of women in society

Society
 Role of women *related to* achievement motivation of
  women

Women
 Role in society *related to* achievement motivation
  of women

Comparison of social conditions of European and Asian immigrant
 families in San Francisco

String:

 (0)* California^d

 (p)* San Francisco^d

 (1)* families $21 immigrant $21 European

 (2)* social conditions $w of

 (t) compared with

(String continues on page 216)

(sub 2↓) (2)   social conditions of Asian immigrant families

(1)*   families $21 immigrant $21 Asian   ⎤ substitute

(2)*   social conditions   ⎦ block

Entries: **California**
San Francisco. European immigrant families. Social
conditions *compared with* social conditions of Asian
immigrant families

San Francisco. California
European immigrant families. Social conditions
compared with social conditions of Asian immigrant
families

Families. San Francisco. California
European immigrant families. Social conditions
compared with social conditions of Asian immigrant
families

Immigrant families. San Francisco. California
European immigrant families. Social conditions *compared
with* social conditions of Asian immigrant families

European families. San Francisco. California
European immigrant families. Social conditions
compared with social conditions of Asian immigrant
families

Social conditions. European immigrant families. San
Francisco. California
compared with social conditions of Asian immigrant
families

Families. San Francisco. California
Asian immigrant families. Social conditions *compared
with* social conditions of European immigrant families

Immigrant families. San Francisco. California
Asian immigrant families. Social conditions *compared
with* social conditions of European immigrant families

Asian families. San Francisco. California
Asian immigrant families. Social conditions *compared
with* social conditions of European immigrant families

Social conditions. Asian immigrant families. San
Francisco. California
compared with social conditions of European immigrant
families

In the last example, notice that what is being compared is "social conditions" of two groups. The final entry actually does this. The other entries run through the changes occasioned by the differencing needed to get all the access points for each group and for the location. In spite of the number of entries, this case is not as difficult as most of the ones in the preceding chapter.

In addition to the types of interrelationships mentioned up to this point, there is one that can be most useful. This is a special format for a different kind of interaction.

TWO-WAY INTERACTIONS INVOLVING TWO KEY SYSTEMS AND A MUTUAL, RECIPROCAL ACTION

Another kind of double theme can be treated in a single string. This is the case when two-way interactions of some kind take place. There are two main kinds of such interactions: those that are system-initiated and those that are author-initiated. We have just seen the author-initiated ones, which called for the special operator (t). The system-initiated actions are amenable to treatment via a separate routine with the string pattern:

> (1)*   entity
> (2)*   action
> (1)*   entity

The routine is like the one with operator (t) and, like (t), it is one of the few cases where operator (1) may be repeated in a string. Basically, the routine repeats the action with the entity on either side of it and invokes the Predicate Transformation with the second key system:

Communication between physicians and patients

String: (1)*   physicians
                        (2)*   communication $v with $w with
                        (1)*   patients

Entries: **Physicians**
                        Communication with patients

                        Communication.   Physicians
                        With patients

                        Communication.   Patients
                        With physicians

                        Patients
                        Communication with physicians

If the action Term had not been marked as a *lead*, only the first and last entries would have been obtained.

Various kinds of relations — foreign, cultural, social, and others — are most amenable to treatment with this useful reciprocal (1)(2)(1) routine:

Foreign relations between Canada and Mexico

String: (1)* $\overset{d}{\text{Canada}}$

(2)*   foreign relations   \$v with   \$w with

(1)* $\overset{d}{\text{Mexico}}$

Entries: **Canada**
Foreign relations with Mexico

Foreign relations.   Canada
With Mexico

Foreign relations.   Mexico
With Canada

Mexico
Foreign relations with Canada

Two-way actions like this are reciprocal relations. At this point, we shall look at another kind of relationship called "directional properties."

DIRECTIONAL PROPERTIES

A directional property is defined as a *property* that belongs to some *possessor* and is directed toward some *object*.[2] This property is expressed through words such as or similar to the following:

attitudes

liability

accountability

responsibility

and by extension through the following words when considered in a general, not a specific, sense:

theories

policies

Directional properties, as a rule, come in four types:

1)   *Directional property by itself*
These are coded as key systems and include terms like:

personal liability

public accountability

They tend to take the broadest of themes and cannot invariably be singled out as belonging to some specific (as opposed to vague or equitable) possessor.

2) *Directional property + Possessor*
These tend to be less ambiguous than the first type because one may now attribute property to a possessor:

String: (1)*   students
                    (p)*   attitudes

Entries: **Students**
                  Attitudes

             Attitudes.   Students

The one-to-one relationship is preserved here without the use of function words for disambiguation.

3) *Directional property + Possessor + Object*
In this type of directional property, the property is treated as the possession of some individual or group and directed towards some object. In coding it, the role operator (s) is used to show clearly which is which. The possessor is coded as agent:

String: (1)*   examinations
                    (s)   group attitudes $v of $w toward
                    (3)*   students

Entries: **Examinations**
                  Group attitudes of students

                  Students
                  Group attitudes toward examinations

String: (1)*   funds
                    (s)   accountability $v of $w for
                    (3)*   trustees

Entries: **Funds**
                  Accountability of trustees

                  Trustees
                  Accountability for funds

4) *Directional Property + Object (possessor understood)*
In this case, a directional property and an object are present, but the possessor is implied rather than explicit. An explicit possessor may be supplied with a very generalized Term:

4) String:

(1)* disadvantaged
(s)* responsibility $v of $w for
(3) society (NU)

Entries:

Disadvantaged
Responsibility of society

Responsibility
For disadvantaged

The responsibility in this instance is assumed to be that of society as a whole. Take note that no entry is wanted under "society" and the Term may not even be needed in the *qualifier*, hence the use of (NU).

There have been some problems with this type of directional property. In some cases the possessor is not stated and "society" as a whole is not satisfactory as an explanation. Therefore, the rules for the role definer operator have been altered so that (s) is not required to be followed invariably by operator (3) agent. Note in the string below that the role definer (s) is accompanied by only one connective when it does not precede the agent.

String:

(0) Great Britain
(2)* science
(s)* policies $w on
(4)* Socialist viewpoints

Entries:

Science. Great Britain
Policies — *Socialist viewpoints*

Policies. Great Britain
On science — *Socialist viewpoints*

Socialist viewpoints
Great Britain. Science. Policies

Here, the first entry followed Standard Format; the last followed the Inverted Format, and the middle one, the Predicate Transformation — with the (s) Term in the *lead*, the connective ($w) and its Term plus the Term to which it pointed, "science," were dropped into the *display* (leaving the unconnected "Great Britain" in the *qualifier*). This is an unusual routine, to be followed only where there is an unstated possessor of a directional property, and even then with great care so that the ensuing entries mean what they are supposed to mean.

Complex Directional Properties

The situations above are not considered to be particularly complex. However, things can get ambiguous. Assume a subject like this:

Accountability of individual students for the behavior of student groups

Three things are involved:

    students

    behavior

    accountability

Who is accountable? Individual students? Students as a group? Society? This kind of directional property may, in fact, be two kinds of directional property:

String:		
	(x)(1)*	students
	(y)(r)*	groups
	(y)(2)*	behavior
	(y)(3)	accountability of individual students
	(x)(1)	student groups
	(y)(p)	members $w of
	(y)(q)*	individuals
	(y)(p)*	accountability $v for
	(y)(p)	group behavior

Entries:

    Students
      Groups. Behavior. Accountability of individual students

    Groups.   Students
      Behavior. Accountability of individual students

    Behavior.   Groups. Students
      Accountability of individual students

    Individuals.   Members of student groups
      Accountability for group behavior

    Accountability.   Individuals. Members of student groups
      For group behavior

Note that in the first theme, "accountability" is of individual students for their own behavior, even in a group. The second theme concerns the accountability of the individual student for the behavior of the group. It would be an understatement to say that either this string or its resultant entries are self-evident!

To understand the use of operator (3) in the first part of the string, it is necessary to go back to the definition of the concept of an *agent*, which was defined specifically as the *subject initiating* the action and thus became one of the basic operators selected for inclusion in PRECIS as a role operator. The full concept covers:

1) the agent of a transitive action

2) aspects

3) factors

When the agent is *directly* responsible for the action immediately preceding it, there is no problem:

<pre>
(1)*   houses
(p)*   roofs $w of
(2)*   damage $v by $w to
(3)*   wind
</pre>

When the agent is *indirectly* responsible, a Blank Field Insert is used between it and the action (replacing the missing direct action and preventing the Predicate Transformation from taking place):

<pre>
            (2)*   science
            (2)   research
(sub 2↑)   (2)   scientific research
            (2)
            (3)*   grants
</pre>

The Term, "grants," is an indirect agent because grants are awarded to people, whose action is to do research.

Where "aspects" or "factors" are involved, the agent again is indirect with respect to the action:

<pre>
(2)*   unemployment
(2)*   compensation
(2)
(3)*   social aspects
</pre>

The direct agent of "compensation" obviously is some public or private organization providing the compensation. "Social aspects" are side effects, an indirect relationship of other factors to the action.

In the string for "student accountability" the first theme invokes the notion of "accountability" and involves the *role* of the agent, "individual students," as being accountable for the action, "behavior." The problem here is that the word "accountability" itself is directional: someone is accountable for some action (and to some authority, often unstated). In this case the authority is not stated, but the action is clearly stated. The phrase "accountability of individual students" replaces a more explicit indirect action:

<pre>
(2)*   behavior
(s)   accountability $v of $w for
(3)*   individual students
</pre>

Use of such a phrase, however, is common in cases of two themes.

The second theme answers the question, "Why should anyone even think that students are accountable for the behavior of groups?" This theme establishes the relationship of the individual student to the group. So this rather long collection of dependent Terms establishes that individual students are *members* (part) of a group. As members, they have the property of accountability for the group's behavior. The group's *behavior* is a function of the *group*. The group exhibits a behavior (another way of saying a group acts in some way). But an individual member in that group possesses responsibility. In both parts of the string, individual students are possessors of the directional property, "accountability," and in both cases "group behavior" is the object of the directional property. Theme 1 establishes the role of the individual. Theme 2 establishes the individual's membership in the group as reason for his or her role. The problem is the degree of responsibility, which depends on the degree of identification with the group.†

The definition of "complex" is helpful here. A *subject* is considered complex if:

1) it has a concept below a (t) or as an agent (3) below a gated action (2) or role definer (s)

(2) two or more terms are involved

(3) all or part of the concept is wanted in the *lead*

A complex *agent* tends to consist of:

1) an entity and part

2) an entity and property

3) an entity and environment (*if* environment applies to the entity and not to the string as a whole)

4) an entity and action

Complex agents usually require theme interlinks (though most are amenable to handling with downward-reading substitutions). In the string above, the first theme Term, "accountability of individual students," is a complex agent. This is apparent after rewriting the string with a role definer (s).

The word, "attitudes," is widely used. This may be a directional property and may be used in four different ways:

1) the attitude itself	(1)*	attitudes
2) The possessor of the attitude	(1)*	adolescents
	(p)*	attitudes
3) "Attitudes" as a directional property	(1)*	criminals
	(s)*	attitudes $v of $w toward
	(3)*	society

---

†Probably every reader has had the painful experience of being penalized for the actions of a subgroup in a group to which the reader belonged.

In this case, the entries are:

Criminals
Attitudes of society

Attitudes.   Society
Toward criminals

Society
Attitudes toward criminals

4)   "Attitudes" as an agent

(2)*   Olympic Games^b
(2)
(3)*   athletes
(2)*   performance

(sub 4↑) (2)   performance of athletes in
Olympic Games
(s)   effects $v of $w on
(3)*   national attitudes

Entries: **Olympic Games**
Athletes. Performance. Effects of
national attitudes

Athletes.   Olympic Games
Performance. Effects of national
attitudes

Performance.   Athletes. Olympic
Games
Effects of national attitudes

National attitudes
Effects on performance of athletes
in Olympic Games

The latter string is interesting because it has a Blank Field Insert. There is a missing direct relationship, probably "competition," between "athletes" and "Olympic Games." It also has a substitution for four Terms, which makes smoother reading and less complex construction in the final entry.

In matters involving directional properties expressed as accountability, attitudes, awareness, liability, responsibility or theories/policies relating to a specific subject — when an author considers a directional property of one group of people with reference to some other people, thing, or event — the situation is complex and must be analyzed with care. Although grammatically in the dative case, the directional property is almost transitive in the sense of a transitive action. From the point of view of the object, the directional property can almost be considered as a kind of effect or result of action. For this reason, the object of a directional property is treated as a key system (1), in cases where it is not plainly an action.

The role operator (s) conveniently expresses the name of an attitude when the object is present:

String: (1)   man
                     (2)*   conflicts
                     (q)*   war
         (sub 3↑) (2)   war
                     (s)*   attitudes $v of $w toward
                     (3)*   pacifists

Entries: **Conflicts.** Man
                     War. Attitudes of pacifists

                     War. Conflicts. Man
                     Attitudes of pacifists

                     Attitudes. Pacifists
                     Toward war

                     Pacifists
                     Attitudes toward war

When a phrase is used in what appears to be a directional property, the indexer should check for an (s) operator as in the "accountability" case presented earlier.

In all cases where operator (s) introduces a role definer there must be both a higher *and* a lower Term; *both* connectives and the lower Term must be coded (3). In some cases where (s) introduces a directional property with an unstated possessor, the lower Term and the $v connective may be omitted. Where there *is* a lower Term, however, it must be coded (3).

Before concluding this chapter, one more directional property needs to be explained. This is the case in which *viewpoint* is a subject and not just a form.

VIEWPOINT AS SUBJECT

Sometimes there can be more than one viewpoint attached to a work. The viewpoint of one author may be directed toward the viewpoint of another author or group. If the author's viewpoint is not required as a *lead*, this may simply be handled with operator (4), viewpoint-as-form. One viewpoint concerned with another is a more complex matter. The following example is taken from the *British National Bibliography*:†

*Aims of Industry viewpoints on Labour Party proposals on
    nationalisation of industries*

("Aims of Industry" is a group speaking for industrialists)

String: (1)*   industries

                     (2)*   nationalisation $w of

(String continues on page 226)

---

†Reproduced courtesy of the Bibliographic Services Division, The British Library, London, England.

String (cont'd)   (s)   proposals $v by $w on

(3)*   Labour Party
     ^c

(4)   Aims of Industry viewpoints

Entries: **Industries**
             Nationalisation. Proposals by Labour Party
             — *Aims of Industry viewpoints*

           Nationalisation.   Industries
             Proposals by Labour Party — *Aims of Industry viewpoints*

           Labour Party
             Proposals on nationalisation of industries — *Aims of*
             Industry viewpoints

If operator (4) had been tagged as a *lead*, the resulting entry could have been ambiguous:

           Aims of Industry viewpoints
             Industries. Nationalisation. Proposals by Labour Party

   This suggests that the topic could as easily have been "Labour Party proposals on Aims of Industry viewpoints on nationalisation of industries." To get an unambiguous entry under "Aims of Industry viewpoints" it is necessary to take the two theme path:

String: (x)(1)*   industries

          (y)(2)*   nationalisation $w of

          (y)(s)   proposals $v of $w on

          (y)(3)   Labour Party
                       ^c

          (y)(4)   Aims of Industry viewpoints

          (x)(1)   Labour Party proposals on nationalisation
                       of industry

          (y)(4)*   Aims of Industry viewpoints

Entries: The first three entries are exactly the same as those produced by the original string with no *lead* under "Aims of Industry viewpoints." The second part of the string resolves the ambiguity which resulted when attempt was made to use the (4) Term as a *lead*. Second theme treatment produces:

           Aims of Industry viewpoints
             Labour Party proposals on nationalisation of industry

This is about as unambiguous as one can get! In similar cases, "attitudes" may be used when more than one viewpoint is involved. The point here is to recognize that there are two views involved, one of which is a reaction to views put forth in a proposal. The time dependency feature is significant because the "Aims of Industry" group could not have presented a viewpoint on the Labour Party proposal until the proposal had been made. In addition to having two viewpoints, representing two themes, two time frames are also involved, and the views, themes, and times represent an interaction. The conglomeration of views, themes, and times presents a situation not unlike the one in an earlier chapter where ability to answer reference questions was time-dependent, first, on analysis of the questions, and second, on the necessity for devising a search strategy—making a total of three actions, each dependent upon the previous one.[3]

SUMMARY

Concept interlinks consist of two kinds: role definer or directional property (s), and author-attributed association (t), considered in this chapter. The latter made use of an upward and downward reading of the string in a somewhat different fashion than that used in the former. Connectives are not required with (t) in the same way as with (s), but in many cases the special action—relating or comparing—served as its own connecting device. Not only is this methodology convenient for the indexer, but it also reflects natural language usage. Examples of the downward-reading substitution with (t) were given. A convenient reciprocal (1)(2)(1) interaction was described.

Directional properties of four types were outlined. Since these are rather hard to handle, extended examples were shown. In particular, attention was given to the significant status of operator (s) in some kinds of directional properties and to the identification of possessor and object in interactive situations.

Finally, viewpoint as subject was discussed as a time-dependent directional property.

With this chapter the discussion of techniques of making PRECIS strings comes to an end. The following chapters deal with details of the indexing system as a whole.

PRECIS MANUAL REFERENCES

Concept interlinks and operator (t): Sections 21.1-21.7, pp. 182-88.

Specific types of operators that may be used with (t): pp. 182, 186-87, 199, 467.

Algorithm 16 for operator (t): pp. 467-69.

Two-way interactions: Sections 19.6-19.7, p. 158; Sections 19.15-19.16, pp. 167-69.

Directional properties: Sections 26.1-26.9, pp. 224-27, 229-33.

Viewpoint as subject is among the directional properties: Section 26.6, pp. 227-29.

REFERENCES

[1]Examples of the downward-reading substitution are either taken from (first case) or based on (second case) those in a communication from the Subject Systems Office, Bibliographic Services Division.

[2]Derek Austin, *PRECIS: A Manual of Concept Analysis and Subject Indexing* (London: Council of the British National Bibliography, 1974): 224, 226, 229.

[3]See chapter 10, pp. 286-89. The order would be: analyze the question; devise a search strategy; answer the question.

12
MANIPULATION CODING

In all of the discussion of PRECIS techniques so far, the assumption has been made that the system is being used manually. However, as mentioned in the first two chapters, from the very beginning, PRECIS was planned so that it could be used as an automated system. Care was taken so that the procedures involved would be amenable to manipulation by computer.

In this book, all mention of the computer has been deliberately avoided in discussion of the various operators and other conventions. This was done because these matters are not tied to the computer, and, in fact, make sense by themselves without reliance on such a machine. A good many special collections, archives, or materials requiring careful indexing are not extensive enough to warrant the expense involved with computerization unless such equipment is readily available at low cost. If a computer is at hand, the use of automation procedures does have advantages, such as freeing the indexer from making the entries. Programming may be obtained from institutions already using PRECIS and translated or emulated locally. In some situations, manual indexing will be used until there is sufficient backlog to make automation feasible.[1] Austin suggests a volume of one or two thousand items per annum as the limit to manual operations.[2] Since two thousand items would be about fifty per week, this seems a reasonable recommendation. Skeptics should remember that these items will also have to be accessioned, cataloged, possibly classified and given proper cross-reference back-up. The cross-referencing, in particular, is extremely important for the operation of the system. This topic will be discussed in the next chapter. In this chapter, the codes used to transform PRECIS strings into machine-readable format will be covered.

MANIPULATION CODES

Before any string can be manipulated by computer to produce entries, it must be translated into a format that the computer can "read." This calls for an additional small group of tags called "instruction codes," which apply to each line of the string and "tell" the computer what kind of action is needed to ensure that each part of the Term gets the treatment it requires. Each instruction in the Primary or Secondary Instruction Codes sets off a prepared, pre-stored set of directions on what to do with the data.

All of this sounds very anthropomorphic. Since the computer is a machine, it cannot be *told* anything. Nor can it read or recognize anything. Actually, the codes discussed here must be put into a Binary Code of zeros and ones, usually in groups of eight or sixteen. For instance, the instruction code that starts the process for humans is a $, but for the computer it is 0010 0100, which is the Binary Code Digit 24 in a standardized machine character and operation code called ASCII.[3] The program of instructions stored in the machine, after proper initialization, will begin to work on the string elements following the dollar sign when 0010 0100 is input. Since programs are created at different levels and work in sequential order once they have begun, the $ tag will trigger a series of sequential actions each time it appears in the line of a string. For example, in the Primary Instruction Code (*see* Figure 13), in the first position it signals "start" and the computer begins to read the string element. In the eighth position, it acts as a signal that the next position will contain the character that identifies the Term code (*see* Figure 5, page 72) in the string element being worked on—that is, whether the Term is a normal one or some special subroutine may be needed. A third $ identifies a subfield and brings in the Secondary Instruction Code.

The nine primary code characters are used in a positional block. That is, they always occur in a sequence of nine columns or positions. The first $ is always in the first position, while the second $ is always in the eighth position. If a dollar sign appears in any of the other nine positions, it will be treated as an error and the computer will either stop or signal that an error has been made. This is because the computer has been programmed to find certain codes in certain columns. If they are missing or are not the ones expected, the computer cannot function as programmed. Actually a matching situation is involved. If a computer is programmed to expect "x," "y," or "z" in a column, it will react and follow through as programmed. If anything else is in the column, this will not be the expected "x," "y," or "z"; it will not know what to do, and it cannot proceed. The primary codes and their accompanying instructions are given in Figure 14 (page 232).

The single letter or double numeral secondary code for subfield is an "escape code" signalled by the third dollar sign. Since it occurs *within* a Term rather than at the beginning of a string line for the Term, it acts as a variable or floating field. A whole succession of such fields may occur, as we have seen in the differenced Term in particular.

EXAMPLES OF CODING

Explanations of the coding process for manipulation will be much clearer with examples. Compared with writing strings, manipulation coding is easy—almost but not quite a mechanical process. With optical character recognition equipment to read the entry forms now in use, the indexer's work could be read directly into the computer. The blank format for each line is in this form:

$___ : ___ : _____0$ _____

$___ : ___ : _____0$ _____

$___ : ___ : _____0$ _____

The theme interlink comes first, then the role operator followed by focus-in-*lead*, substitute and *display/qualifier* treated as a unit. The Term Code indicator ends the Primary Code. Any Secondary Codes go on the line with the Term. The work sheet used by indexers is similar to Figure 15 (page 234). Such a sheet both simplifies coding and serves as an aid to memory.

(Text continues on page 233)

Figure 13
Manipulation Codes

Codes used to instruct computer. The first two $ are pre-printed in fixed position; the third * has no fixed position as its location depends on the length of the words which precede it. The zero in the 7th position is fixed and pre-printed.

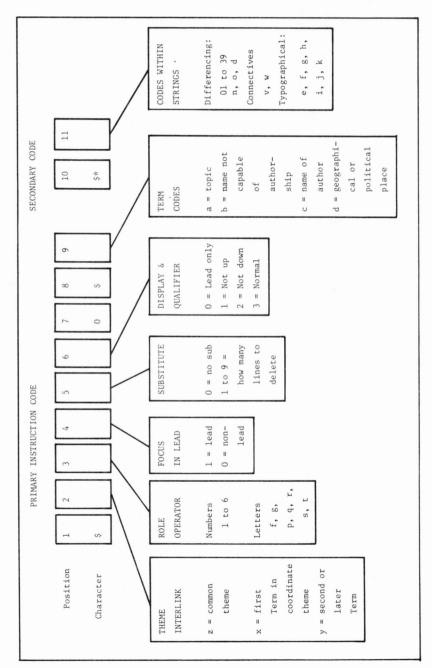

Figure 14
Primary Code Positions and the
Instructions for Them in Brief Form

Column	Acceptable Codes	Instructions
1	$	Start
2	x,y,z	Theme Interlink if "x" or "y", otherwise standard uses
3	0,1,2, 3,4,5, 6,p,q, r,s,t, f,g	Use routine developed for each operator
4	0,1	Wanted in <u>lead</u>? 0 = no, 1 = yes
5	0,1-9	If 0, no substitution involved; if 1-9, replace number of lines above or below as indicated by the numeral
6	0,1,2, 3	0 = (LO) Print only in the <u>lead</u> position 1 = (NU) Do not print above the <u>lead</u> (not in <u>qualifier</u>) If used with numeral 1-9 in Column 5, indicates a Downward-Reading Substitute 2 = (ND) Do not print in display. If used with numeral 1-9 in Column 5, indicates an Upward-Reading Substitute If used with zeros in Cols. 4 and 5, indicates a Blank Field Insert 3 = Normal. Print in <u>Display</u>, and <u>Qualifier</u>, and <u>Lead</u> if a 1 in column 4
7	0	Empty column
8	$	What follows is type of Term code
9	a,b,c, d	a = normal Term b = proper name of something not capable of authorship c = name of person or corporate body capable of authorship; includes artists, composers, etc. d = geographical or political <u>area</u> or <u>place</u>

Most of the rest of this chapter will consist of samples of manipulation codes, many for strings used in earlier chapters. Explanations will be added with the strings so that the reader can see how the manipulation code fits the string. The first example will be a normal and simple string:

Example 1: Normal string

		d
String:	(0)*	Florida
	(1)*	libraries $21 academic
	(2)*	management

Analysis for coding:

Line 1:	1.	Theme interlink? No.	Use	z
	2.	Operator? Environment		(0)
	3.	Focus in *lead*? Yes		1
	4.	Substitute? No		0
	5.	Want in *qualifier* & *display*? Yes		3
	6.	Type of Term? Geog.		d

Coding: $ z 0 1 0 3 0$ d   Florida

Line 2:	1.	Theme interlink? No	Use	z
	2.	Operator? Key system		(1)
	3.	Focus in *lead*? Yes		1
	4.	Substitute? No		0
	5.	Want in *q & d*? Yes		3
	6.	Type of Term? normal		a

Coding: $ z 1 1 0 3 0$ a libraries $21 academic

Line 3:	1.	Theme interlink? No	Use	z
	2.	Operator? Action		(2)
	3.	Focus in *lead*? Yes		1
	4.	Substitute? No		0
	5.	Want in *q & d*? Yes		3
	6.	Type of Term? normal		a

Coding: $ z 2 1 0 3 0$ a   management

(Text continues on page 235)

Figure 15
Sample Indexers' Work Sheet

Type used at British National Bibliography. The printed numbers are MARC codes, 082 for Dewey classification number.

SI	082010 633'.00973	691 0652385
083		

Field crops. Cultivation $b United States

690

$z 0 003 0$dd *United States*

$z 0$a

$z 1 103 0$a *field crops*

$z 0$a

$z 2 103 0$a *cultivation*

$z 0$a

$z 0$a

$z 0$a

$z 0$a

$z 0$a

$z 0$a

$z 0$a   BPK

692 008 1906	692	692
692	692	692
692	692	692

043 *n - US - - -*	050 *SB187.U6*

LCSH

650 Field crops $z United States

693

  02 376720 0

BSD CS5   BL
                                                 BE
                                                 Nuc

In the above case, the subfield requiring the third $ is in the key system line, where "libraries" has been differenced by "academic." Putting all of this together, we get:

$ z 0 103 0$ d	Florida
$ z 1 103 0$ a	libraries $21 academic
$ z 2 103 0$ a	management

Notice that columns 4, 5, and 6 have been written together as a unit. This is a mnemonic form with which indexers soon become familiar. It is easier to think of 103 as "normal entry tagged for the *lead*" than to consider each separately. Most of the time these three columns taken together do have a meaning that is easier to remember when they are grouped. Once the string is input in the manipulation code, the computer program will take care of word order, printing or suppression of parts, spacing and type fonts as the various codes direct.[4]

The rest of the examples will be done without the "analysis for coding" step. The figures for this chapter should be consulted, as well as pertinent parts of this book or the *PRECIS Manual* as the need arises.

Example 2: String element not wanted as a *lead*

String:
        (0) $\overset{d}{\text{Massachusetts}}$

        (p)* $\overset{d}{\text{Salem}}$

        (1)*   houses $d 1675-1699

        (2)*   preservation

Coding:
$ z 0 003 0$ d	Massachusetts
$ z p 103 0$ d	Salem
$ z 1 103 0$ a	houses $d 1675-1699
$ z 2 103 0$ a	preservation

Example 3: Focus code, Predicate Transformation

String:
        (1)*   taxes $21 income

        (2)*   calculation $v by $w of

        (3)*   tax consultants

        (q)*   H & R $\overset{c}{\text{Block}}$ $i (Firm)

Coding: $ z 1 103 0$ a   taxes $21 income

$ z 2 103 0$ a   calculation $v by $w of

$ z 3 103 0$ a   tax consultants

$ z q 103 0$ c   H & R Block $i (Firm)

Example 4: Alternative coding for coordinate concepts (f)

String: (1)*   journal literature
                     (3)*   critical analyses
                     (q)*   review articles $v &
                     (f)*   book reviews
                     (2)   inclusion in journals

Coding: $ z 1 103 0$ a   journal literature

$ z 3 103 0$ a   critical analyses

$ z q 103 0$ a   review articles $v &

$ z f 103 0$ a   book reviews

$ z 2 003 0$ a   inclusion in journals

Example 5: Blank Field Insert

String: (1)*   audiovisual materials
                     (2)*   cataloging
                     (2)
                     (3)*   rules

Coding: $ z 1 103 0$ a   audiovisual materials

$ z 2 103 0$ a   cataloging

$ z 2 002 0$ a

$ z 3 103 0$ z   rules

Notice that the 002 generally indicates the Blank Field Insert and therefore is easy to recognize in the manipulation code.

Example 6: *Lead*-only Terms

String: (1)*   legends $21 French (LO)
                     (g)*   tales $21 French (LO)
                     (r)   French tales & legends

Coding: $ z 1 100 0$ a   legends $21 French

$ z g 100 0$ a   tales $21 French

$ z r 003 0$ a   French tales & legends

The code 100 for *lead*-only is also distinctive and readily recognized, as is the 003 to indicate that a Term is not wanted as a *lead*.

Example 7: Upward-Reading Substitution

String: (1)*   paintings $21 American

                                 c
        (p)*   Homer, Winslow $f 1836-1910

                                 c
(sub 2↑) (1)   Homer, Winslow $f 1836-1910

                                 b
        (p)*   Herring net $e The

        (6)   critical studies

Coding: $ z 1 103 0$ a   paintings $21 American

                                         c
      $ z p 103 0$ c   Homer, Winslow $f 1836-1910

                                         c
      $ z 1 022 0$ c   Homer, Winslow $f 1836-1910

                                         b
      $ z p 103 0$ b   Herring net $e The

      $ z 6 003 0$ a   critical studies

A reminder of the instructional codes for typography would be helpful at this point:

$e   comma, then non-filing part in italics
$f   comma, then filing part in italics
$g   return to bold face roman type, no preceding punctuation
$h   period, then filing part in italics
$i   no preceding punctuation, filing part in italics
$j   period, two spaces then filing part in ordinary roman type
$k   no preceding punctuation, filing part in ordinary roman type

Code ($j) produces two blank spaces before a filing word. It is similar to the kind of spacing that separates the *lead* from the *qualifier* and is used to distinguish between homographs, mainly in cross-references where such words must be identified. As a matter of fact, these codes are used in the Reference File as well as in the creation of index entries by computer.

Example 8: Downward-Reading Substitution

String: (2)*   radiotherapy
               (s)   use $v of $w in
(sub 2↓) (3)   electron beams
              (1)*   electrons
              (r)*   beams

Coding:	$ z 2 103 0$ a	radiotherapy
	$ z s 003 0$ a	use $v of $w in
	$ z 3 021 0$ a	electron beams
	$ z 1 103 0$ a	electrons
	$ z r 103 0$ a	beams

The upward-reading substitution can be identified by the code, 0n2. The 4th coding position is *always* zero for "not wanted as *lead*." The 5th position's "n" indicates the number of lines in the string to be replaced. The 6th coding position is *always* 2 ("not down"). The downward-reading substitution can be identified by the code, 0n1. The 4th position is *always* zero; the 5th "n" indicates the number of lines in the string to be replaced. The 6th position is *always* 1 ("not up").

In both of these cases, the 0n2 and the 0n1 are easily recognizable characteristics for identification; the "2" or the "1" tells you which is which — whether to replace Terms higher in the string or lower. A mnemonic to jog the memory would be "2 for HigHer, 1 for lower" (*higher* has two letters alike; in *lower*, all letters are different).

Example 9: Theme Interlinks

String:	(z)(1)*	students
	(z)(q)*	girls, 14 years
	(x)(p)*	strength $01 physical
	(y)(2)*	measurement
	(x)(2)	activities
	(y)(q)*	sports

Coding:	$ z 1 103 0$ a	students
	$ z q 103 0$ a	girls, 14 years
	$ x p 103 0$ a	strength $01 physical
	$ y 2 103 0$ a	measurement
	$ x 2 003 0$ a	activities
	$ y q 103 0$ a	sports

The use of (x) and (y) shows up well in this example. The economy of the code, as compared with the string, is plain to see in that the code does not require any extra characters. Actually, the (z) is in every normal string but is not listed until the manipulation code is used.

Example 10: Inverted Format plus *lead*

		d
String:	(o)*	Canada
	(1)*	social services
	(p)*	information sources
	(6)*	handicapped persons $01 for
	(6)	directories

Coding:	$ z 0 103 0$ d	Canada
	$ z 1 103 0$ a	social services
	$ z p 103 0$ a	information sources
	$ z 6 103 0$ a	handicapped persons $0 for
	$ z 6 003 0$ a	directories

Once again, the code 103 means "use as *lead*," while 003 conveys the information that the accompanying Term is not to be used as a *lead*.

Manipulation coding prepares the way for input of data into the computer. What happens after input depends on the programs. The logic behind the programs is very helpful in understanding how the string elements are manipulated to become index entries.

ALGORITHMS

The reason for using any code is to set data apart in some way so that it can be used with a prepared routine. Routines and subroutines take the form of a series of step-by-step computer instructions called "algorithms." The algorithms are not the actual programs, but are equivalent to a flow pattern, block diagram or schematic, or summary of what is taking place in actual programs.

These step-by-step instructions have had to be thought out very carefully in order to make the computer do what the system requires of it. It is the job of the indexer to plan out the system. The indexer and programmer work out details. The programmer then writes the actual program routines. Any omitted step impairs chances of producing the desired results. The manipulation coding discussed above is only the beginning. For a system as complex as PRECIS, very sophisticated programs are required.

It is very strongly recommended that the reader become familiar with the algorithms used in PRECIS, as listed in the *Manual*.[5] Although some of these have been slightly modified by the new routines for operators (f), the downward-reading substitution, and so on, the major part of the algorithms is untouched, and all are helpful.

In some cases, one algorithm will call up another as needed. The algorithms are the best summaries of PRECIS operations available. Furthermore, in the *Manual* they are accompanied by examples that give a step-by-step build-up of each index entry. This process, which isolates each bit of the whole procedure, can be invaluable when trying to create strings from title-like phrases, because it enables the indexer to determine the outcome of each tentative string element in achieving the overall set of entries desired.

MORE COMPLEX EXAMPLES

The remaining examples illustrate the coding of more complex strings. These code just like the simpler ones, but they are longer, or have some special manipulations.

Example 11: Role definer (s) for "indirect action" as a *lead* in a
case with an action following an agent, and use of an upward-
reading substitution for clarity

		d
String:	(0)*	United States
	(1)*	welfare services
	(s)*	expenditure $v by $w on
	(3)*	government
(sub 3↑)	(3)	expenditure by government on welfare services
	(2)*	reduction $d 1978
	(6)	investigation reports

Coding: $ z 0 103 0$ d   United States

   $ z 1 103 0$ a   welfare services

   $ z s 103 0$ a   expenditure $v by $w on

   $ z 3 103 0$ a   government

   $ z 3 032 0$ a   expenditure by government on
                welfare services

   $ z 2 103 0$ a   reduction $d 1978

   $ z 6 003 0$ a   investigation reports

Entries: **United States**
   Welfare services. Expenditure by government.
   Reduction, *1978 — Investigation reports*

   Welfare services.   United States
   Expenditure by government. Reduction, *1978*
   — Investigation reports

   Expenditure.   Government. United States
   On welfare services. Reduction, *1978*
   — Investigation reports

   Government.   United States
   Expenditure on welfare services. Reduction, *1978*
   — Investigation reports

   Reduction.   Expenditure by government on welfare
            services. United States
   1978 — Investigation reports

The complex parts here are the Terms tagged with operators (s), (3), and (2)
with a date. The manipulation code gives the correct tags for each part of the
code that the computer is being called upon to manipulate. The actual arranging,
however, is indicated in the rules in the previous chapters and the abbreviated
form in the algorithms. For example, the algorithm for date as a difference has
three instructions:

a) the element prefixed by the secondary code $d is always the last part of a term.

b) The code $d can occur only once in a term.

c) The element following $d is always printed in italics.[6]

And in this example the date is in the *display*, even with the Term to which it is attached in the *lead*. If there had been a Term below "reduction," however, the date would have gone along with "reduction" into the *qualifier*, still at the end of the Term, when the lower Term came into the *lead*.

In this case, when the (s) word "expenditure" was the *lead*, "(3) government" went up into the *qualifier*, and the rest of the (s) phrase, "On welfare services," dropped into the *display*, as called for with the Predicate Transformation. This Transformation also was used with the (3) word "government." The upward-reading substitution replaced three elements in the string when "reduction" moved to the *lead* position.

Example 12: System-initiated two-way interaction

String:
    (1)*   man
    (2)*   communication $v with $w with
    (1)*   animals

This is a system-initiated two-way action and with such an action the connective preposition is invariably the same word. A (1)(2)(1) relationship like this has been programmed so that the action takes place twice, once in each direction. This is automatic and the manipulation code does not have anything but the normal coding:

Coding: $ z 1 103 0$ a   man
           $ z 2 103 0$ a   communication $v with $w with
           $ z 1 103 0$ a   animals

Entries: **Man**
           Communication with animals

           Communication.   Man
           With animals

           Communication.   Animals
           With man

           Animals
           Communication with man

The identical algorithm is used for this and for the Predicate Transformation because the same principle is involved, even though the initial appearance is different.

Example 13: Operator (f) for coordinate Terms with differences

String:
                d
          (0)*   Canada
          (1)*   cows $21 Guernsey $v &
          (f)*   horses $21 Arabian
          (2)*   exhibitions

Coding: $ z 0 103 0$ d   Canada
        $ z 1 103 0$ a   cows $21 Guernsey $v &
        $ z f 103 0$ a   horses $21 Arabian
        $ z 2 103 0$ a   exhibitions

Entries: **Canada**
        Guernsey cows & Arabian horses. Exhibitions

        Cows. Canada
        Guernsey cows & Arabian horses. Exhibitions

        Guernsey cows. Canada
        Guernsey cows & Arabian horses. Exhibitions

        Horses. Canada
        Guernsey cows & Arabian horses. Exhibitions

        Arabian horses. Canada
        Guernsey cows & Arabian horses. Exhibitions

        Exhibitions. Guernsey cows & Arabian horses. Canada

Example 14: Upward-reading and downward-reading substitutions in the same string

Influence of climate and per capita income of developing countries on allocation of foreign assistance for developing countries by developed countries

String:
          (1)*   developing countries
          (2)*   foreign assistance $v by $w for
          (3)*   developed countries
   (sub 3↑) (2)   foreign assistance for developing countries
                  by developed countries
          (2)*   allocation
   (sub 4↑) (2)   allocation of foreign assistance for developing
                  countries by developed countries
          (s)   influence $v of $w on
   (sub 1↓) (3)   climate of country $v &
          (3)*   climate $v &
          (g)*   per capita income

Coding:

$ z 1 103 0$ a	developing countries
$ z 2 103 0$ a	foreign assistance $v by $w for
$ z 3 103 0$ a	developed countries
$ z 2 032 0$ a	foreign assistance for developing countries by developed countries
$ z 2 103 0$ a	allocation
$ z 2 042 0$ a	allocation of foreign assistance for developing countries by developed countries
$ z s 003 0$ a	influence $v of $w on
$ z 3 011 0$ a	climate of country $v &
$ z 3 103 0$ a	climate $v &
$ z g 103 0$ a	per capita income

Entries:

Developing countries
   Foreign assistance by developed countries. Allocation.
   Influence of climate of country & per capita income

Foreign assistance.   Developing countries
   By developed countries. Allocation. Influence of
   climate of country & per capita income

Developed countries
   Foreign assistance for developing countries. Allocation.
   Influence of climate of country & per capita income

Allocation.   Foreign assistance for developing countries
      by developed countries
   Influence of climate of country & per capita income

Climate.   Developing countries
   Influence on allocation of foreign assistance for
   developing countries by developed countries

Per capita income.   Developing countries
   Influence on allocation of foreign assistance for
   developing countries by developed countries

This string, which is a modification of a sample from the Subject Systems Office, British Library, has several interesting features. The two upward-reading substitutions are there to improve the English when Terms below "developed countries" and "allocation" come into the *lead*. The downward-reading substitution replaces "climate $v &" when Terms earlier than "climate $v &" are in the *lead*. When "climate" itself is in the *lead*, it is still part of the "g" block, so that each of the last two Terms is led without the other. The first substitution upward is standard procedure in this kind of string. The second one, 042, was added so that "developing countries" could be used in the *qualifier* for the last two entries. (This is not obvious at first glance. Count tag by tag up the manipulation code version of the string and replace.) When starting with "climate" or "per capita income,' first read upwards and drop the two preceding lines into the *display*:

$ z s 003 0$ a	influence $w on
$ z 2 042 0$ a	allocation of foreign etc.

then last, to the *qualifier*:

$ z 1 103 0$ a	developing countries

This leaves the first element of the string intact and usable. The downward-reading substitution is used to improve the sense of the entry by adding "of country."

Another example illustrates the "aspects" problem.

Example 15: Aspects

Genetic aspects of diseases of the musculoskeletal system

String:	(1)	man
	(p)*	musculoskeletal system $w in
	(2)	diseases $w of
	(2)	
	(3)*	genetic aspects

Coding:	$ z 1 003 0$ a	man
	$ z p 103 0$ a	musculoskeletal system $w in
	$ z 2 003 0$ a	diseases $w of
	$ z 2 002 0$ a	
	$ z 3 103 0$ a	genetic aspects

Entries:	**Musculoskeletal system.** Man
	Diseases. Genetic aspects
	Genetic aspects. Diseases of musculoskeletal system
	in man

This string of five elements produced only two entries. Notice the Blank Field Insert to prevent the Predicate Transformation from occurring. This was necessary because the "aspects" nature of the agent indicates that it is an *indirect* one.

The remaining two examples are taken from the *British National Bibliography*.†

Example 16: Complex topic

Techniques for testing the toxicity of toxic chemicals such as petroleum and petroleum dispersants on organisms

String:	(1)*	organisms
	(3)*	toxic chemicals
	(q)*	petroleum $v &

(String continues on page 245)

†Reproduced courtesy of the Bibliographic Systems Division, The British Library, London, England.

String (cont'd)	(g)*	petroleum dispersants
	(p)*	toxicity
	(2)*	testing
	(p)	techniques

Coding:	$ z 1 103 0$ a	organisms
	$ z 3 103 0$ a	toxic chemicals
	$ z q 103 0$ a	petroleum $v &
	$ z g 103 0$ a	petroleum dispersants
	$ z p 103 0$ a	toxicity
	$ z 2 103 0$ a	testing
	$ z p 003 0$ a	techniques

By this time, it should be quite apparent that the string is obtained from the coding by reading down the third column and attaching the words in the data section. Whether to *lead* or not depends on whether there is a 1 or a 0 in the fourth column. The fifth column is used only for a substitute and the sixth is always 3 unless it is a case of (LO), (NU), or (ND). The entries for this code are:

Organisms
Toxic chemicals: Petroleum & petroleum dispersants.
Toxicity. Testing. Techniques

Toxic chemicals.   Organisms
Petroleum & petroleum dispersants. Toxicity. Testing.
Techniques

Petroleum.   Toxic chemicals. Organisms
Toxicity. Testing. Techniques

Petroleum dispersants.   Toxic chemicals. Organisms
Toxicity. Testing. Techniques

Toxicity.   Petroleum & petroleum dispersants. Toxic
chemicals. Organisms
Testing. Techniques

Testing.   Toxicity. Petroleum & petroleum dispersants.
Toxic chemicals. Organisms
Techniques

The last example is a case of an author-attributed association with complex parts. A case like this required theme interlinks until the downward-reading substitution was adopted. Here it will be done both ways.

Example 19: Author-attributed association with complex parts

Equality of opportunity for promotion of personnel in British industries compared with that in industries of other developed countries #

Original string:	(x)(0)*	Great Britain ^d

Original string:

(x)(0)*	Great Britain
(y)(1)*	industries
(y)(p)*	personnel
(y)(2)*	promotion
(y)(p)*	equality of opportunity
(y)(t)	compared with
(y)(2)	equality of opportunity for promotion of personnel in industries in developed countries
(x)(0)*	developed countries
(y)(1)*	industries
(y)(p)*	personnel
(y)(2)*	promotion
(y)(p)*	equality of opportunity
(y)(t)	compared with
(y)(2)	equality of opportunity for promotion of personnel in industries in Great Britain

Coding:

$ x 0 103 0$ d	Great Britain
$ y 1 103 0$ a	industries
$ y p 103 0$ a	personnel
$ y 2 103 0$ a	promotion
$ y p 103 0$ a	equality of opportunity
$ y t 003 0$ a	compared with
$ y 2 003 0$ a	equality of opportunity for promotion of personnel in industries in developed countries
$ x 0 103 0$ a	developed countries
$ y 1 103 0$ a	industries
$ y p 103 0$ a	personnel
$ y 2 103 0$ a	promotion
$ y p 103 0$ a	equality of opportunity
$ y t 003 0$ a	compared with
$ y 2 003 0$ a	equality of opportunity for promotion of personnel in industries in Great Britain

The bracketed areas on the strings above represent the "t" blocks — the actual comparison in each part of the string. Each such block ends a theme. Using this clue, it is possible to make a more compact string using substitutions.

		d	
Second string:	(0)*	Great Britain	
	(1)*	industries	
	(p)*	personnel	
	(2)*	promotion	
	(p)*	equality of opportunity	
(sub 5↑)	(2)	equality of opportunity for promotion of personnel in industries in Great Britain	
	(t)	compared with	
(sub 5↓)	(2)	equality of opportunity for promotion of personnel in industries in developed countries	
	(0)*	developed countries	
	(1)*	industries	
	(p)*	personnel	
	(2)*	promotion	
	(p)*	equality of opportunity	

Coding:

$ z 0 103 0$ d	Great Britain
$ z 1 103 0$ a	industries
$ z p 103 0$ a	personnel
$ z 2 103 0$ a	promotion
$ z p 103 0$ a	equality of opportunity
$ z 2 052 0$ a	equality of opportunity for promotion of personnel in industries in Great Britain
$ z t 003 0$ a	compared with
$ z 2 051 0$ a	equality of opportunity for promotion of personnel in industries in developed countries
$ z 0 103 0$ a	developed countries
$ z 1 103 0$ a	industries
$ z p 103 0$ a	personnel
$ z 2 103 0$ a	promotion
$ z p 103 0$ a	equality of opportunity

Entries: **Great Britain**
Industries. Personnel. Promotion. Equality of opportunity
compared with equality of opportunity for promotion of
personnel in industries in developed countries

Industries. Great Britain
Personnel. Promotion. Equality of opportunity *compared
with* equality of opportunity for promotion of
personnel in developed countries

Personnel. Industries. Great Britain
Promotion. Equality of opportunity *compared with* equality
of opportunity for promotion of personnel in industries
in developed countries

(Entries continue on page 248)

Promotion.   Personnel. Industries. Great Britain
Equality of opportunity *compared with* equality of
   opportunity for promotion of personnel in industries
   in developed countries

Equality of opportunity.   Promotion. Personnel. Industries.
   Great Britain
compared with equality of opportunity for promotion of
   personnel in industries in developed countries

Developed countries
   Industries. Personnel. Promotion. Equality of opportunity
   compared with equality of opportunity for promotion of
   personnel in industries in Great Britain

Industries.   Developed countries
   Personnel. Promotion. Equality of opportunity *compared*
   with equality of opportunity for promotion of personnel
   in industries in Great Britain

Personnel.   Industries. Developed countries
   Promotion. Equality of opportunity *compared with* equality
   of opportunity for promotion of personnel in industries
   in Great Britain

Promotion.   Personnel. Industries. Developed countries
   Equality of opportunity *compared with* equality of
   opportunity for promotion of personnel in industries
   in Great Britain

Equality of opportunity.   Promotion. Personnel. Industries.
   Developed countries
compared with equality of opportunity for promotion of
   personnel in industries in Great Britain

These entries are identical, whether made with the theme interlinks string or with the downward-reading and upward-reading substitutions string. The actual number of elements in the second string is greater than in the original string. Which is easier to use? The question is moot. The repetitiousness of the "t" block may be annoying in the original string. On the other hand, in the second string one has to remember that the "substitute" block, like the (x)(y) process, may have a second operator (0). These are the only situations where this is permitted. One also has to remember that with an author-attributed association (t) like this there are two comparisons:

a)   The first comparison is between what may be called the *upward-reading substitute block*:

d

(0)* Great Britain ⎤
(1)* industries ⎥
(p)* personnel ⎥ block
(2)* promotion ⎥
(p)* equality of opportunity ⎦

and . . . . (t)

the downward-reading substitute itself:

(sub 5v) (2)   equality of opportunity, etc.

b)   The second comparison is between the downward-reading substitute block:

(0)* developed countries ⎤
(1)* industries ⎥
(p)* personnel ⎥ block
(2)* promotion ⎥
(p)* equality of opportunity ⎦

and . . . . (t)

the upward-reading substitute itself:

(sub 5↑) (2)   equality of opportunity, etc.

The indexer, in a case like this, probably should use the system that comes easiest. In cases where it obviously is more advantageous, as in some of the cases in chapter 10, to use the downward-reading substitution, then this should be done. Probably it is advisable to analyze a two-theme topic with care, in case there is a time-dependency involved in addition to the apparent two themes.

SUMMARY

The manipulation codes are a "shorthand" to enable PRECIS strings to be put into machine-readable form for computer production of entries. The design is for the indexer to do the part of indexing that takes brains and the computer to manipulate the elements in the indexer's strings into desired entries for the printed index (or for an index via cathode-ray tube terminal). In other words, in an equitable situation, the human does the brain work and the computer does the drudgery. Any reader who verified the statement about the entries from the two strings in example 19 should have a very good idea of the type of drudgery that it is a pleasure to donate to a computer.

It remains now to describe the reference files and indicate how they are made.

PRECIS MANUAL REFERENCES

Manipulation coding: Sections 28.1-28.20, pp. 245-61.

Algorithms 1-18: Appendix 3, pp. 437-75. In the re-programming minor changes have been made to some of these algorithms, but in general, they are still valid.

Various matters relating to automatic data processing in PRECIS are covered in Appendix 5, pp. 481-85.

Details of how to correct entries, to add and delete, and so on, are in the *Manual* but are not included in this book because the author's experience in working with six different computer programmers has been that each uses a different method and does not like the others'.

REFERENCES

[1]Audrey Taylor, "Manual Applications of PRECIS in a High School Library," *International PRECIS Workshop, University of Maryland, October 15-17, 1976* (New York: H. W. Wilson, 1977): 157-68.

[2]Derek Austin, *PRECIS: A Manual of Concept Analysis and Subject Indexing* (London: Council of the British National Bibliography, 1974): 245.

[3]There are actually three codes involved: "$," which means "start" to a human; "24," which is a decimal code for "$"; and "0010 0100" representing the decimal numerals "2" and "4," respectively, in binary arithmetic. The computer gets the "0010 0100" as a pattern of on (the 1) and off (the 0) electrical pulses. It is designed to interpret these patterns according to the digital logic built into its components.

[4]The fifth Appendix in the *PRECIS Manual* (pp. 483-85) includes a check routine called "Validation of Strings." This routine checks to see that the Primary Instruction Code has been filled in completely and with valid codes. It looks for Terms preceding or following, as required by the rules, and other equivalent presences or absences. The x_1, x_2, and x_3 are used in this validation to represent theme coding, term coding, and the second digit of the secondary code, respectively. There are minor changes in the validations as a result of the new additions.

[5]Austin, *PRECIS: A Manual*, pp. 439-75. Of these algorithms, number 5, "Salient difference: Operator j," and number 8, "Salient focus," have been deleted. Algorithms 9 and 10 have had slight revisions.

[6]*Manual*, Algorithm 7, p. 447.

13

The rationale for the reference structure in PRECIS was given in chapters 1 and 6. To recapitulate briefly, there are three relationships:

Equivalence

Hierarchy
- generic
- whole-part
  - geographical regions
  - systems and organs of the body
  - areas of discourse (i.e. disciplines)

Association

When indexing, the indexer must, to a considerable degree, be influenced by the collection and the clientele. Thus, indexing in an engineering facility or for an archive in a local historical society is not the same as that for a public or academic library. In each case the users are oriented differently with regard to the collection, and the subject matter varies from highly specific to virtually universal. In general, the index should be reasonably specific, allowing the reference function to carry the burden of the more general terms.

EQUIVALENCE

In PRECIS, for synonyms, near-synonyms, and sometimes antonyms, the standard "see" reference is used to refer from the word not used to the one preferred for the system; this is the *equivalence* relationship. While linguists debate, with considerable justification, whether any words are truly equivalent, in an index, for practical purposes, a decision must be made. Several kinds of conditions require decisions:

1)   When a popular word is to replace a technical one:

Felis *See* **Cats**

Cerebrum *See* **Brain**

2)   When more than one term is commonly used:

Fourth of July *See* **Independence Day**

Paranormal *See* **Supernatural**

(Examples continue on page 252)

Illness *See* **Sickness** (and sometimes,
Health *See* **Sickness**)

Implements *See* **Tools**

Wetness *See* **Dryness**

The words in this last case in PRECIS are called "quasi-synonyms," which describe cases in which there is a choice between descriptive antonyms that are equivalent — for instance, "half empty or half full." Not all antonyms will fit the requirement of being descriptive. There are situations in which both antonymous words are desirable:[1]

inferior - superior

injurious - beneficial

coarse - refined

overthrow - support

Probably all index systems require decisions concerning the equivalence of words.

HIERARCHY

Hierarchy, as we have seen, takes different forms. The pure generic form is a biological one, based on a rigid classification system and taxonomy:

Plants
  Trees
    Conifers
      Firs
        Douglas firs

"See" references are made from Latin names to the vernacular.

The whole-part kind of hierarchy can be illustrated in several ways. The feudal system is a classic sociopolitical-military kind of hierarchy. There are also geographical types:

North America
  Canada
    Ontario
      Toronto
        Don Valley

Systems and organs of the body are another classic example:

Cardiovascular system
  Blood vessels
    Arteries
    Veins
    Capillaries

Again, "see" references are made from Latin or technical names.

Hierarchy in Areas of Discourse is limited to relationships among disciplines:

Behavioral Sciences
  Psychology
    Educational psychology
    Genetic psychology
    Industrial psychology
          etc.
            (+ tool subdisciplines such as
                  Psychometrics
                  Experimental psychology)

In addition, whole-part relationships cover areas other than these three. For practical indexing purposes there are other breakdowns:

Spanish literature
    Drama in Spanish
    Fiction in Spanish
    Poetry in Spanish

"Generic" relationship is taken much more broadly than the biological definition above would indicate, including such relationships as:

Emotions
    Depression
    Ecstasy
    Grief
    Happiness
    Hate
    Love

These are literally *kinds* of the whole: depression *is* an emotion. In most cases they can be recognized by asking:

  "Is x a *kind* of y?"

  "Is x a *part* of y?"

The first question identifies a "to be" situation, the second a "to have" one.

ASSOCIATION

The area of associative relationship is huge. Depending on the context, the only limits are those set by the equivalence and hierarchical functions. In PRECIS the associations have to be fairly obvious:

England - Periodicals on England

Engineering - Mining

Recreation facilitiees - Piers

Foetuses - Abortion

Sociology - Social psychology

Emigration - Immigration

In these cases, neither "kind of" nor "part of" applies; the association is more vague than that. A very large proportion of the references in PRECIS, judging by the content of the Subject Indexes in the *British National Bibliography*, are of the associative type.[2] Fortunately for the user, both the hierarchical and the associative relationships are expressed as "x *See also* y," so that it is not necessary in using the reference to stop and determine whether hierarchy or association was intended.

For the indexer, this happy situation does not exist, because the indexer does have to put the references together into a network. In fitting words into a network, one must be very conscious of what kind of relationship is involved. Networks of words abound with polyhierarchies, for one thing. (This is true also with the "Broader term — Narrower term" relationships used in standard thesauri.) Networks can also be drawn up by tracing relationships between words connected by "see also." Where the reference says "**Horticulture** *See also* **Gardens**," an arrow is drawn from "Horticulture" to "Gardens" because that is the direction in which the user is being led.

An example of a network, *as it would appear to a user*, is given in Figure 16. Since all of these relationships appear to the user as "*see also*" from one term to another, the user has no way of telling which were hierarchical references and which were associative. Only the indexer, who has access to the tracing in the files, and the expert in the discipline to which the terms relate, know the difference. For the average user it makes little difference whether the connection is made from one word to another by hierarchical or associative relationships, so long as the connection is there.

Similarly, there are omitted links between some of the words in the network. In PRECIS, a special bypass routine has been developed so that the user is not led through empty classes on the way to an appropriate term. "Empty" is used in the sense of literary warrant: if there is no book on the subject corresponding to a class, that class is passed over (unless connections have to be made for semantic reasons). The bypass routine is *transparent* to the reader. It takes place within the computer. That is, a leap from class A to class D takes place without the user's being aware that classes B and C have been skipped.

Figure 16
Arrowgraph to Show Network of Associative and Hierarchical Relationships
for the Word "Waves" as Seen by the User

Kinds of relationship are not specified because the system is "transparent" to the reader. Intervening steps are telescoped into shorter leaps when no books were received on the topics represented by them. Both of these shortcuts save the time of the user. Based on "See also" references, *British National Bibliography* Interim Cumulation, May-August 1975.

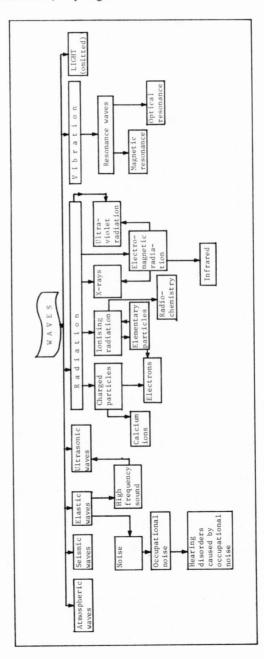

After all, the user is not particularly interested in *how* the reference system gets to the desired class, only that it does get there quickly and easily. The bypass routine can obviously only be used for words occuring in a hierarchy. It is never used with associative terms. Furthermore, a thesaurus of relationships, such as the reference file underlying PRECIS, is used for back-up purposes rather than as a classification system. It purposely delineates some of the non-hierarchical relationships that may prove helpful to the user.

In *analyzing* an existing network, it is necessary to consider all the possible relationships that may be involved. Because of the use of "blanket" references — ones with the instruction:

x *See* **names of individual x's**

and references for pseudo-classes:

Ducks *See also* **Rubber ducks**

and the device of bypassing empty hierarchical classes — a PRECIS network is very hard to analyze at present. When the thesaurus is published, and assuming that the coding (tracing) will be included, it should be much easier because the implicit relationships will then be explicit. In the face-value analysis of Figure 16, for example, some of the relationships that look slightly circular are undoubtedly representing two different kinds of relationships. The arrows, each of which stands for the words, "see also," make it appear that one hierarchy is present, whereas the diagram is actually a collection of little hierarchies joined together by associative relationships. "Radiochemistry," "high frequency sound," "noise," "hearing disorders caused by occupational noise," and some of the odds and ends under "radiation" which have multiple arrows attached to them undoubtedly represent associative connections. In PRECIS, as we shall see, directional signals are tagged for the computer, so that the form of relationship can be found in the coding, even if it is not apparent in the results.

Although it may appear that everything is connected to something else, actually this is not the case. It is estimated that 30% of the words used in PRECIS are "orphans."[3] Judging by the number of definitions per word in any standard dictionary, this may turn out to be an overestimate.

At this point a digression will be made in order to discuss types of relationships used in modern thesauri and in subject headings. The reader may or may not be familiar with the topic, but since it influences what will be discussed later in this chapter, it is added to serve as background information. Following the digression, relationships in PRECIS will be covered in greater detail.

DIGRESSION ON TYPES OF RELATIONSHIPS IN THESAURI AND SUBJECT HEADINGS

The systematic creation of "see also" references between words makes what Charles Ammi Cutter called a "syndetic structure."[4] A syndetic structure underlies all indexing systems containing cross-references, whether subject headings, thesauri, or whatever the organization is. Syndetic structures have within them a concealed classification.[5] In less sophisticated indexing systems than PRECIS, there tends to be a grand mixture of generic, whole-part, and associative relationships, rarely identified, and even then only roughly. In a *standard* thesaurus,[6] for example, one may have a series of narrower and related terms which descend stepwise (*see* Figure 17).

Figure 17
Sequence of Relationships

When a Narrower Term (NT) becomes the headword (T), the former headword (T) becomes a Broader Term (BT). The diagram illustrates a sequence (Hierarchy I) connecting to another sequence (Hierarchy II) where the connection is made with an associative relationship (RT). Terms from the *Thesaurus of Engineering and Scientific Terms* (New York: Engineers Joint Council, 1967).

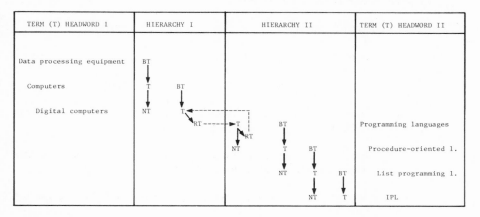

In skeletal form the sequence looks like this:

BT ---- Computers (T) ---- NT
      BT ---- Digital computers (T) ---- RT (into another hierarchy)
           Programming languages (T) ---- NT
                           ---- RT (back to "digital
                                    computers")
           BT ---- Procedure-oriented languages ---- NT
              BT ---- List processing languages ---- NT
                 BT ---- IPL (programming language)

Going horizontally, each word in turn goes from broader term to narrower term, unless or until there is nothing more above or below. Reading the series of sequences vertically, as in Figure 17, it will be seen that the same word may be broader and/or narrower, depending on how many levels there are to the total sequence. As a rule in thesauri, not more than seven or eight levels of hierarchy are given for any term and, of course, many do not have more than one or two.

In the example, it is obvious that "digital computer" is a kind of "computer" and "IPL" is a kind of "programming language." The relationship between the two hierarchies is an associative one. In addition, there are other associative words such as "programming" (the action) and "programmer" (the agent). In standard thesauri, associative relationships of all kinds are labelled *Related Terms* (RT), but many are so plainly cross-categorical that their purpose in the thesauri—to suggest other places to look—tends to follow Peter Roget. In a thesaurus for information retrieval, words are clustered by alphabetization so that "look-alikes" tend to appear together. Terms *related* to homographs may be collected under a single headword. A "related term" cluster has the effect of splintering the headword into its various meanings.

The problem with dealing with words as words, without consideration of their relationships, except in a very superficial manner, has produced thesauri that scramble relations, in spite of using differentiating devices such as "broader term," "narrower term," and "related term." There are at least nine different kinds of relationships, and probably more:

1) Synonymous terms, handled with "see" references to the synonyms of choice—equivalence relationship.

2) Terms related by hierarchy—generic, "to be" relationship.

3) Terms related by part or property—possessive, "to have" relationship.

4) Terms related by association—interactive, "to do" relationship.

5) Terms related by association—homographic (100% identical spelling) relationship (bear, classify, bore, ice, press).

6) Terms related by association—linguistic root or stem and/or grammatical relationship (program, programming, programmer).

7) Terms related by association—cross-categorical relationships, generally across hierarchies.

8) Terms related by association—words related *to each other* in a hierarchy in forms analogous to societal relationships (siblings, cousins, etc.).

9) Terms related by association—suggestion-of-where-else-to-look type of relationship (Roget-type).

The opportunity of reading multiple meanings into words may be diminished by use of bound terms: terms always used in a predetermined order. Or standardized definitions may be used, though this rarely is more involved than agreeing to use a given dictionary. However, things like metaphor, deliberate use of imagery, allusion, and other literary devices, as well as neologisms or even old words with new meanings, all creep into living language. If every term had one meaning and one meaning only, there would be no need for a syndetic system.

The syndetic structure is concealed in subject headings and semi-concealed in thesauri. In either system, one can work out the direction of relationships with arrows, as above. Theoretically, in correct subject heading practice, the direction is from general to specific, going from level to level downwards as the subject may require. However, "general" and "specific" can be in different categories. (This even happens in thesauri among the broader and narrower terms.) Little attention has been paid to the *type* of relationship involved, probably because to do this systematically, even with a small collection, takes a disproportionate amount of effort for the results achieved. When attention is not paid to the separation of categories or of levels in individual categories, the result can be, to put it politely, muddled. The types of relationships in a sequence have not been analyzed systematically. Nor is there an objective means of term selection and definition other than literary warrant. In some cases, as mentioned above, the related terms may redefine a headword such as a homograph.

The physical layout of subject headings is not the same as that used in a thesaurus. Relationships, other than the ones needed for synonyms, are scarcely considered, although, as with standard thesauri, blatant homographs are defined:

Mercury (metal)

Mercury (planet)

The alphabetical listing of both thesaurus terms and subject headings works against easy recognition of the relationship of subordinate word to headword. In standard subject heading practice, there are conventional methods, more or less adhered to, which indicate the direction of "see also" cross-references. They are described in relation to the heading itself. A reference from a "higher" or equivalent term is a "see also" *to* or a "see" *to* the term but is traced as a "see" *from* or a "see also" *from* the upper term. That is, a reference leading *to* a term from another term is traced in relationship to the central term. By the same token, a reference *away* from the term is called a "see" (s.) or a "see also" (s.a.) in the tracing (*see* Figure 18). The tracing is always made from the point of view of the central term — in anthropomorphic terms, "to me" and "away from me." The actual pattern in the finished index looks like a series of "see" and "see also" references; only the tracing (with its codes x, xx, s., s.a.) shows the structure in the subject headings.

Figure 18
Outline of Syndetic Structure

Relationships are centered on the TERM, being towards it or away from it, but a record (tracing) of what has been done is kept with the term itself.

Higher in hierarchy	Central term	Lower in hierarchy	
See also toward---------	TERM-----------------	See also away	(function)
xx-----------------	TERM-------------------	s.a.	(code)
See also from-----------	TERM-----------------	See also to	(tracing)
Broader term-----------	TERM-----------------	Narrower term	(theory)

This normal method of indicating references in subject headings is in marked contrast to the method to be described in the following pages. The PRECIS thesaural method will now be covered in detail. Although mentioned throughout this book and a brief indication of its basic semantic foundations given, the full system has to be understood to see its significance in the creation of the index.

TREATMENT OF DEFINITIONS IN THE PRECIS THESAURUS

In the PRECIS reference structure, attempt has been made to correct some of the abuses of standard thesaural method. As each new word appears as a string Term to be used in the *lead* position, it is looked up in dictionaries and other aids.

If need be, scope notes are added. The general source used in PRECIS is *Webster's Third International Dictionary.* The indexer making the reference could, if desired, record the number of the specific definition used. For example,

chaos 1) (Obs.) A chasm or abyss;
2) The confused state of primordial matter before the creation of orderly forms;
3) Any confused collection or state of things, complete disorder.

If the item being indexed is defined by the second definition, the record will say:

chaos def. 2

000 000 0

The number is the Reference Indicator Number (RIN) for that particular word. Every word used in the *lead* has its unique identification number. If "chaos" turns up as definition 3, a new record will be made, and a different identification number assigned to this second definition of "chaos." The RINs run from zero to 999 999x, so that it is possible at any time to tell how many different words have been used as headwords.

The notion of defining each word systematically was suggested by Calvin Mooers.[7] He called such defined terms "descriptors." Unfortunately, *descriptors* soon became a synonym for any kind of index word, without the very specific definition attached, as required by Mooers. While the PRECIS definitions are not exactly created in Mooers' style, they are more nearly like it than is the case in other systems made up of words.

At this point, an explanation of the rationale for the method of reference-making used in PRECIS must be made. This can be a source of confusion if not understood clearly.

THE PRECIS METHOD OF BUILDING A SYNDETIC STRUCTURE IN THE FORM OF A THESAURUS

The syndetic structure in PRECIS is built from the bottom up. This is the *inductive* method. The *results* look exactly like a system made from the top down by logical division, which is the *deductive* method for making such a structure. The references say "see also," which is the same as in a deductive system. However, the tracing on the records, to be described in the next section, is an inductive tracing. The coding tag used, '$o', is an upward-pointing one.

Since the reference structure in PRECIS is made by inductive means, the *tracing* of references goes from the lower term to the higher term, making a chain of upward-reading references. The *actual index* turns the direction around so that the "see also" references read from top to bottom. PRECIS makes allowance for sideways references in or out of a category, called "crossing" references. There are no exact equivalents in subject headings, although reciprocal cross-references are similar in physical arrangement:

Narcotics *See also* **Analgesics**

Analgesics *See also* **Narcotics**

In considering chains of references in the PRECIS system, the reader should remember "upward for input — downward for output." Tracings are upward or sideways, while references in the index proper go downward or sideways.

It is unfortunate that the words, "see also," are used for so many different types of relationships. Probably this affects the user only indirectly. In a way, the collection of "see also" references serves a double purpose. It guides the user from term to term in a hierarchy or associative word network and it serves as a Roget-type of thesaurus in suggesting other words to use in searching.

RELATIONAL CODES

Five kinds of relationships are recognized in PRECIS. These and their relational codes are:

$m   Equivalence *(See)* Non-preferred word ——▶ Preferred word

$o   Hierarchy *(See also)* Generic or whole-part covering *degree* of

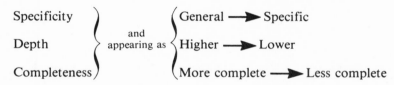

For association, there are three kinds, all represented as *"see also."* The first is:

$n Association *(See also)* One-way cross-categorical (Non-reciprocal)

These are commonly found in references such as

Snakes
   See also
     Herpetology

In the bypassing procedure mentioned earlier, these '$n' codes are never eliminated. Only hierarchical ones, '$o', are subject to elimination when empty classes occur.

The second associative code is:

$x Association *(See also)* Collateral association: sibling or collateral words; common immediate ancestor (same category); common category.

And the third is:

$y Association (*See also*) Cross-categorical association: interactive across categories (different categories)

Category 1 ⇄ Category 2   Botany ⇄ Gardening

Though '$x' and '$y' go both ways — they are reciprocal cross-references — in making actual references only one appears if only one of the words was used as a headword in the index. If both words appear as *leads* in the index, references are made going both ways. That is, these references are two-way by definition, but if only one is actually used as a *lead*, the reciprocal reference is not made.

Distinguishing between *cross-categorical* relationships represented by '$n' (one-way) and '$y' (two-way) can be a problem. In general, if one of the terms can be explained without the other, use '$n', but if both are needed, use '$y'. For example, the word "ships" implies "voyages" and also "sea." It is impossible to discuss "voyages" without "ships," whereas it is quite possible to discuss the "sea" without mentioning "ships." Therefore, one would use

ships $y voyages
voyages $y ships
ships $n sea

In summary, *"see also"* can cover the following relationships in a PRECIS index:

'$n'   cross-categorical association between terms in two different categories involving hierarchical chains — one-way.

'$y'   cross-categorical association between terms in different categories
        — one-way if only one of the terms is a *lead*
        — two-way if both teams appear as *leads*

'$o'   hierarchical relationships between words in a chain

'$x'   collateral relationship between sibling terms in an array (same category)

The state of knowledge at the present is such that no clear statement has been accepted generally for use of associative relationships or even to define them clearly; certainly, there are many kinds.[8] For PRECIS, two above, "collateral" for sibling within a category and "cross-categorical" for words in separate categories, are singled out and applied. They have been recognized as reciprocal arrangements, even when only one reference has been made.

BUILDING THE NETWORK

To see how the references are put together in PRECIS, a specific example will be used. The reference-building process starts from the bottom and is created upward. The finished network references are read from top to bottom, but they were constructed originally in the opposite way. This is not as complicated as it sounds.

Let us begin with the noble "mouse." The first thing needed is an equivalence reference:

Mouse *See* **Mice**

This is done because countable things (with a few exceptions) are, according to the standards for thesaurus structure, in the plural. If needed, the Latin term from accepted taxonomy should also be added. In large systems, the reference file would be separated from the string compiling operation, and created by different personnel. The small system will necessitate one person doing both. Either way, familiarity with both procedures is recommended.

The next step upwards is to recognize the collective category to which mice belong: "rodents." A card is made for each word and an identification number is assigned:

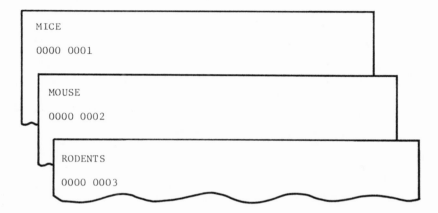

The links between these words are then made and transcribed on the card with the word to which they apply:

```
MICE            $m  MOUSE        $o   RODENTS

0000  0001         0000  0002        0000  0003
```

The next move is to build upwards from "rodents" with words related to it (the intervening one-term-on-a-card step will be omitted). The second reference card will be:

```
RODENTS         $o   MAMMALS

0000  0003            0000  0004
```

Then a third level is recognized and made, and so on until it is impossible to go any higher:

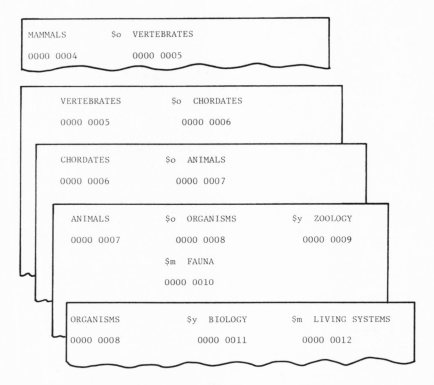

"Organisms" is the end of the line upward from "mice." On each card, the word tagged '$o' leads upward to the next higher link. The '$y' represents a sideways relationship to a word in another, parallel vertical line. "Animals" has a cross-categorical connection with "zoology" and, similarly, "organisms" with "zoology." The card for "zoology" supplies the linkage to "biology" and the one for "biology" to "science":

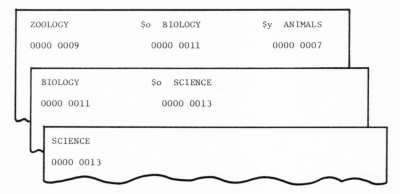

There is no upward connection from "science."

To avoid confusion, in the RIN file when there is only one Term on a card, words like "science" (which would be the chosen Term) are printed in black, while words like "mouse," "fauna," and "living systems" (which are rejected synonyms) are printed in red, meaning "do not use!"

Although the "see also" references all look alike in the index, they are of two different types:

Science
　　See also　　　　represents a generic connection
　　　Biology

Biology
　　See also　　　　represents a cross-categorical connection
　　　Organisms

The cross-categorical connection between "zoology" and "animals" is a reciprocal (two-way) one. It is the only one given below which does not represent a generic cross-reference.

Organisms	**Animals**	**Chordates**
See also	*See also*	*See also*
Animals	**Chordates**	**Vertebrates**

Biology	**Zoology**	
See also	*See also*	
Zoology	**Animals**	

Vertebrates	**Mammals**	**Rodents**
See also	*See also*	*See also*
Mammals	**Rodents**	**Mice**

There are three synonym-type cross-references:

Living systems *See* **Organisms**

Fauna *See* **Animals**

Mouse *See* **Mice**

Although the computer has this chain of steps in its storage, actually to print each step, whether it is full or empty, is very annoying to the user. Therefore, in individual indexes, only the Terms that apply to needed entries are employed, plus a minimum of intervening words required for logic. This minimal skeleton for bypassing prevents the generation of entries like **"Science See also Mice."**

In working out relationship strings manually, a diagram is advisable, because it is much easier to visualize than a series of '$o's and such. The bottom line is the base index word—the one that appeared on the document, in this case (mouse =) mice. The diagram appears as Figure 19 (page 266).

Figure 19
The Finished Network of Thesaurus Cross-Reference Structure
(which began with the word "mouse")

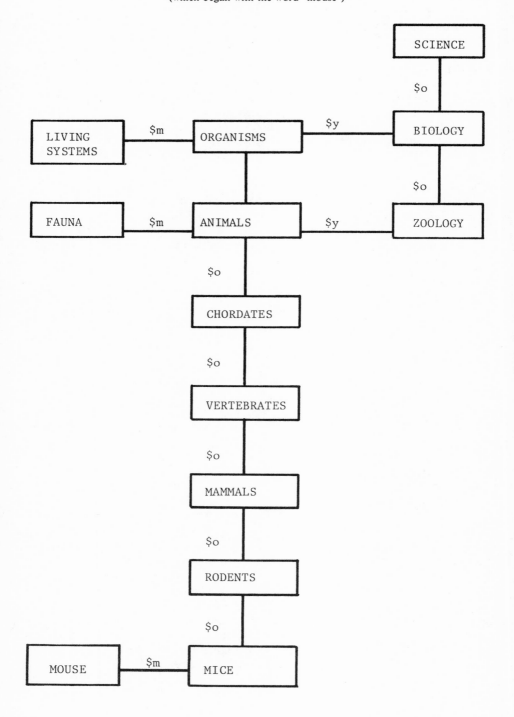

This type of build-up is easiest to show with biological entities. The same type of pattern is followed for all other words, but the networks developed can be quite extensive because of the associations.

In string-writing, the first general rule is: *Avoid writing strings for Terms where there are two classes and one is a subclass of the other.* In such cases, a reference is used for the class (if common) and a string Term for the subclass. This rule does not apply to cases where a quasi-generic group (q) or study region/study example (5) is involved. Nor does it apply in situations where a general class word, such as "constituents," "elements," "collections," "curriculum subjects," and so on, is added for a part or property or similar thing to be connected to a whole.

The second rule for string-writing is:

When two or more words relate to a word of greater generality

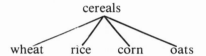

make a reference entry for the thesaurus rather than a string Term for the general word.

Both of these rules have to be used with a touch of common sense. In many, but not all, situations discussed in this book the need of such a reference has been indicated. A file can have too many references, just as an unsubdivided classification number can become overburdened.

Some common references include things that are not strictly hierarchical. Thus one may have:

Italian paintings
  See also
    **Books containing graphic reproductions of
    Italian paintings #**

Libraries
  See also
    Documents on management of libraries

These *following* references should be used sparingly. They are associative and logical but not very easy to fit into a classified system. Another type of reference covers the non-existent generic form:

Ships
  See also
    Model ships

Words like this, and "artificial flowers," "petrified wood," and so on, are syncategorematic (or pseudo-categories). Nevertheless, they are needed in indexes and have to be associated with the nearest real category. Similarly, blanket records can get out of hand. This type of reference may make life easier for the indexer, but how is the user to know which words have been chosen? Of course, the names of states, provinces, the local counties and so on would be known to the local clientele. A situation where "everybody knows" certain terminology would support a blanket reference.

THESAURUS MAKING

In making the thesaurus, every *lead* Term in every string is a candidate for possible references. The indexer uses the Term as entry point and looks both up and down a potential hierarchy to see where it belongs. After an index has been going for some time, obviously new Terms or alterations of old Terms do not occur as frequently as when the thesaurus was first being compiled.

A thesaurus can be made from the top down, deductively, using logical division. However, for the PRECIS type, an inductive approach is preferable so that Terms can be added and relational networks constructed. The initial presence of a Term means that it actually has been found or is required for the material being indexed. Literary warrant is a constraint on the system. It guarantees that there will be few empty classes or unused index words. It also guarantees a complex network or series of complex networks as the structure becomes more complete. New Terms will not be added until a work has been processed through the system.

A good many concepts can belong to more than one class at a time. This causes as many problems in indexing as it does in classification. One of the unique features of PRECIS is that it attempts to define the relationships that can be found with the polyhierarchies created by placing concepts in all the places to which they apply.

The reference structure for PRECIS is open-ended in that any reference is identified by a location in storage. It is the *address* of that location that forms the identification number. The content of the address can be altered, as when a Term is replaced by a more modern one, without changing its address. This means that the content of the addresses can be updated as more precise vocabulary comes along, while the relationships remain intact. All that is added is a cross-reference from the old Term. This is a feature that takes advantage of the unique properties of the computer. For example, if the word "chairman" is replaced by "chairperson," in a computer-held reference network one simply changes the word "chairmen" to "chairpersons," adds a *see* reference from "chairmen" and all the interrelationships built into "chairmen" continue with "chairpersons." Of course, in changes of other words, the interrelationships may have to be cut, augmented, or redefined in the new context.

What has been described to this point comprises the bare bones of the reference system. There are a number of message input codes for initial input as well as codes for updates, corrections, deletions, and so on. There are also typography codes for output. When improved computer access via the MERLIN system has been completed it will be possible to call up the computer-held network. Also, the thesaurus can be either printed or used via console.

The system is well-adapted for use in making a thesaurus according to accepted standards. The upward-leading relationships can easily be converted to broader (BT) and narrower (NT) terms, which would preserve the hierarchical lines. The associative factors, '$n', '$x', and '$y', are all related terms (RT), but the differentiation for various types of relationships made in PRECIS should be preserved because it is very helpful. This probably would necessitate using (RN), (RX), and (RY), a small but important additional step. The intellectual advances achieved to this point deserve to be preserved.

SUMMARY

A brief overview has been made of the reference back-up in PRECIS. This is an integral part of the whole indexing system. In fact, without it, it would be much harder to make the strings and entries, since all the relational factors would have to be built into the syntactic part. Several of the types of relationship present in any index have been differentiated and defined for use. The system can be used manually or with a computer. Either way, PRECIS is a system designed for the future.

PRECIS MANUAL REFERENCES

Semantic aspects in general: Sections 29.1-29.20, pp. 268-83. (Some of these have appeared earlier.)

Data files: Sections 30.1-30.11, pp. 284-90.

Construction and coding for references: Sections 31.1-31.24, pp. 291-309.

Parts of the sections on changes and updates, as well as other codes: Sections 32.13-32.17, pp. 320-24; 33.1-33.22, pp. 330-45. The latter set should be read primarily for information rather than for coding.

Auxiliary uses for the file appear briefly in Section 34, pp. 351-55.

The various codes are brought together in Appendix 9, pp. 541-42.

REFERENCES

[1]A useful book in decision-making about such words is *The Random House Vest Pocket Dictionary of Synonyms and Antonyms,* edited by Lawrence Urdang (New York: Random House, 1960).

[2]Most of the examples in this chapter were taken from the *British National Bibliography* for 1975.

[3]Derek Austin, *PRECIS: A Manual of Concept Analysis and Subject Indexing* (London: Council of the British National Bibliography, 1974): 352.

[4]Charles Ammi Cutter, *Rules for a Dictionary Catalog* (Washington: GPO, 1876): 15, 48-49; 3rd ed. (1891) 57-58; 4th ed. (1904) 79-80.

[5]Julia Pettee, *Subject Headings: The History and Theory of the Alphabetical Subject Approach to Books* (New York: H. W. Wilson, 1946): 25, 57-60, 73-80; George Scheerer, "The Subject Catalog Examined," *Library Quarterly* 27 (1957): 187-98; Phyllis A. Richmond, "Cats: An Example of Concealed Classification in Subject Headings," *Library Resources & Technical Services* 3 (1959): 102-112.

[6]*Thesaurus of Engineering and Scientific Terms* (New York: Engineers Joint Council, 1967): 90, 115, 225, 308, 310.

[7]Calvin N. Mooers, "Analysis of the Hexagon of Notification," *Journal of Documentation* 30 (June 1974): 181-82.

[8]J. E. L. Farradane, "A Scientific Theory of Classification and Indexing," *Journal of Documentation* 6 (1950): 83-90; and his "Further Considerations," *Journal of Documentation* 8 (1952): 73-92. His relational diagram has been reproduced many times, perhaps most recently in A. C. Foskett, *The Subject Approach to Information*, 3rd ed. (Hamden, CT: Linnet Books, 1977): 75, 77.

14
ANALYSIS FOR STRING WRITING

Now that the basics of PRECIS are covered, it is possible to develop an outline of decisions that have to be made during the process of string writing. While this would have been helpful in chapter 3, at that point the potential indexer did not know what *options* were available. And until the fundamental options had been explained, it would have been impossible to make informed and sensible decisions. There still are fine points and details of PRECIS beyond what has been covered in this book. Only the more fundamental decisions will be covered here.

When the first step in indexing has been accomplished—a preliminary title-like phrase has been composed, rewritten in the passive voice, and reduced to telegraphic form—the indexer can begin thinking about string writing. The preliminary title-like phrase may suggest a format for the string, but before coding, a number of questions need to be asked and answered.

It has already been indicated that the first thing to do is to *look for the action*. The first decisions to be made, therefore, concern the action. What is it? What object is it performed upon? Who or what (if anything) performs it? When these basic questions have been answered, a series of preliminary decisions follow.

PRELIMINARY DECISIONS: ELEMENTS

At this stage, a listing should be made to consider whether the major functional elements are present in the title-like phrase. The following checklist may be helpful.

1) Environment
   a. Is the environment obviously a geographical or political area? — Operator (0).
   b. Does it have sub-parts? — Operator (p).
   c. Is it, itself, actually a sub-part? — reassign operators.
   d. Is it an example of a larger area? — Operator (q).
   e. Are parentheses and/or italics needed? — add parentheses and/or typographical code, AND remember the Term code d.

2) Entity (key system)
   a. Is the entity a unit or a whole? — Operator (1).
   b. Does the entity have parts or properties? — Operator (p).
   c. Is it an entity that is a focus and can be differenced? — apply differencing operators.
   d. Does the entity have a definite and limited time span? — consider $d.
   e. Does the entity call for a Term code other than a? — check for possible use of b, c, or d.

f. Could the entity have other, equivalent names? — if so, use a "see" reference.

g. What relationship does the entity have to other entities (especially ones with possible hierarchical relations) — consider generic and/or associative relationship patterns.

h. Will the entity require other Terms to explain its relationship to the action? — consider the possibility of a vital and unstated link between the entity and the action or the need for a role definer.

i. Is the entity a place? If so, is something portable involved? — consider place as key system.

j. Is the entity a member of a quasi-generic class? — Use (q).

3) Action

a. What kind of a word expresses the action? noun? gerund? word ending in "-ion"? select the most fitting.

b. Is the action *word* the best available for expressing that particular action? — think again.

c. If a word ending in "-ion" represents the action, does it express the action itself or the result of action? — a result of action may necessitate further consideration of the nature of the action.

d. Is there a hidden action relating indirectly to the stated action? — look for an indirect action, especially if the agent does not seem to be the direct instigator of the action.

e. Is there an obvious consequence of the action? Is it the object? Another action? — look again very carefully.

f. Is there a synonymous term for the action word from which it must be differentiated? — make a "see" reference.

g. Is the action named in a word that is a homograph? — define it, probably with a (q) operator.

h. Is the action an entity that may be differenced? — if so, take appropriate steps.

i. Does the action have its own properties or parts? — use Operator (p).

j. Is the action specifically as well as generally identified? — use (q) for the specific sub-part.

k. If the action word may be both transitive and intransitive (words like "sing"), which of the possibilities is actually present? — make the proper construction so that the key system is identified if the action is transitive.

l. Does the *action* occur as a sequence of actions or all at once? — a sequence may take different treatment in the string.

m. Is the action a quasi-generic class member? — Use Operator (q).

4) Agent

a. Is the agent clearly performing the action? — if not, look for an indirect agent.

b.   If the agent is not directly related to the stated action, is another agent present that is so related? — change agents.

c.   If the agent is not the agent of the action, is there an unstated action to which it is directly related? — consider a blank field insert.

d.   Does the agent have parts or properties? — use Operator (p).

e.   Is the agent described so that differencing operators may be used? — apply them.

f.   Is the agent a general designation for a temporary (as opposed to a generic) class? — identify with Operator (q).

g.   Is the agent an aggregate or a vague term like "man" or "society"? — consider not using it as a *lead*.

h.   Is the agent's apparent relationship to the action and the entity (if there is one) a logical one? — think this through again.

5) Viewpoint as form
   a.   Is the work being indexed written (painted, compiled, composed) from a distinct point-of-view or as a viewpoint (method) of a particular school of thought? — consider identifying it.

   b.   Does the point of view influence the content of the work to such an extent that it makes it distinctive? — use Operator (4).

   c.   Is the viewpoint a reaction to another viewpoint and therefore more than form? — consider viewpoint as subject.

6) Special illustrative case
   a.   Is the subject presented through an example? A special grouping? A limited study, case, or survey which represents the whole? — consider identifying the topic rather than the whole.

   b.   Is the example (etc.) so obvious that it constitutes the theme of the work? Use Operator (5).

7) Target and/or Form
   a.   Is the content of the work aimed at the specific target group of potential users? — identify the target and use Operator (6).

   b.   Is the content written in a readily identifiable form such as a bibliography, guidebook, etc.? — identify it as such and use Operator (6).

   c.   Would the form make a difference to the potential user in deciding whether an item is suitable for use or not? — in cases where the form or format is out of the ordinary the potential user probably would appreciate having this option; use Operator (6).

   d.   Is more than one form or target present? — use both.

   e.   If both a form and a target are present, which order is best? — make the determination on logical grounds.

The above questions identify and define the Main Line operators. They are not the only queries that may be asked, but they are enough to point up some of the possible things to consider in determining what additions or impediments accompany these operators. Furthermore, the relationships between operators should be more apparent after this stage of analysis. With these clarifications out of the way, further preliminary decisions may be made.

PRELIMINARY DECISIONS: LOGIC

A fundamental factor in decision-making is the determination of what kind of order is involved in the exposition of the topic of the material being indexed. Several questions help with this.

1) Syntactics
   a. In making the string from the telegraphic style listing, are the tentative Terms in their syntactical order in the passive voice?
   b. Is there a one-to-one relationship between the various Terms in the string?
   c. Are connectives needed to clarify the syntax?

The answers to these questions may involve rearranging, adding, or completely rewriting the string. This logical set of questions may have to be asked more than once in the process of building the final string. The logic in PRECIS is extremely important.

2) Semantics
   a. After the tentative string has been rearranged according to its syntactic order, are there places where *meaning* will have to be considered? In this connection, the following should be kept in mind. Are there:
      i.   differences?
      ii. equivalence relationships?
      iii. generic relationships?
      iv. hierarchical relationships?
      v.   quasi-generic relationships?
      vi. cross-references?
   b. Are disambiguating connectives needed to clarify any of the relationships?

(If some of the questions in the several parts of the decision making analysis seem repetitive, it is because the viewpoint changes with each section, and what was passed over originally may appear valid in a different setting or context.)

3) General relationships
   a. Is a "to be" situation present?
      Four kinds are identifiable:
      i.   a priori, generic, context-independent (names of animals, plants, minerals, etc.)
      ii. a posteriori, quasi-generic, such as:
           — a situation occurring with special contexts and not holding under all circumstances

         — a member of a class in THIS SPECIFIC CASE or condition
         — context-dependent relationship (sine qua non — literally "without which nothing")
         — cases where a class and its member must both be in the same string

    iii.   an aggregate situation with several members
    iv.   a difference

b.   Is a "to have" situation present? — five kinds are possible:

    i.   possession of parts or properties (actual or attributed) in the classic forms: quality, quantity, adornment, content, and acquisition. (In PRECIS, the sixth classic form, "something that is part of us" — hand, foot, etc. — is treated as a kind of hierarchy; *see* chapter 6).
    ii.   dependent situations that call for a possessor
    iii.   terms recognized as interposed
    iv.   whole-part relationships *except* those that are
         — hierarchical whole-part
         — geographical regions
         — systems and organs of the body
         — areas of discourse (disciplines)
    v.   aggregates and combinations of parts, properties, and entities considered as separate interposed Terms

c.   Is a "to do" situation present?
This is somewhat complex. In general it applies to actions that are or tend to be:

    i.   performed on, by, with, or to something
    ii.   a process going on within something (in the physiological sense)
    iii.   a study (representing things which themselves are part of something)
    iv.   transitive or intransitive, with or without dependent elements or connectives
    v.   expressed in words that are in
         — noun form (management, performance, flow, change)
         — gerund form when a suitable action noun does not exist (shipping, teaching, programming, fishing)
         — an ambiguous form representing both the process and the product of the process (science, education, explanation, generalization)
    vi.   used with agentive or role definer functions
    vii.   initiated by a system (one- and two-way actions)
    viii. occurring sequentially in time.

d.   Are further relationships present, such as:

    i.   interposed operators?
         — dependent elements (part, property, quasi-generic group membership, aggregate)
         — concept interlinks (role definers, author-attributed associations)

          —coordinate concepts [for standard (g) and alternate (f) types]

  ii.   connectives (between string Terms)?
  iii.   theme interlinks (two themes in one string)?
  iv.   differences relating to
       —*lead* or non-*lead*?
       —spaced out or closed up?
       —level (direct, indirect, very indirect, etc.)
       —*lead* and non-*lead* parenthetical differences?
       —date as difference?
       —following differences?
  v.   places where substitutions are needed?

  e. Are there other kinds of things to be considered:
    i.   situations in which a time dependency is involved?
    ii.   presentations that only apply in a special context?
    iii.   limitations or constraints that may prevent use of a solution that seems applicable at first glance?
    iv.   nature of the work: critical? creative? mainly pedagogical? in an unusual medium?
    v.   intellectual level of the work and its intended audience?

4) Formats
  a. Are there features that suggest a format other than the standard one may be required?
  b. Will this format call for some additional care in making the string? (e.g., if operators (3), (t), (s), or (1)(2)(1) are present).

By the time all of these questions are answered and the various other points noted, plus anything else that the indexer may think of, the analysis of the work being indexed should be almost complete. The next stage is that of making the final decisions.

FINAL DECISIONS CONCERNING BASIC STRING ORDER

First of all, the string elements that are the Main Line Operators should be set down, as they are applicable, with enough space between them to add any interposed operators that may be needed. The analysis should have revealed whether a "to be," "to have," or "to do" situation was present.

1) If a "to be" situation is present, consider
  a. the *thesaurus* solution when
    i.   an obvious hierarchy is involved and it is possible to make a reference from a higher, more general word to the string Term
    ii.   a multiple word Term is present
    iii.   a false generic Term is present (rubber duck)
  b. the *sequencing* solution when a member of a quasi-generic group or aggregate is involved
  c. the *differencing* solution when a "kind of ..." descriptive word is basically in adjectival form, *provided*
    i.   a part is not differenced by its whole

      ii.   levels of relationship can be determined and identified with delimiter tags ($01, etc.)

      iii.   one or more differences is wanted as a *lead* in addition to the focus

      iv.   a difference is wanted in preference to the focus

      v.   an undifferenced multiple word Term is inadequate

      vi.   the inner part of a closed-up Term is wanted as *lead*

2) If a "to have" situation occurs, consider
   a. the use of sequencing with as many part/property operators as the hierarchy within the possessive system requires
   b. whether a quasi-generic relationship or an aggregate would be preferable

3) If a "to do" situation exists, consider which type may be present:
   a. an action alone in noun or gerund form
   b. an action involving a simple environment or an entity with or without interposed or differenced Terms
   c. the above plus an agent
   d. some or all of the above plus complex relationships such as indirect agent, indirect action, role definer, author-attributed association, etc.

After these various kinds of action situations have been settled, the next step involves more answers to questions more specifically stated.

FINAL DECISIONS CONCERNING VARIATION IN STRING ORDER

The normal shunting process may be interrupted in several ways:

1) Are some of the Terms wanted as *leads* only under certain circumstances? Consider changing the order by using:
   a. LO (*lead* only)
   b. NU (not up)
   c. ND (not down)

2) Are some Terms wanted as *leads*, but consolidation or even elimination of them would be preferable when not in the *lead*? If so, consider using
   a. upward-reading substitutions (sub n↑)( )
   b. downward-reading substitutions (sub n↓)( )
      Remember the manipulation code for each
          upward = 0n2
          downward = 0n1
   c. blank substitutions

Before proceeding to discussion of more complex questions to be decided, a brief summary of the most significant rules in PRECIS will be made.

RECAPITULATION OF THE MAJOR RULES IN PRECIS[1]

1) The object of action comes before action.

2) The name of an action precedes its agent.

3) The numbered Main Line operators determine the overall structure of every string.
   a. Every string must begin with (0), (1), or (2).
   b. Every string must contain a Term prefixed by (1) or (2).
   c. Interposed operators may be introduced into a string at any point, but they may not start one.
   d. The word attached to the connective ($w) may not begin the *qualifier.*
   e. Connective ($w) does not appear in entries until the string Term *following* the one to which it is attached comes into the *lead.* ($v) appears in entries when the Term *to which it is attached* or any *earlier* Term is in the *lead.*

4) An asterisk (*) is used to indicate when a Term is wanted as a *lead*; its use may be limited by conventions LO, NU, and ND.

5) Upward- and downward-reading substitutions may be made to produce clearer understanding or better syntax or to cut down on the number of individual operations needed when a string is read.

6) Operators (0), (1), and (2) take the Standard Format. Operators (3), (s), and a *lead* Term immediately below an (s) or a (t) invoke the Predicate Transformation when tagged as *leads*. Operator (3) *must* be preceded by an action Term (2), however. Operators (4), (5), and (6) call for the Inverted Format, when tagged as *leads*.

7) Interposed operators (2), role definer, and (t), author-attributed association have special rules for their use, their place in the string and the entries resulting from them. The other interposed operators (p) part or property, (q) member of a quasi-generic group, (r) aggregate, (f) coordinate concept in non-standard combinations, and (g) coordinate concept for standard combinations, are less complex.

8) The Blank Field Insert is used to defeat the Predicate Transformation in cases where operator (3) agent, is not *directly* the instigator of the action given in the string.

9) Theme interlinks are used in cases where a subject consists of two or more distinct themes.

10) Differencing is used to make access points for descriptive words under certain conditions.

11) For general structural definition, a thesaurus of references contains each Term used in the index. All concepts except "orphans" generate relationships of the generic or associative type. Any Term, including "orphans," may require equivalence relationships.

FINAL DECISIONS CONCERNING
COMPLEX CONCEPTUAL RELATIONSHIPS

Since there is no particular order in which complexities turn up, these decisions are made ad hoc. For convenience, they are listed alphabetically, according to the name of the concept involved. They tend to be more complicated than the type of relationships that can be identified by asking "Where?," "When?," "What?," "What action?," "By what?," or "By whom?," and "How?"

1) **Action.** Two-way Action, Reciprocal Action (1)(2)(1)
    Is there a system-initiated interaction whereby an action by A on B results in a simultaneous and reciprocal action by B on A?

    Is there any dependent element between either element (1) and the action (2) other than the concept (g)? If so, this voids the reciprocal action.

    Is there a substitution after the action (2)? This also voids the action. A two-way action must answer the first question above in the affirmative so that the second entity (1) may act like an agent (3) and thus invoke the Predicate Transformation.

2) **Agent.** Special Rules for *Aspects & Factors*
    Is the agent (3) accompanied by an unstated action resulting in a two-way action of some kind between the system named higher in the string and the concept accompanying the word "aspects" or "factors"? (The accompanying concept word for "aspects" may be "social," "psychological," "cultural," "meteorological," etc. The accompanying "factors" may be "safety," "economic," "environmental," etc.)

    In such cases the Blank Field Insert should be put in the string before the agentive Term (3) to prevent the Predicate Transformation from occurring.

    Aspect. *See* **Agent**

3) **Chinese Plate Syndrome.**
    Does a literary work (or equivalent) occur in the same index as works that are history and/or criticism of it?

    "Products of the imagination" (literary, artistic, musical) have the name of the writer, artist, or composer put into the string, after the name of the genre, representing a subset of the genre; the *form* of the work is added (6):

    (1)*   poetry in English

             c
    (p)*   Donne, John

    (6)   texts

    The *critical* study of an individual work is treated as follows:

    a.   Name the subject or topic (key system).

b.   Name its maker or author (as part of the key system).

c.   Make a substitution for these two elements to use when reading upward into the *qualifier*. This should include only the name of the maker, author, etc.

[e.g., (sub 2↑)(1)   Homer, $\overset{c}{\text{Winslow}}$ $f 1836-1910].

d.   Name the work; tag it as "b" (class-of-one, incapable of authorship).

e.   Indicate the form of the study (*critical studies*, etc.).

4)   **Concept Interlink**: Author-attributed Association (t).
Are concepts in the string related to each other by the action of an author who put them in juxtaposition?

If so, are they one-way or two-way action types?

one-way = explanation, exposition

two-way = comparison, relationships

If these conditions are met, note that operator (t)

a.   tends to have no value as a *lead*

b.   May be accompanied by connectives ($v), ($w) as needed

c.   is always in italics in entries

d.   may not be accompanied by a dependent element *except* when such an element is found on either side of the (t) and *both* dependent Terms relate to the next higher Term above the sequence containing the (t):

Term x

Part of Term x

(t)

Another part of Term x

Things being compared are usually put in alphabetical order.

5)   **Concept Interlink**: Role Definer.
Is the agent's role obvious with respect to the action and object? If not, consider the possibility that one of the following may be involved:

a.   the *unusual* role, in which the action described is not one with which the agent normally is associated.
  — Very often the *unusual* role was one of the reasons for writing the document.

b.   the *indirect* agent, in which the Term labelled as agent may not be directly responsible for the action but is a tool or instrument used by some other entity in performing the action

c.   the indirect action, in which the action is not performed on the object in any direct sense, but rather in the sense of

the $\left\{\begin{array}{l}\text{effect}\\\text{influence}\\\text{implications}\end{array}\right\}$ of (some action) on (something)

d.   "role definer" explains the function of the next *lower* Term in the string

6) **Connectives.**
   If the answer to any of the following questions is "yes," use connective symbols:
   a. Is ambiguity present in the string?
   b. Does readability deteriorate as entries are made from string elements?
   c. Is it desirable to shunt several Terms as a block?
   d. Is the operator (s) present?
   e. Could using ($v) and/or ($w) make it unnecessary to write a substitute phrase?

7) **Coordinate Concepts**: Operator (g).
   Are there several Terms present that share some kind of common relationship (e.g., properties, sub-categories) with a higher Term? Or are they gathered by a lower Term that acts as a *binding* Term? Are entries for the coordinate parts needed separately but not jointly when each separate Term is in the *lead*? If this is the case, the coordinate concepts may be treated as a block. Alphabetical sequence is used except in the presence of
   a. a time-dependent sequence

    e.g., (1)*   grain
          (2)*   planting
          (g)*   cultivating $v & ⎤
          (g)*   harvesting   ⎦   "g" block

   b. canonical order

          (1)*   breakfast
          (p)*   pancakes $v & ⎤
          (g)*   maple syrup   ⎦   "g" block

   c. one Term has a difference that does not apply to the others

          (1)*   office machines
          (p)*   typewriters   ⎤
          (g)*   fans $21 electric ⎦   "g" block

   (reverse order would imply "typewriters" were also electric)

8) **Coordinate Concepts**: Non-standard Treatment (f).
   Are coordinate Terms needed both as separate entries and jointly *in every entry*?

   If this is the case, use operator (f). Remember that with (f), differenced Terms do *not* have the whole Term repeated in the *display* when the focus of each is in the *lead*:

   Frogs
   Spotted frogs & brown toads

   not

   Frogs
   Spotted frogs. Spotted frogs & brown toads

In the relatively rare situation where a single difference applies to what would be two different foci, the *lead*-only (LO) method may be utilized. It is preferable to use the (f) operator if there is even the slightest chance that the combined Term might be misinterpreted (i.e., if "muffins" below were made of anything except corn):

(1)*   bread $21 corn (LO)
(g)*   muffins $21 corn (LO)
(r)*   corn bread & muffins

"*Lead* only" is literally *lead only*, with no repetition of the whole differenced Term in the *display*.

9) Differences.

Is only the focus of a compound Term wanted as *lead*?

If standard differencing is involved, code the parts unwanted as entries as either

$0 (spaced) or $1 (closed up)

and the second digit according to the level of relationship to the focus.

Is the focus not wanted as *lead*?

Either do not tag the string element with *, but mark the first digit of the difference for a *lead* [e.g., (1) roots $21 square] or, preferably, write the focus and "difference" as a multiple word Term [e.g., (1)*   square roots].

10) Differences: Special Case.

Do you have a place name used as an adjective?

If the focus is something portable (may appear in a different location), use a difference:

(1)*   cars $21 Japanese

otherwise use operator (0):

(0)*   Japan
(1)*   temples

11) Directional Properties: Attitudes, Accountability, Liability, etc.

When a situation involving an attitude, etc. occurs, is it

a.   a phenomenon, with neither holder nor object being named? Treat as a key system.

b.   a phenomenon belonging to a holder or group, but with no object named? Treat as a "to have" situation, with attitude as property of the holder.

c.   a phenomenon belonging to someone or a group with the object named? Treat the object as key system, with the holder as the agent who directs the attitude toward some thing or some group.

d. a case where phenomenon, object, and possessor are all present? Use the Predicate Transformation for both the (s) and the (3) Terms, and for any dependent Terms that may be in the "3" block.

e. a phenomenon with an *implied* possessor and an object? This "implied" possessor is used with operator (s) to resolve the ambiguity present when there is no obvious possessor. Since the operator cannot be used without connectives ($v) and ($w) *and* since it must have Terms above and below, the implied possessor is treated as an agent. This implied possessor is marked (NU) because it is not wanted as *lead* or in the *qualifier*. Failure to mark it (NU) would put it into the *qualifier* in an unnecessary one-to-one relationship to the *lead* when or if the (s) Term was tagged for the *lead* position. For example, take "attitudes to old people":

String:
  (1)* old people
  (s)* attitudes $v of $w to
  (3)   society(NU)

Entries:
  Old people
  Attitudes of society

  Attitudes
  To old people

(Normally, when (s) is in the *lead* the (3) Term goes into the *qualifier*, but here (NU) is used to prevent that.)

f. a phenomenon where there are two *systems*, one as a possessing system and the other as a system toward which the directional property is directed?

If the directional properties are

  accountability

  liability

  responsibility, etc.

and they occur in title-like phrases such as

  the accountability of steel industries for
    atmospheric pollution

use the following order:

  — object toward which the directional property is aimed

  — the directional property

  — its implied possessor

    (1)* atmosphere
    (2)* pollution $w of
    (s)   accountability $v of $w for
    (3)* steel industries

g. a situation with "policies" or "theories" as directional properties?

All theories associated with a specific person call for a string in the form:

$$
\begin{array}{l}
\qquad\qquad\text{c} \\
(1)^* \quad [\text{name}] \\
(p) \quad \text{theories}
\end{array}
$$

If the theories are in a given field, however, the directional property becomes apparent:

(1)* economics

(s) theories $v of $w on

$$
\begin{array}{l}
\qquad\qquad\text{c} \\
(3)^* \quad [\text{name}]
\end{array}
$$

Factors. *See* **Agent**

Following differences. *See* **Differences**

12) **Quasi-Generic Relationships:** Homographs.

Is the selected Term for a string element a homograph?

If so, it should be disambiguated by supplying the name of the class of which it is a member. The class itself should not be used as a *lead* if the Term is a true generic form.

Example: "cranes" as birds and as lifting equipment.

Use   (1)   birds
                             (q)* cranes $21 whooping

This will give the entry:

> **Cranes.** Birds
> Whooping cranes

And it should be included among the members of the class, "birds":

> **Birds**
> *See also*
> **Cranes**
> **Ducks**
> **Warblers**

13) **Relationships** (Thesaural).

Aside from the normal class-subclass relationships for which "see also" references are made, are there relationships where concepts stand in sibling relationship to each other, as in cases of members of an array, or where they are related, but as "cousins" or by another, less close degree of relationship?

These various kinds of relationships may call for one- or two-way relationships in the thesaurus. In making such a file, it is helpful to work out as many of the relationships of individual Terms as may be possible. Since the network of relationships is built up inductively, additions have to be tested for their logical fit with respect to the words already in the thesaurus. In the early stages of thesaurus-building, there will be many more additions than when the reference file has been used for some time and is fairly complete.

14) **Substitutions.**

Another disambiguation method involves supplying substitutions.

Do the entries from the string make less sense when

— being read up into the *qualifier*?
— being treated according to the Predicate Transformation?
— they involve comparisons or two-way interactions?
— they become redundant, too wordy, or unnecessary in later entries?
— two themes are necessary to express the content of the item being indexed?

In all of these cases it probably will be helpful to substitute other terminology or blanks for the elements that would normally occur in entries if left to be formed according to rule. Substitutions may take the following forms:

a. upward-reading into the *qualifier*.

Use

i. connective ($w) to disambiguate two or more adjacent lines of the string in standard format or to retain related concepts in the *display* in Predicate Transformation, limiting the content of the *qualifier*.

ii. upward-reading substitutes consisting of either a replacement word or phrase or a blank, as the situation dictates.

b. downward-reading into the *display*.

Use downward-reading substitutes in cases where there is a very complex situation rather than one with two distinct themes (see chapter 10):

i. a case with a dependent Term that is in colloquial form and involves a dual and reciprocal action.

ii. a case, embodying a role definer, where economy in a two-way, gated action may be obtained.

iii. a case where a role definer may be needed as a *lead* in a complex two-way theme.

iv. a case with a role definer requiring a retained environment.

v. a case with an extended string.

Two-way Interactions. *See* **Actions: Substitutions**

SUMMARY

The reader should bear in mind that the process of making a string is not automatic, although it may appear to be so on the surface. At each stage, the indexer must consider alternatives, based on subject analysis of each individual theme. This list of decisions should serve to remind the reader that there is a vital intellectual step between the analysis that produced the title-like phrase and the actual writing of the string. The procedures used in subject analysis include recognition of blocks, subroutines, and even adding sequential types of logic in the progression from the first to the last statement in the string. In PRECIS such blocks and sequences have already been built into the system, along with the order determined by the string. Because indexing, like writing, has always been a very subjective operation (except when attempted automatically by computer with little or no human intervention), anything that increases objectivity is helpful (other than completely abandoning any attempt to ascertain and retain *meaning*). PRECIS has made a significant beginning toward such a goal by its careful identification of some of the steps.

REFERENCES

[1]The reader may find it helpful to consult A. C. Foskett, *The Subject Approach to Information*, 3rd ed. (Hamden, CT: Linnet Books, 1977) chapters 5-9. Some of the basis for decision-making may have been taken for granted in this discussion, so that the reader may wish to refer to the background, which is well explained in Foskett.

15
CONCLUSION

In summing up the basics of PRECIS, first it is necessary to return to the purposes for which it was made. It was designed as a stand-alone index to be used with all kinds of cataloging and classification systems, as well as all kinds of subjects in almost any format. It also was designed to take advantage of the computer's ability to deal with dull and repetitive operations. That is, the indexer would provide the brain work and from that the computer would make the actual subject index. At the same time, each entry would have to be constructed so that it would be intelligible to the user without requiring instruction on how to use the index. These objectives have been achieved.

The indexing method was devised to enable the indexer to establish the subject of the item being indexed in some kind of verbal statement, allowing four such statements per item. The statements, in turn, provided the basis for a string. Each line of the string contained a Term made up of one or more words and various connective devices if needed. The Terms were each identified by a coded operator, reflecting the syntax of the parts of the string. The operators were arranged in the string according to a standardized order.

The order had to be in this standard form so that a full set of intelligible entries could be made without disturbing or distorting the original statement. A method of handling compound Terms was added. The various formats and procedures of PRECIS were developed in order to achieve some degree of consistency among indexers as well as to make a comprehensive index.

All of this was not aided by the vagaries of the English language. In normal language usage, for example, there is terminological scatter—the same idea expressed in different words—and terminological concentration—the same words expressing different ideas. There was also syntax scatter—the same message carried with different structures in different voices (active, passive)—and syntax concentration—use of noun-verbs (gerunds), nouns made from adjectives, and nouns derived from other parts of speech.

In general, for other than compound Terms, the rules of the string became the determining factors for entries to be made from that string. These tended to encourage consistency.

Since the PRECIS system was based on the notion of context dependency, the relationships between words, between Terms in a string, and between words in their ultimate combining order have been extremely important. Insofar as it has been possible, logic and reason underlie choices governing the grammar and syntax of indexing. The system has dispensed with all unnecessary words on one hand and supplied missing but vital connecting words on the other. Only such words as were necessary for production of an unambiguous index entry were retained.

Some of the rejected words, especially ones of great generality, were put into a reference file, to be developed ultimately into a thesaurus. This reference file was also designed to handle synonyms and their equivalent.

While semantic relationships could be handled by a reference file or thesaurus, syntactic relationships resolved themselves into predicative (to be), possessive (to have), and interactive (to do) types. (Sometimes a single theme can be expressed in all three ways in either active or passive voice.) In general, however, logic and the statement of relationships among concepts contained in the item being indexed determine the method for building and displaying relationships.

For PRECIS, therefore, five general rules were adopted:

1) Predicative relation: kind or category is stated before the name of an individual or member belonging to that category.

2) Possessive relation: the whole is expressed before the part or property.

3) Interactive relation: the object affected is stated before the action and the action before its agent.

4) The passive voice produced this order and thereby reduced syntactic complexity.

5) In general, if a choice is possible, the logical rather than the grammatical object is preferred.

By this time, the reader who has used this book and the *PRECIS Manual* should be aware of the differences in usage of the English language in the United Kingdom and on this continent. Part of the reason for writing this account was an awareness of the need to "translate" British terminology. As a result of teaching PRECIS for several years, the author developed some samples, examples, and simple explanations in familiar words for assisting North American students in learning this innovative system.

The terminological problems are social and cultural in origin. For example, "working classes" may be used in Britain but not in the United States. A number of words used in PRECIS, as exemplified by the indexes to the *British National Bibliography* have somewhat different connotations on this side of the Atlantic. For example, "explaining" has been substituted for "expounding" because in British usage the word has not acquired the derogatory meaning of "pontificating." Another word with an adverse connotation is "negroes" which here would be "blacks."

In somewhat different vein, British libraries have "stock" rather than "collections" and stores sell "goods" rather than "stock." "Vacation homes" are "holiday residences"; "cabins" are "chalets"; "mobile homes" are "caravans"; "field trips" for children are "educational visits." And so it goes.

A convention in the *British National Bibliography* is to place literary forms of all kinds under language and then by nationality of the writer:

English literature
  African writers
  American writers
  Australian writers
  Canadian writers
  Irish writers

Poetry in English
  American writers
  Burmese writers
  Canadian writers
  New Zealand writers
  Scottish writers
  Yemeni writers

The term "English writers" is not used, the assumption being that only writers outside of England need be identified. There are, however, allowances for groups of writers both in and out of England:

American negro writers
Athlone writers
Civil service writers
East Anglian writers
Richmond upon Thames writers
Thurrock writers
Women writers

Since the Standard Format permits an entry under each of these kinds of writers, there is no entry as such under "American literature," "Canadian literature," "Brazilian literature," or any other literary forms with the nationality coming first.

A convention is also used with art and music forms, where the form is given first and then the nationality of the artist or musician second:

Sculptures
  African metal sculptures
  English sculptures
  French bronze sculptures
  Italian sculptures

Music
  American music
  Austrian music
  Czechoslovakian music
  English music
  French music
  German music
  Hungarian music

Here the language is not involved and the headings are similar to subject headings. In most of the literary, fine art, and music forms, a date or span of dates is given to cover the period and often the name of an individual writer, artist, or composer is attached. An example of this was given in chapter 8, with discussion of problems, using as an example the paintings of Winslow Homer.

These conventions used in the *British National Bibliography* should not be rejected out of hand because they are not ordinary North American practice. There are advantages to listing by language, form, or medium first. Currently, there is considerable unhappiness among minority groups because their contributions are lumped with majority work by either language or country. Formerly Displaced Persons (now American and Canadian citizens) writing in the Ukrainian language, exiles writing in their native languages, Americans living and writing abroad while retaining their American citizenship and American audience, and others in similar categories are all special cases that do not fit the norms used in either classification or subject heading systems.

Another point of interest concerns the abundance of multiple-word index entries, so that although only one word serves as the specific entry point, its companion words are irrevocably joined to it and are not available as headwords themselves unless they are tagged as differences. For this reason, an authority file is needed with PRECIS—not to determine which words are legal for use, but to find out what configurations of words have been used. Like any other indexer, the PRECIS practitioner wants to bring like words together.

This collocation process requires the indexer to pay more attention to the filing order of words. The actual choice of operators and string order can be determined in part by the need for collocation of words. Some of the routines in PRECIS are made for achieving maximum collocation, and to avoid scattering entries all over the index. In looking at the entries in the subject index of the *British National Bibliography*, one is impressed by the frequency of use of "bound terms" in preference to use of differencing or dependency. The effect is to index by grouped words and either cross-reference by noun or omit the noun. This does not mean, of course, that the majority of index words are not single ones. It means that the indexer has not felt constrained to find a single word if possible.

Another feature of PRECIS is affected by the European practice of classifying the main sequence of works, using alphabetical lists or catalogs as supplementary forms of access. North Americans as a rule alphabetize everything: dictionary catalogs, divided catalogs, book catalogs, microfiche catalogs, unit record indexes, etc., etc., etc. This book has omitted those features of PRECIS that are necessitated by use of classification as the basic file order.

On the other hand, being used to an alphabetical approach, North Americans expect a file somewhere containing every word used as entry to every work so that it would be possible to tell how many items are indexed by each variety of configuration of Terms that make up a string. Or to tell how many times each individual *lead* has occurred.

These and similar considerations have led to emphasis upon PRECIS as a *technique* for indexing. Since the vocabulary is avowedly "open-ended," there is room for the indexer to develop terminology according to the language, customs, and conventions of the prevailing society. It is unlikely that a major institution like the Library of Congress or National Library of Canada could take over PRECIS indexes directly and unchanged from the British Library. This would cause as much grief as is now found with Library of Congress subject headings. But a judicious adaptation to the linguistic practices of each country in no way would spoil or diminish the power of the PRECIS system. The system can stand by itself and is adaptable to reasonable changes to make it acceptable to different kinds of users.

Another advantage is that the librarian, archivist, information scientist, or anyone else with a file to index can make good use of PRECIS without waiting for a national body to standardize the vocabulary to be used with it. PRECIS can make use of "natural language" (the language in a document). This can be rationalized by means of the cross-referencing system to be used with it. Again, the cross-referencing system is built from the ground up, relating one "natural language" to another to take care of synonymous words or new usage of old words in different context. Thus the indexing can be adapted to very special situations, to "in-group" terminology and acronyms, to all kinds of materials in many different media, and, in fact, particularly to the type of file to which standard indexing, classification and thesaural techniques are poorly applied, if they are applicable at all. PRECIS is a portable system in that it does not require expensive reference tools or external bibliographic support from centralized offices. The indexer can carry the technique in head and briefcase.

In a day when costs of bibliographic organization and control are so high that nationwide and international cooperation and networking seem to be the only practical solution, it is a blessing to find one system that can be applied almost anywhere, to about anything, by only one person in many cases, and, at the same time, be geared to the satisfaction of the user because it treats subjects with the user's own vocabulary. The system is not a panacea, but it does throw its light into hitherto dark corners and adds one more bit of organization for areas where formerly there was disorder and chaos.

Appendix A
GLOSSARY

Action
Representation in noun form of the type of activity described grammatically as a verb. Words derived from verbs, usually gerunds or nouns indicating that some kind of function or effect has been produced or performed, generally involving the expenditure of energy or exertion or motion. Actions may be directional in one or two (reciprocal) ways.

Agent
A person, thing, or cause of an effect; normally something or someone producing an effect. An agent may act upon an object directly or indirectly.

Aggregate
A word having a grouping or combining connotation: gang, herd, committee, pack.

Author-attributed association
An association between two or more elements created by an author and not necessarily occurring in the nature of things.

Binding Term
A Term used to connect a block comprising two or more words representing individual concepts that are mutually related to some other Term. This other Term cannot refer to any of the single concept Terms in the block, but only to their aggregate, which represents the block as a whole.

In a classified catalog, the binding term is used where the class numbers for each individual concept (Term) differ from the class number representing these concepts as a whole (i.e., the next higher level in the hierarchy to which each single class belongs).

Binding Term and "bound term" are not related.

Blank
Empty, as in Blank Field Insert or Blank Substitution Insert; replacement of word or phrase by a blank (representing nothing). Used to change string order under certain conditions.

Block
A sequence of string elements (lines, Terms) gathered into a unit for operational purposes.

Bound term
An indexing term consisting of two or more words that must always be used as a unit for semantic reasons. Originated when it was discovered that freely combined single words could have entirely different meanings according to their order: fish food, food fish. Used in this

book wherever two or more words appear as a unit. Bound term and "binding Term" are not related.

Canonical Term

A bound term in which the components are normally used in a given and customary order: ham and eggs, man and wife, mother and child.

Chinese Plate Syndrome

Descriptive of a situation in which both the subject (i.e., a creative work) and a work about it (i.e., criticism, paraphrase, parody, abridgment, etc.) are both indexed in the same collection.

Class-of-one

Class with a single member, as with individual people, paintings, symphonies, etc.

Closed-up difference

A multi-part word that is coded as two separate differences, but printed as a single word; as in the case:

(1)   joints $21 metal $21 welded $33 arc-

which, for the index permits an entry under both "welded" and "arc-welded." The indicator for "closed-up" is either a $1 for non-*lead* or $3 for *lead* and, as shown above, is the first digit in the 2-digit differencing code. This produces the entry: **Arc-welded metal joints.**

Codes

Numerical or letter designation for different forms of differences, Terms, string concepts, etc. Used as tags or triggers to identify a concept and/or to initiate some action involving the concept. Code types in PRECIS consist of those identifying Blocks, Connectives, Differences, Operators, References, Terms, Themes, and Typography. In this book, a set of conventional marks is utilized to distinguish between codes where the same letter may be in different types of codes. In PRECIS itself, as a rule, only parentheses ( ) or $ or both are needed to differentiate between the various codes.

Compound term

Term with two major parts: focus and difference; multiple-word terms. For example: Stretch orlon knit fabrics.

Focus = fabrics

Differences = knit
                      orlon
                      stretch

(1)*   fabrics $21 knit $21 orlon $01 stretch

The focus is a class and the differences are sub-classes of that class.

Concept
Single idea or unit of thought, expressed in one word or several; in PRECIS, natural language Terms that can be matched logically by one of the role operators in the system.

Concept Interlink
Special types of operators used to indicate roles, directional properties, and author-attributed associations (associations made by an author and not necessarily occurring naturally).

Conceptual types
Entities, namely "things" (either concrete or abstract) and activities (matters concerned with action or the results of action). Expressed in noun form if possible or, if activities, in gerund form when a suitable noun is unavailable.

Connectives
Words used to connect other words into a unit. In PRECIS, introduced by operators ($v) for a downward connection and ($w) for an upward one. In most cases, connectives are prepositions.

Coordinate concepts
Terms that bind or connect; copulating terms that pull together related higher or lower terms. Terms that are grouped in the document or matter being indexed by being related to a *common* higher or lower term, but not necessarily to each other. Listed in alphabetical order in a string provided they are not canonical (q.v.).

Date as Difference
In many instances, the subject being indexed covers a limited period of time. In such cases, the extent of time covered is treated as a difference. Such periods can be many things:

centuries $d 1800-1899

wars $d 1914-1918

events $d 1776

a few years of a person's life $d 1973-1975

The lifespan of a person is not treated as a difference, but is added after the name. In print, all dates are italicized.

Smith, John $f 1896-1959

Definition
A phrase giving a thing's fundamental attributes, or essence.

Dependent elements
Parts, properties of things, grouping into a class of disparate items, aggregates.

Difference
That part of a compound Term which represents a subclass of a class called the *focus*. A difference may be an

adjective or adjectival phrase or a prepositional phrase. In the Term, "quick banana bread," the focus is "bread" and the differences "banana" and "quick," in the order:

(1)*   bread $21 banana $21 quick

Differences of this type may be direct, indirect, very indirect, etc. up to nine levels of directness. A difference is preceded by a $ and coded either numerically (using a matrix), as in the above case, or with letters, as in the case of date $d, and the rarely used parenthetical differences, $n and $o.

See also. **Direct difference, Following difference, Indirect difference, Preceding difference, Date as difference, Differencing operators and Focus**

Differencing

The logical action of describing a focus in order to bring out a "to be" or "kind of" or "part of" relationship; equivalent to use of adjectives in grammar and syntax. A part is *never* differenced by its whole.

Differencing operators

These operators are used to modify a focus or to add a time factor that is of limited duration. The operators are: numerically coded normal differences (roughly, adjectival ones) $01 to $39, non-*lead* and *lead* parenthetical differences $n and $o, and date as difference $d.

Differentia

That part of the essence (fundamental attribute grouping which distinguishes a thing) which separates the species from other species in the same genus; those factors that differentiate.

Direct agent

An agent that acts directly upon an object. Grammatically, the subject of a transitive action.

Direct difference

A difference that directly modifies a focus; equivalent to an adjective applying directly to a noun. In the example

(1)   curtains $21 damask $21 ruffled $21 white

all differences can be used directly with the focal word, "curtains." Any number of words can be direct differences for a single focus.

Direct object

An object acted upon directly by an agent. Object of a transitive action by an agent.

Directional properties

Properties associated with some words whereby the property is distinguished by being "pointed" toward something. Words such as "attitude" or "accountability" or "responsibility" have this property.

Disambiguate	Render unambiguous.
Display	Successively narrower relationship with respect to the *lead* (headword) in a two-line index entry.
Element	Generally a line in a PRECIS string; otherwise one word in a phrase or in a collection of words.
Environment of action	A place where an action takes place; used with following differences of certain types (e.g., betting at race tracks, the track being the environment for betting).
Essence	The set of fundamental attributes that are necessary and sufficient conditions for every concrete thing to be a thing of that [some particular] type (Cohen & Nagel).
Focus	The noun or substantive component which specifies the class of ideas or concepts to which a compound term belongs, literally the focal point of the descriptive matter: "sky" in "blue sky," "bridges" in "truss bridges."
	The noun or noun-phrase being differenced.
	A focus must be either an entity or equivalent and represented by a substantive [noun, verbal noun, or a noun-verb (gerund)]. Focus and difference make up a *compound Term*.
Following difference	A difference that, in normal grammatical usage, follows its focus: "diets for food allergies" ("diets" is the focus, "for food allergies" is the difference, in this case a prepositional one); with "conditions indicating deterioration," the following difference after "conditions" is an adjectival phrase starting with a gerund.
Formats	Three methods for basic arrangement of string terms when rewritten as index entries: Standard, Inverted, and Predicate Transformation. Standard Format has normal shunting procedures. In Inverted Format, when operators (4), (5), or (6) are used as *lead* (headword), elements of the string are read from top to bottom and dropped into the *display* position of the entry. For Predicate Transformation, parts of the string are reformatted in order to retain the sense of the original context.
Forms	Format of presentation, such as biography, bibliography, list, anthology, dictionary, encyclopedia, pictures, etc.
Gating	The use of connectives ($v) and ($w) to join words to make a grammatical phrase in an index entry. Use of only one of these connectives (with its appropriate word) is called "half gating," while both constitute "full gating."

Generic Relationship A term whose only function is to specify the class of objects or action; an a priori (natural, existing) relationship; a relationship that holds under all circumstances.

Generic term A term representing an existing ("to be") relationship of the kind representing the basic type of an entity: "Turbulence" as the fundamental form in cases where more specific words, such as "clear air turbulence," form the index term. Generic types of words are used in the thesaurus as cross-references rather than as index terms, to increase specificity in indexing:

> **Turbulence**
> *See also*
> **Clear air turbulence**

Genus The category of essence of a number of things exhibiting differences in kind. By definition, *genus* consists of two parts, genus proper and differentia (Cohen & Nagel).

Gerund The "-ing" form of a verb, used as a verbal noun.

Homographs Words with identical spelling but different meanings. Differentiated in PRECIS by use of the quasi-generic operator (q), which places each word in the context of the class to which it may be assigned.

Indirect agent An agent acting upon an object that is unstated and not included in the PRECIS string. The identification of an indirect agent normally calls for use of a Blank Field Insert to prevent the Predicate Transformation from occurring. Otherwise there would be a false impression of the originator of the action upon the key system as object.

Indirect difference An Indirect difference is one that modifies another difference (the one immediately preceding) rather than the focus. The first Indirect difference modifies the Direct difference, which is considered the first level of difference. The first Indirect difference is the second level of difference; the second Indirect difference is the third level of difference; and so on to a limit of eight indirect levels in a pattern of decreasing directness.

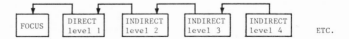

(1)* curtains $21 lace $22 woven $33 hand

Entries under: Curtains, Lace curtains, Woven lace curtains, Handwoven lace curtains.

Indirect object

An object acted upon indirectly; one possessing an indirect relationship to a stated agent in a PRECIS string. Normally the agent, rather than the object (key system), is treated as indirect, and the object is retained even though the direct agent is "understood" rather than stated.

An object in the active voice (dative case) which has been transformed into a key system, even though it is only acted upon indirectly. Or, where the direct action lacks an agent, the agent present being that of an *unstated* action and object.

Interposed operators

Operators interpolated into the sequence of Main Line operators to complete the full sense of the context. These operators are (p), (q), (r), the concept interlinks (s) and (t), and the coordinate concepts (f) and (g).

Key system

The object of a transitive action; the subject (agent) of an intransitive one. Used in PRECIS as the first element in a string after the locale (geographical or political area as setting). Identified after transforming a grammatical sentence into the passive voice and reducing it to a title-like phrase.

Lead

Headword, filing word or phrase. The name given to the position in the two-line PRECIS shunting format which identifies the term to be used as the filing word(s) in an index entry.

Level

Degree of directness of differences.

    Level 1 = direct difference
    Level 2 = first indirect difference
    Level 3 = second indirect difference
    etc. to 9 levels

Level is taken in terms of relationship to the *focus*; thus, if the word "very" represented the degree of indirectness from the third to the ninth level, the indirect differences would be:

    Level 3 = very indirect difference,
    Level 4 = very, *very* indirect reference,
    Level 5 = very, very, *very* indirect difference, etc.

Location

Geographic or political area, locale, environment, place.

Manipulation code

A special code of instructions which indicates to the computer what predetermined format is required during the creation of index entries. The code covers words, typefonts, spacing, etc.

Manipulation string

A string written in manipulation codes, ready for computer processes which will produce the index entries.

Observed system Topic of the work being indexed; the work itself if objects are being indexed; subject of written discourse.

One-to-one relationship Words which are in juxtaposition (contiguous words, adjacent words) bear this kind of relationship to each other. Each is dependent upon the preceding word in context and provides context for the following word. Meaning thus conveyed by sentence or phrase is incomplete until the final word has been reached and there are no more.

Part A functional piece of a thing, belonging to it by reason of being connected to it.

Place Normally environment or location. In special cases may be a key system or the environment of an action.

Preceding difference A difference that precedes the focus, such as "On-the-job training," "Intermittent flow," "training" and "flow" being the respective foci.

Predicate Transformation A special format invoked by the presence of an action Term immediately followed by the Term representing its agent; invoked to avoid ambiguity in index entries.

Property (Logical definition) A property is a predicate that does not indicate the essence of a thing yet belongs to the thing alone. Property is an attribute that follows necessarily from the definition. The roles of property and definition are interchangeable, but absolute in a given system (e.g., in mathematics, the properties coming from the definition are the axioms) (Cohen & Nagel).

Property (Operational definition) A quality belonging to a key system, action agent, location. Distinguished from "part" by reason of belonging in the sense of possession.

Qualifier The area in the two-line index entry which is occupied by a term higher in the string, but still in a one-to-one relationship with the *lead* term; representing a broader context with respect to the *lead*.

Quasi-generic category The category to which a quasi-generic group belongs. Homographs are treated as quasi-generic categories because their variant meanings assign them to different categories.

Quasi-generic group A grouping formed by an author; any grouping not occurring in nature; a group of members whose relationship to each other is not a true generic one (not a priori, not once-and-for-all).

Quasi-generic relationship

An a posteriori relationship conferred upon members of a group in PRECIS by context-dependency; must have been based on the context of the work being indexed and not on nature; a relationship that does *not* hold under all circumstances.

Role definer

A special routine that identifies the role played by an agent in some kinds of situations, such as an unusual role, an indirect agent, or an indirect action. Typical words involved are "role of ... in," "participation of ... in," "applications of ... in," "use of ... in," "influence of ... in," "effects of ... in," and "implications of ... in."

Role operator

The primary means of indicating the basic function of each word or set of words in the string according to the formal outline of the PRECIS system. These operators, for example, identify some 25 kinds of terms used in the PRECIS syntax. At the same time, the codes applied to the operators trigger specified routines to be applied with each operator. These routines, in turn, create the index entries in a predetermined format.

Sample population

Term used for a selected instance or special grouping as the type of emphasis used in a work.

Shunting

The clockwise method of presenting elements of a string in successive entries made for an index. The order is from *display* to *lead* to *qualifier*. Individual Terms in a string are shunted until all those destined to be headwords have been used.

Space-generating

Also called "spaced" or "spaced-out." A form of difference code which puts a space between two words in an entry. Spaced code is $0 for non-*lead* words and $2 for words wanted as *leads*. This code (and the closed-up differencing code, $1 and $3, for non-*lead* and *lead*, respectively) provides the first digit of the 2-digit difference code.

Substitutions

Terms used to replace other terms when ambiguity could otherwise result.

Targets

Users, readers, special groups toward whom a work is aimed; potential users whose interests are especially covered by the context.

Term

Verbal representation of a concept. Commonly a synonym for "word"; in PRECIS a string element of one or more words considered as a unit, and identified and tagged by a role operator. Terms may contain differencing and connective operators as well. Used with a capital T in this book except when serving as a synonym.

Theme interlinks
Two special role indicators, (x) and (y), added before regular role indicators when a string contains two themes or more. Each theme begins with an (x) role operator and continues with (y) operators until the theme comes to an end. Common themes are represented by (z), used only at the beginning or at the end of the whole sequence of themes. For example, the title:

Insulation of public buildings and ventilation for schools in New York: a manual for civil engineers

might well yield a string such as:

```
                    d
(z)(0)*   New York $i (N.Y.)
(x)(1)*   public buildings
(y)(2)*   insulation
(x)(1)*   schools $21 public
(y)(2)*   ventilation
(z)(6)    manuals $01 for
(z)(6)    engineers
```

Viewpoint as form
A situation in which a work is written or treated from a particular point of view.

Viewpoint as subject
A situation where a viewpoint is the subject of a work.

Appendix B
SPACING

SPACING OF INDEX ENTRIES

Instructions	Results
Use two spaces between *lead* and *qualifier*:	**Mice.** Pests
First line of *display* is indented 2 spaces: entry begins at the third position.	**Mice.** Pests Extermination
An overrun on the *qualifier* begins after eight spaces, starting on the ninth position	**Designs.** Adhesive-backed floral wallpaper Appliqued designs
An overrun on the *display* begins at the fifth position, after four blank spaces	**Houses.** Cities. Canada Building plans for clustered housing

PRECIS REFERENCES:
"See" references

Use one space on either side of the word *See*, which is in italics. Both Terms are in bold face. Overrun begins on the ninth space, after eight blank spaces.

Prehistoric civilization *See* **Pre-Columbian civilization**

PRECIS REFERENCES:
"See also" references

Use one line for the base Term, a second line for the words "*See also*" and a third line for the Term referred to. "See also" begins at the fourth position (after three blank spaces). The Term referred to begins in the sixth position after five blanks, while any overruns start at the ninth position, preceded by eight blanks. Both Terms are in bold face.

Blood transfusion
See also
Diseases transmitted by blood transfusion

SPECIFIC DETAILS

Index Entries

Use two spaces between *lead* and *qualifier*:

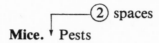

First line of *display* begins at the *third position*, after two blanks:

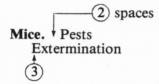

An overrun of the *qualifier* starts in the *ninth position*, after eight blanks:

Designs.   Adhesive-backed floral
⑨————►wallpaper
   Appliqued designs

An overrun of the *display* begins at the *fifth space*, after four blanks:

Houses.   Cities.＼Canada
   Building plans for clustered
 ⑤—►housing

Normally there is one space between words. Any further overruns in the *display* start at the *seventh position*.

References

Use one space on either side of the word "See," which is in italics. Both Terms are in bold face. Overrun begins in the ninth position, after eight blanks.

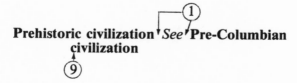

Use the first line for the base Term, a second line for the "See also" (in italics) and a third line for the Term referred to. The "See also" starts in the *fourth position*, after three blanks. The Term referred *to* begins in the *sixth position*, after five blanks. An overrun starts at the *ninth position*, preceded by eight blanks. Both Terms are in bold face.

Blood transfusion
④———►*See also*
⑥———►**Diseases transmitted by blood**
⑨————►**transfusion**

Appendix C
CONVENTIONS USED IN THIS BOOK
FOR REPRESENTING VARIOUS PRECIS CODES

Blocks	"g" block, "3" block, "s" block, etc.
Connectives	($v), ($w)
Differencing	$01, $02, $11, $12, $n, $o, $d, etc.
Operators	(0), (1), (p), (g), (s), (t), etc.
References	'$m', '$n', '$o', etc.
Terms	"a", "b", "c", "d"
Theme Interlink Operators	(x)( ), (y)( ), (z)( )
Typography	($e), ($f), ($g), ($h), ($i), ($j), ($k)

Some codes use the same letters for different purposes. In PRECIS strings they may appear with ( ) or $. For convenience in the text, additional tagging has been added for Connectives, References, Terms and Typography:

Parenthetical Difference Codes (formerly called operators)	**Reference Codes** (' ' added)
$n	'$n'
$o	'$o'

Operator Codes	**Reference Codes** (' ' added)
(x)( )	'$x'
(y)( )	'$y'

Operator Codes	**Typographical Codes** ( ) added
(f)	($f)
(g)	($g)

Manipulation Code groups such as 003, 103, 0n1, 0n2, etc. are used without quotation marks or parentheses.

Appendix D
STRINGS AND ENTRIES FOR EXAMPLES
USED IN CHAPTER 3

1) *How to Buy a House* (*see* chapters 6 and 7)

2) *The World of M. C. Escher* (*see* chapters 6 and 7)

3) *Speakeasy Manual: the Speakeasy III Reference Manual.*

**Programming languages for digital computer systems,
Speakeasy, level Nu, manuals**

String:
    (1)*   digital computer systems
    (3)*   programming languages
    (q)*   Speakeasy III language
    (p)   level Nu
    (6)   manuals

Entries:
Digital computer systems
    Programming languages: Speakeasy III language.
    Level Nu — *Manuals*

Programming languages. Digital computer systems
Speakeasy III language. Level Nu — *Manuals*

Speakeasy III language. Programming languages.
    Digital computer systems
Level Nu — *Manuals*

4) *Preselectors for high frequency shortwave radios: Holstrom
Associates model SK-20, assembly manual*

String:
    (1)*   radios $21 shortwave $21 high frequency
    (p)*   preselectors
    (q)   Holstrom Associates model SK-20
    (6)*   assembly manuals

Entries:
Radios
    High frequency shortwave radios
        Preselectors: Holstrom Associates model
        SK-20 — *Assembly manuals*

Shortwave radios
    High frequency shortwave radios. Preselectors:
        Holstrom Associates model SK-20 — *Assembly
        manuals*

(Entries continue on page 308)

High frequency radios
High frequency shortwave radios. Preselectors:
Holstrom Associates model SK-20 — *Assembly manuals*

Preselectors. High frequency shortwave radios
Holstrom Associates model SK-20 — *Assembly manuals*

Assembly manuals
High frequency shortwave radios. Preselectors:
Holstrom Associates model SK-20

5) *Manufacturer's catalog for Rustrak miniature strip chart recorders*

String: (1)*   recorders $01 chart $22 strip $22 miniature $01
                        c
                        Rustrak

                 (6)*   manufacturers' catalogs

Entries: **Recorders**
                Rustrak miniature strip chart recorders —
                Manufacturers' catalogs

                Strip chart recorders
                Rustrak miniature strip chart recorders —
                Manufacturers' catalogs

                Miniature chart recorders
                Rustrak miniature strip chart recorders —
                Manufcturers' catalogs

                Manufacturers' catalogs
                Rustrak miniature strip chart recorders

6) *Practical information on applications of Motorola field-effect transistors*

String: (1)*   electronic equipment
                 (2)   construction $w of
                 (s)   applications $v of $w in   c
                 (3)*   transistors $21 field-effect $01 Motorola
                 (6)   practical information

Entries: **Electronic equipment**
                Construction. Applications of Motorola field-effect
                transistors — *Practical information*

Transistors
  Motorola field-effect transistors. Applications in
    construction of electronic equipment — *Practical
    information*

Field-effect transistors
  Motorola field-effect transistors. Applications in
    construction of electronic equipment — *Practical
    information*

Cross-references:

FET *See* **Field effect transistors**

Semiconductor devices
  See also
    Transistors